The Library
of World
Biography

Books by Elizabeth Longford

QUEEN VICTORIA: BORN TO SUCCEED

WELLINGTON: THE YEARS OF THE SWORD

WELLINGTON: PILLAR OF STATE

VICTORIA R.I.: A PICTURE BOOK

WINSTON CHURCHILL: A PICTORIAL LIFE STORY

THE ROYAL HOUSE OF WINDSOR

BYRON'S GREECE (*Photographs by Jorge Lewinski*)

THE LIFE OF BYRON

By the same author writing as Elizabeth Pakenham

JAMESON'S RAID

The Life of Byron

by Elizabeth Longford

THE LIBRARY OF WORLD BIOGRAPHY
J. H. PLUMB, GENERAL EDITOR

Little, Brown and Company — Boston — Toronto

FIRST EDITION

T11/76

The author wishes to thank John Murray, controller of Byron copy-
rights, for permission to reproduce extracts from Byron's poetry and
prose as well as from Byron's journal and letters. Excerpts from Byron
letters in The Lovelace Papers and in The Byron Collection at the
Bodleian Library, Oxford, are reproduced by the kind permission of
Viscount Knebworth.

Library of Congress Cataloging in Publication Data
Longford, Elizabeth Harmon Pakenham, Countess
   of, 1906–
   The life of Byron.
   (The Library of world biography)
   Bibliography p.
   Includes index.
   1. Byron, George Gordon Noël Byron, Baron,
1788–1824—Biography. I. Title.
PR4381.L6   821'.7 [B]   76-22714
ISBN 0-316-53192-8

Published simultaneously in Canada
by Little, Brown & Company (Canada) Limited

PRINTED IN THE UNITED STATES OF AMERICA

To Frank

Acknowledgments

"I AM GENERALLY CONTENT to be a listener when important questions are introduced, such as the English Parliament and Lord Byron!" The Russian playwright Griboyedov put these words into the mouth of his hero in *The Misfortune of Being Clever*, and they aptly illustrate the talismanic function of Byron in his own day. I am indebted to Miss Ludmilla Kranidova for bringing them to my notice, and I hope to show in the following pages that Byron today still possesses relevance and magic as man and poet.

I would also like to thank most warmly Lady Mander, Mrs. Elma Dangerfield, Mr. Michael Rees, Mr. Cecil Roberts, Mrs. Beatrice Hanss, Mrs. Helen Lloyd, Miss Lucy Edwards and Mrs. Gwen Beaumont. I am very grateful to Professor John D. Jump and Professor Jack Lindsay for personal kindness, and to Professor Paul Fleck and Professor and Mrs. John Clubbe for many stimulating discussions, previews or copies of their published work, and their companionship, whether in Byron's Italy, Greece or Switzerland. My special gratitude is due to those great Byronists, Mrs. Doris Langley-Levi Moore and the Earl of Lytton (Byron's great-

great-grandson) for many enlightening conversations; and to Mr. John Murray for his generosity in keeping me up to date with new publications and in extending hospitality in *the* room where so much Byronic history was made. I am grateful to Miss Annabel Jones for information from the Longman archives. Like so many others, I am indebted to Professor Leslie Marchand's great work on Byron. Last but not least, Mr. Arnold Houldsworth, through the original kind offices of, Mrs. Jane M. Barker, has allowed me to print as an appendix his full and hitherto-unpublished account of the opening of Byron's tomb in 1938. Mr. Houldsworth, at the time a church-warden of St. Mary Magdalene, Hucknall Torkard, is now the only living eyewitness of that dramatic event on June 15. My warmest thanks are due to him.

This is the ninth book that Mrs. Agnes Fenner has typed for me, and I thank her again for her skill and stamina. My friends Professor Plumb and Christopher Falkus have given me invaluable advice when reading the manuscript, as have Francis Bennett and Jean Whitnack. My daughter Antonia Fraser has once more written critical notes in the margins which Byron would have enjoyed. To my husband I am as always deeply grateful for criticisms and suggestions at every stage, and for sharing my pleasure in this opportunity to study the life of a great poet.

Introduction

WHEN WE LOOK BACK at the past nothing, perhaps, fascinates us so much as the fate of individual men and women. The greatest of these seem to give a new direction to history, to mold the social forces of their time and create a new image, or open up vistas that humbler men and women never imagined. An investigation of the interplay of human temperament with social and cultural forces is one of the most complex yet beguiling studies a historian can make; men molded by time, and time molded by men. It would seem that to achieve greatness both the temperament and the moment must fit like a key into a complex lock. Or rather a master key, for the very greatest of men and women resonate in ages distant to their own. Later generations may make new images of them — one has only to think what succeeding generations of Frenchmen have made of Napoleon, or Americans of Benjamin Franklin — but this only happens because some men change the course of history and stain it with their own ambitions, desires, creations or hopes of a magnitude that embraces future generations like a miasma. This is particularly true of the great figures of religion, of politics, of war. The great creative spirits, however, are used by subsequent generations in a reverse manner — men and women go to them to seek hope or solace, or to confirm despair, reinterpreting the works of imagination or wisdom to ease them in their own desperate necessities, to beguile them with a sense of beauty or merely to draw from them strength and understanding. So this series of biographies tries in lucid, vivid, and dramatic narratives to explain the greatness of men and women, not only how they managed to secure their niche in the great pantheon of Time, but also why they have continued to fascinate subsequent generations. It may seem, therefore, that it is paradoxical for this series to contain living men and women, as well as the dead, but it is not so. We can recognize, in our own time, particularly in those whose careers are getting close to their final hours, men and women of indisputable greatness, whose position in history is secure, and about whom the legends and myths are beginning to sprout — for all great men and women become legends, all become in history larger than their own lives.

Keats, Shelley, Byron are the great romantic poets of early nineteenth century England who created legends as well as great poetry. They all died young — Keats of tuberculosis, Shelley by drowning, Byron of fever: all were rejected by society or themselves rejected the responsible world of authority in politics and in literature. They were dropouts, Bohemians, adored and despised, feared and honored. They represented a new force in the world of letters — the unfettered genius, unconstrained by life's conventions. This is more true of Shelley than of Keats, truer still of Byron. Byron was born to be a romantic hero, the driven individualist; sensitive to wrong yet capable of diabolic personal behavior: saint and sadist in one impulsive heart.

As often happens with great men, Byron's age awaited him. The turmoil of the French Revolution and the dramatic success of Napoleon, followed by his disastrous fall, had helped to breed a sense of a doom-laden age that called out for heroic aspirations and fortitude towards disaster. Fated lovers locked in an inexorable destiny; an unfeeling, uncomprehending, crass world of authority that stifled creativity, this was the imagined world in which Byron's heroes lived, driven inscrutably to their own self-destruction. This world was as mythical as the romantic beauty-sodden world of Keats's *Eve of St. Agnes,* but one which Byron's poetic gifts made almost real, real enough at least for readers to lose themselves in it and feel it to be true.

Such beliefs, such imaginings, wild, dark, compelled, needed a sustaining life-style. Byron's riven temperament created his tempestuous poetic world but to give a dimension of truth to his fantasies his life had to be fantastic. It was. Love affairs made horrendous by hints of incest, sodomy and murder, hints whose truth was deliberately obscured. Journeys to what were then the remote lands of the Middle East, which became pilgrimages of the spirit, threaded with ecstasy and despair. Everything that Byron could take to excess he did, whether it was starving to reduce weight or drinking himself into a stupor or rioting in love. It seems impossible to overpaint Byron's life. And certainly Elizabeth Longford never diminishes the wild excesses to which she knows Byron was prone.

But as she so subtly portrays, there is far more in Byron than the extravagant romantic, far more than Childe Harold on a tragic pilgrimage. Byron resonated with his age. He remained a huge best seller, read by some with shudders, by most with delight. Technically he was less skilled than Shelley or Keats, far less profound, more remote from that haunting unforgettable quality of the greatest poetry that seems to take us unblinkingly to the truth of ourselves and of our world. And yet his success was far from superficial, far from being merely an aspect of his time. He possessed compassion, a deep empathy for those who were victims of fate, whether poor stocking-frame weavers from Nottingham or the downtrodden, brutalized peasants of Greece. He attacked their oppression, and by implication all oppression, with savage satire that still burns with indignation. There was, too, in his life as in his poetry a lyricism, a yearning for the freedom of the spirit.

Like anyone with an overheated, Gothick imagination he could be tedious, he could, indeed, be absurd, but Byron was saved from the worst excesses of his imagination by a capacity for self-mockery — nowhere better displayed than in his letters and journals, of which Elizabeth Longford makes such excellent and telling use.

It would be easy to make Byron appear to be the most detestable of men: the treatment of his wife was abominable, the lack of a sense of personal responsibility shocks even today. Nevertheless his life radiates, in spite of the cruelty and sadism, with warmth, compassion, exceptional generosity and gusto. Oddly enough, with as much gusto for death, for suffering, as for life and happiness. Byron lived to excess in all things. Only a skilled and practiced biographer could grasp the essence of such a man: in this short book he is all there.

— J. H. PLUMB

Contents

The Life of Byron

ONE

"Hot Youth"
(1788-1809)

NOTHING REMAINS of the London street in which Byron was born except the name, Holles Street. "The glory and the nothing of a Name" — as Byron himself was to write of a poet's gravestone. Today there is no longer even a stone to commemorate Byron's birthplace, though in 1864 the first of London's blue plaques, erected to mark the homes of famous people, was placed there in his honor. Since then the brick eighteenth-century house in whose rented back room the poet made his debut has become the concrete cliff of a department store.* Yet if Byron had to be born in London, Holles Street was appropriate.

Like the adjacent streets and squares it had been called after the nobility whose money built them. Lady Henrietta Cavendish Holles was an heiress who married the Earl of Oxford, head of the Harley family. Holles Street joins Oxford Street to Cavendish Square, and so to Harley Street and Devonshire Street and Place. When Byron reached manhood these names of interrelated families flourished in Whig society, and their bearers scattered thorns or roses in his path.

* John Lewis, the store in question, has a Byron Room.

The niece of Georgiana Duchess of Devonshire, Lady Caroline Lamb, supplied the thorns, while the Countess of Oxford shared a bed of roses.

Now and then throughout history a particular society has offered its lucky members all that can be imagined of civilized perfection, whether it be fifth-century Athens, the antebellum South in the United States, or the British aristocracy in Byron's youth. In each case, however, Paradise had been flawed: in the first and second by slavery, in the third by the economic enslavement of the British working class. Byron did not live to see the power of the aristocracy diminished in the great reforms of the 1830's. But he did grow up in the shadow of the gigantic event that set in motion these and so many other changes — the French Revolution. In its turn the Revolution had been deeply influenced by the European Enlightenment and especially the French *philosophes.*

Clever young men like Byron read the skeptical philosophy and history of Voltaire, Locke and Hume, and the romantic *Nouvelle Héloïse, Confessions* and revolutionary *Social Contract* of Jean-Jacques Rousseau. But they could not fully have appreciated the desperate nature of French poverty during the *ancien régime:* how it was officially graded — or rather, degraded — into the poor, the necessitous, the indigent and the destitute, each group in deadly fear of the one below. Nevertheless when the English poor tried a little violence in 1812 Byron knew how to respond. Not with fetters and the gallows but an impassioned plea to Parliament for sympathy and mercy.

His mother gave him as a child a favorable impression of Liberty, Equality and Fraternity. "I am quite a Democrat," she would say, "and I do not think the [French] King, after his treachery and perjury, deserves to be restored." He was a schoolboy when Liberty and Equality slipped imperceptibly into Order and Hierarchy, Bonaparte taking over the revolutionary wars and turning them into French imperialism. Goethe, the greatest of Byron's literary contemporaries (though born many years before him) whose youthful *Sor-*

rows of Werther launched the Romantic movement — Goethe for a time saw in Napoleon Bonaparte the principle of order. To Byron as to many of his fellow Whigs, Napoleon stood for no such abstraction. At the very least he was the Opposition mascot. The Tories flaunted their King and country; the Whigs romanticized the enemy Emperor. That Napoleon was interested in toppling reactionary thrones was also of interest to the Whigs. Dying in exile when Byron was himself an exile, the Emperor had been at times a macrocosm of the young rake.

Napoleon was not chivalrous about women, nor was Byron; Napoleon loved his sister, as did Byron; Napoleon was a superstitious skeptic, as was Byron. They were vanquished within a year of one another by orthodoxy, Napoleon by the military establishment, Byron by the social establishment. At each stage of his pilgrimage Byron could measure his ideals against Bonaparte's career.

At first Byron felt the glamour of Napoleon's success. Disillusion followed, with the banishment to Elba instead of heroic death: *"So abject — yet alive!"* The Hundred Days brought renewed admiration, followed by empathy with the exile of St. Helena. Finally recognition dawned that Napoleon had betrayed himself by his lust for conquest. Historians of the future, wrote Byron, would prize wisdom above valor and exchange "ten thousand conquerors for a single sage." Many of his generation, in their ultimate disenchantment, were to choose like him the sages — Prometheus in myth, Washington, Franklin, Goethe or Bolívar in life.

The English Romantic poets had been among the most loyal disciples of the young Revolution. Byron led the middle or "Regency" wave of Romantics, preceded by the "Lake Poets," Wordsworth, Coleridge and Southey, and followed by Shelley and Keats. It was no surprise to Byron that after Waterloo public opinion became disillusioned, especially with the politics of patriotism. He extended his disenchantment to poetry itself. All but satire. He admitted that he would like his merry masterpiece *Don Juan* to live.

Freed from the twin cults of popularity and ostracism, Byron finally returned to the pure ideal of liberty. He died for it. This act belonged neither to the spirit of the Enlightenment nor of the bloodstained Revolution, far less of Bonaparte. Only partly inspired by the Romantics, it was a step into nationalism during its age of innocence. It took a poet to see the way. But then, as Byron's friend Shelley had written, "Poets and philosophers are the unacknowledged legislators of the world."

It is debatable whether Byron was more affected by his ancestry or his deformity. Professor Marchand, his biographer royal, plumps for the latter: "George Gordon, the sixth Lord Byron, was born with a lame foot on January 22, 1788." Certainly the lame right foot, today thought to be dysplasic or clubbed, distorted Byron's life. From earliest childhood he learned to bear pain. In proud youth his deformity taught him shame and concealment. When he grew to manhood, it introduced him to the whole problem of evil — who or what caused such inherited suffering? Without deformity he might never have developed his compensatory talents for boxing, swimming, riding, target shooting and lovemaking. Would there have been any need to rival Leander at the Hellespont? Or Philoctetes, with his mortal wound and immortal bow, a legendary leader of the embattled Greeks?

The most important thing about Byron's ancestry was the Celtic strain on both sides. The poet's grandfather Vice-Admiral Sir John Byron came of a North Midlands family going back to the Norman Conquest, and married his first cousin Sophia Trevanion of Cornwall. She was a bluestocking of true Celtic sprightliness greatly valued in Dr. Johnson's circle. Celtic appreciation of consanguinity may have accounted for the many loves between siblings and cousins among the Byrons. The admiral himself had been remarkably fond of his sister Isabella.

Known as "Foul-weather Jack" or "Hardy Byron," he had been shipwrecked off the coast of Patagonia. The kindly young castaway from the *Wager* adopted a stray Indian dog which he named Boxer. But despite his protests, his starving mates made Boxer into a stew, compounding their offense by offering none to his master. Eventually young Jack Byron dug up the remains and ate the skin and paws — a comically macabre incident which the admiral's grandson transferred from "grand-dad's" diary to his own *Don Juan*.

The head of the family was the fifth Lord Byron, the admiral's elder brother and the poet's great-uncle. He had earned the title of "Wicked Lord" after killing a relative and neighbor, Mr. Chaworth of Annesley Hall, in a duel. Horace Walpole said he was mad. Though the House of Lords acquitted him of murder, he lived henceforth as a scandalous recluse at Newstead Abbey, the family home in Nottinghamshire, with "Lady Betty," a servant girl.

The poet's father was another black sheep. This "Mad Jack," the admiral's son, had all the dash of a Guards captain, but he proved more adept at capturing heiresses than enemies. He eloped with the wife of Lord Carmarthen. After her divorce they were married, and in 1783 a daughter called Augusta Mary was born — the poet's half sister. The mother died, but as long as her fortune lasted, "Mad Jack" disported himself in France. Then he came back for another heiress. Within two spring months of 1785 he met and married in Bath a Scottish lass of twenty with an overbuxom figure, a burr, and a moderate fortune of £23,000. This was Catherine Gordon of Gight, Byron's mother.

A Celt, it seemed, if ever there was one. She once bit a piece out of a saucer and her temperament would produce hysterics at the theatre, an excitability which her little boy probably inherited. While watching *The Taming of the Shrew* he jumped up and loudly contradicted the bullying Petruchio. Catherine Gordon's ancestry was bursting with romance and drama: royal descent from Annabella Stuart, daughter of James I of Scotland; five murders; two hangings; one excommunication; and a possible suicide.

The whirlwind which had swept Catherine into matrimony soon scattered her fortune. She loved and lashed her Johnny Byron when they met, but he dared not meet her too often for fear of meeting his creditors also. Having lived with him three months in France, Catherine took the lodgings at 16 Holles Street for her confinement because they were relatively cheap. Afterwards she dodged about the Home Counties with her baby until 1789, when the family moved to Aberdeen. There they tried to live together at opposite ends of Queen Street. Byron, though under three, always remembered the "domestic broils," which led to his own early "horror of matrimony." Of his father he wrote: "He seemed born for his own ruin, and that of the other sex" — a judgment which Byron transferred to his own destiny. The captain decamped once more to France in 1790, where he poured out his love upon a woman far dearer than his wife — Mrs. Frances Leigh, his sister. He died in 1791 aged thirty-six. It was a fatal age for the Byrons. Both the poet and his daughter Ada were to die at that age.

Mrs. Byron's lawyers had been able to retrieve less than £150 a year out of her fortune. Gight, of which Catherine was the thirteenth and last "laird," was sold. Some of her son's suspicions of the number 13 stemmed from this fact — and from his parents' marriage date, 13 May. Meanwhile his mother, now living alone with him and his nurse, Agnes Gray, in Aberdeen, proved to be as provident economically as she was unstable emotionally. Moods of depression alternated with bursts of intense tenderness or furious temper: "Ah, you little dog, you are a Byron all over." She once called him a "lame brat" — an infamous taunt, particularly as her son came to believe, though mistakenly, that his deformity had been caused by her false modesty at his birth. But her successful management of the pence enabled her to acquire on Aberdeen's best thoroughfare, Broad Street, a six-room apartment. Her four-year-old son was sent to "Bodsy" Bower's neighborhood school, where Geordie, obstreperous but prepossessing in red jacket and nankeen trousers, learned by rote, "God made man, let us love him." God's love for man, however, was given a disastrous twist in Geordie's mind by his Calvinistic nurse, Agnes Gray. She taught him that some people were sinners predestined to damnation, a doctrine which darkened his life. At the same time she introduced him to the beauty of Biblical language.

After acquiring from tutors a "grand passion" for history, he entered Aberdeen Grammar School at seven under the name of "Geo. Bayron Gordon." (His father had taken his mother's name on marriage.) Geordie was therefore correct when he later declared himself as "half a Scot by birth, and bred a whole one." He was a whole Scot in his wide reading (he preferred Eastern travel and Gothick tales) and in his love of the hills and waters. He would swim in the "black deep salmon stream" which widened into a pool under the "Brig o' Baldounie." In his speech he was all Scot, and not a few of his sayings have survived in their Aberdonian vitality: "Dinna speak of it!" (to a woman who pitied his lameness); "Come and see the twa laddies with the twa club feet going up Broad-st!" (of himself and a lame school friend); and when he was in one of his rages he became "Mrs. Byron's crookit deevil." Above all he was a Scot and a Gordon in his earliest love affair with Mary Duff, a cousin, when both were seven, an idyll to be celebrated in one of his first love poems, "When I Roved a Young Highlander."

Soon after his tenth birthday it all ended and, strangely, he never saw Scotland again. The "Wicked Lord" died on 21 May 1798. His only grandson had been killed in Corsica and George was heir to the barony. So Geordie Gordon became "Dominus de Byron" at the school roll call, and though the first shock of his new identity caused him to burst into tears, he was not displeased to be a lord and a Byron. "Trust Byron," he had once proudly declared, quoting the family motto when about to repay a debt of honor by thrashing a schoolfellow. *Crede Byron* also stood for his truthfulness, loyalty and sense of justice. And now for his English inheritance.

Newstead Abbey might have been created for Byron and his mother. Stuffed as they both were with Gothick tales like Mrs. Radcliffe's *Mysteries of Udolfo,* it was their dream of a perfect ruin. They arrived at the end of August 1798, thus exploring it in the autumn, most Gothick of seasons. They were entranced by the lofty stone façade of the ancient priory (never in fact an abbey). Behind the "yawning arch," traceried windows, high gables and carved finials was — nothing. All hollow. What else should a Gothick ruin be? To the left of the church stood the "battlemented" mansion. There were state rooms, cloisters and the ghost of a headless monk, alternatively of "Little Sir John with the Great Beard," a medieval Byron who haunted the library. But only the scullery had been inhabited. Here the "Wicked Lord" had communed with his tame crickets.

Before the dilapidated mansion stood a fountain, and beyond that a long sheet of water complete with waterfall and the required eighteenth-century forts and follies. The remains of Sherwood Forest surrounded the denuded three thousand acres of the estate. The young lord fell headlong in love with Newstead's haunting beauty and was to fight a losing battle for many years to avoid selling. His mother's income had fallen to £135, and though Byron's elevation to the peerage produced a Civil List, or state pension, it was only £300.

Since his lameness had not improved, he was sent early in 1799 to Nottingham, where he attended a quack named Lavender, trussmaker to the Infirmary, who screwed his leg into a painful wooden frame. His nurse, the bibulous May Gray, sister of Agnes, varied her affairs with chaise-boys by hopping into bed with Byron. "My passions were developed very early," he recalled. He complained of her to his solicitor and agent, John Hanson, who had described him as "a fine sharp Boy," and he was sent away to Dr. Glennie's school in Lordship Lane, Dulwich.

During the holidays his mother still scolded and boxed his ears when he bit his nails, but there were some "brisk gambols" with the Hanson family in Kensington. John Hanson fell for his charm, and so did Hanson's daughter, who noted at once that their guest was "a pretty Boy." His Dulwich schoolfellows found him somewhat too lordly; but Byron may have thought that in selecting a school for him in Lordship Lane his guardian, Lord Carlisle, had been guided by a proper respect for his rank.

The summer days of 1800 and the dark eyes and long lashes of Margaret Parker, a first cousin, produced his "first dash into poetry." Byron long remembered her "*transparent*" beauty, evanescent as a rainbow. She died of consumption in 1802.

Dulwich had become "this damned place" and in the spring term of 1801 Byron went to Harrow, a "public [private] school with 250 boys at it," as he proudly informed his cousin George Byron.

Today it is equally hard to conceive of the deference paid by masters to schoolboys of rank, and the ruffianly behavior of schoolboys towards one another. At the Aberdeen Grammar School Byron's peerage had been announced by the headmaster over congratulatory wine and cake. Dr. Drury, headmaster of Harrow, made a special point of drawing out the spirited but shy young lord — "a mountain colt," as he called him, who could be led if at all only by "a silken string." There was nothing silken in the attitude of Byron's schoolfellows. They would have ridiculed his deformity but for his own effective resort to fisticuffs. Soon it was he who protected boys less bellicose than himself by "licking" or "thrashing" their bullies.

Byron was not happy. "I always *hated* Harrow until the last year and a half," he wrote. He hated the "drill'd dull lesson" and the school discipline. Turbulence was the keynote of his public activities. Even as an orator on Speech Day he himself referred complacently to "my turbulence." His private melancholy would express itself in reverie under an elm in the churchyard, where he lay on a gravestone.

His beloved Newstead had to be let if it was to be restored in time for his twenty-first birthday. Mrs. Byron could at first provide no settled holiday home for her son. At thirteen and fourteen his innate restlessness was exacerbated by continual travel from one holiday base to another: from Piccadilly to Kensington in London to Cheltenham in Gloucestershire to Half Moon Street in London to Bath in Somerset. He liked wearing Turkish costume at a Bath masquerade, but this passing pleasure could not compensate for the presence of "my tormentor" — his mother. When he was fifteen and a half Mrs. Byron rented Burgage Manor at Southwell, twelve miles from Newstead, to be his home for six years. Burgage Manor is a pleasant villa with a sunny garden at the back and in front tall trees and a smooth green. Standing at the remote end of the village, it seems still to enjoy a Jane Austen–like dignity and peace. To Byron it was stagnation. He soon found some greener grass on the other side of the hill.

"Hills of Annesley, hills of Annesley!" Annesley Hall was conspicuous on a rise close to the steward's house at Newstead, where Byron had found a refuge and plenty of pistol shooting away from Southwell. His lovely cousin Mary Chaworth, the heiress of Annesley, was waiting to marry John Musters, a hunting squire and the owner of some of the new stocking frames; but this did not prevent Byron from falling desperately in love with her. Mary treated him as something between a brother and a swain. This might have been endurable, since Byron's etherialized longings for the unattainable were no less imperative than his animal passions. But he heard Mary say to her maid, "Do you think I could care any thing for that lame boy?" The remark was like "a shot through the heart," he said; and some of the lead was to remain in his heart like the Snow Queen's icicle in Kay's, destroying his self-confidence and creating the Byronic myth of love's fatality. By September 1803 he was distraught. His mother considered his state serious enough to warrant his missing the whole of the next term at Harrow. Meanwhile he had been invited to live at Newstead Abbey by his tenant, the personable Lord Grey de Ruthyn.

From this relationship stemmed nothing but trouble. Poor, harassed, misguided Mrs. Byron made advances to

Grey; Grey made advances to a disgusted Byron; while from the past emerged the one human being among these frustrating, infuriating or lascivious people who seemed to understand him. Byron may have met his half sister Augusta during a London holiday in 1802. Now he began writing to her as "a Friend in whom I can confide." He confided the fact of Grey's offense, though he could not bring himself to name its specific nature, even to her.

It would have been happier for Augusta and her "baby Byron," as she called this brother four years her junior, if their relationship had developed from now on uninterruptedly, and therefore in all probability normally. But Augusta was engaged to her first cousin George Leigh. Byron felt it was a mistake. "Can't you drive this Cousin of ours out of your pretty little head?" Augusta, however, was determined on "the matrimonial clog." She married Leigh in 1807, by which time the intimate correspondence with Byron had lapsed. Instead of remaining a true sister and steady confidante she was to become yet another of his "evanescent" dreams, but one which was to reappear in the fatal guise of a lover, gilded by the second separation.

Byron's last, successful year at Harrow was fortunately under way and he could sometimes forget Mary in his protective love for the young lords Clare, De La Warr and Dorset, or commoners of his own age like Edward Noel Long and Thomas Wildman. His lame foot was no longer bandaged but merely supported by an inner shoe. He played in the Harrow–Eton cricket match, scoring eighteen, though with a runner, and got riotously drunk with the team afterwards. He could find mental stimulus in unorthodox philosophical reading, but felt he had to fight one of his schoolfellows for writing "Atheist" under his name. Finally, it was in his last year that he showed his talent for organized rebellion. He had often fired abuse at individual masters. Now he led a mutiny against a new headmaster. To join in the "barring-out" of an unpopular master was not uncommon in those unruly days. To take the lead is always remarkable.

Byron wound up accounts at Harrow by carving his name

in July 1805 on the traditional school wall. He was ready to make a new and deeper mark on the world. As he had written with youthful bombast to his mother the year before: "I will cut myself a path through the world or perish in the attempt. . . . I will carve myself the passage to Grandeur, but never with Dishonour. These Madam are my intentions."

In *Childe Harold* Byron was to speak of his "repugnant youth" and in *Don Juan* of his "hot youth." It was on entering Trinity College, Cambridge, on 24 October 1805 that "repugnant" changed into "hot." Not that he warmed up rapidly. "Yesterday my appearance in the Hall in my State Robes," he wrote on arrival, "was *Superb,* but uncomfortable to my *Diffidence.*" Before he could adjust, the eight-week term was over and Cambridge did not see him again until the summer of 1806: "this place is the *Devil*" — a hell of drunken, disputatious, punning Fellows and licentious undergraduates. No doubt there were exceptions. Edward Noel Long had come up with Byron from Harrow. Together they would ride, swim, lounge, listen to music, "occasionally read" and drink much soda water. John Edleston, a fair-haired, dark-eyed choirboy of Trinity, inspired Byron with a "violent, though *pure,* love and passion," during this, "the most romantic period of my life" — despite Byron's self-confessed "changeable Disposition."

Yet Byron's changeability was uppermost. His hot youth found other congenial outlets. "College is not the place to improve either Morals or Income," he wrote sententiously to Hanson. So whither must he go but London, where his morals immediately took a dive into debauchery and his finances into the clutches of the usurers. Like other young sparks of his day he referred to the latter as "*sordid Bloodsuckers*" and "*Tribe* of *Levi*"; nevertheless his philosophy of sensation did not allow him to live without them.

He stayed first at 16 Piccadilly. The great architect John Nash had not yet built the new Regent Street at the end of

Piccadilly, under whose splendid arcading would soon gather hordes of prostitutes. (The arcades had to be demolished.) But "Paphian goddesses," as Byron called his collection of blue-eyed Carolines and Coras, were never in short supply, and he could rehabilitate himself by frequenting the Bond Street rooms of "Gentleman" Jackson, the boxer, and Henry Angelo, the equally gentlemanly fencing instructor. His landlady, his sister, his mother, and Hanson were all called upon to help raise loans. "Your last Letter, as I expected," he wrote to Hanson, "contained much Advice but no Money." It was all to be in *Don Juan:*

> *Let us have wine and women, mirth and laughter,*
> *Sermons and soda-water the day after.*

Hanson's thankless task included freeing a Byron family estate at Rochdale in Lancashire from the legal entanglements created by the "Wicked Lord," and selling it before the young lord's majority. Hanson never succeeded; but twice while at Cambridge Byron was excited by the news of an imminent sale, first for £30,000, then for £60,000. With such a prospect tantalizingly within reach but never in his grasp, his debt of £10,000 to the moneylenders seemed less outrageous.

Nor was his squandering always selfish. John Edleston and Francis Hodgson, an older Cambridge friend training for the Church, were both indebted to Byron for gifts of money. London, however, was always to suck him into a life-style which neither his income nor his temperament and constitution could sustain. He returned to Cambridge for a second term in May 1806 as a dandy equipped with a carriage, a liveried servant and personal trinkets of silver and gold. Necessity forced him back to Burgage Manor for the rest of 1806, even though his relations with his mother were appalling. For her part, she was worried to death by his extravagance — ". . . ruined; at eighteen!! — Great God . . ." — while he referred to her at best as "Her Ladyship," "the Dowager" or "the old lady"; at worst as "my amiable Alecto" (a Fury with serpent locks), "my Hydra" (a venomous monster with a dog's body), "that Upas Tree" and "the *Beldam*."

Fortunately for both of them Byron found a second home in Southwell with the Pigot family across the green, especially Elizabeth, six years his senior and a sister-substitute for Augusta. We can still see a Byronic trademark there — his name inscribed on the wallpaper — and picture him leaving rapidly by the french window when Elizabeth signaled the approach of callers.

For the next three terms when Byron should have been studying at Cambridge he was agreeably occupied in seeing his first volumes of poetry through the press. *Fugitive Pieces* was privately printed and handed around Southwell by him on 26 November 1806, but later called in and burned, all but four copies. Byron's literary adviser, the Reverend John Becher, had found his description of "panting" in a mistress's arms "rather too warmly drawn." Today Becher's tombstone in Southwell Minster still recalls for us that earliest example of what Thomas Moore, Byron's first full-scale biographer, called Byron's pliability.

Nothing daunted by the all-too-fugitive nature of his *Fugitive Pieces,* Byron was ready with a second version, also privately printed, in January 1807: *Poems on Various Occasions.* Some of the vigorously erotic poetry had been replaced by new verses which even Becher must have realized were now rather too tepidly drawn. It was not till the summer of 1807 that Byron at last submitted his poems to the test of publication. "I have passed the Rubicon," he wrote in the preface, immediately covering himself with the announcement that poetry was "not my primary vocation." This third version, allegedly the fruit of depression, was called *Hours of Idleness.* But the youthful author had been far from idle in other fields.

He had instituted his famous regime of dieting, violent exercise, "*much* physic, and *hot* bathing," which was to reduce his inherited portliness from an incredible 203 pounds to an elegant 147 pounds. From this transformation emerged a slim youth of 5 feet 8½ inches with dark-chestnut curls, blue-gray eyes, cleft chin, marble brow, and a mobile Grecian beauty.

Thus armed with two irresistible assets — enchanting looks and a published oeuvre — Byron returned to Cambridge in the autumn of 1807 for his third and last term. His successes enlarged his friendships. The brilliant John Cam Hobhouse — Byron's much-loved "Hobby" to the end — sharpened his interest in the world of politics, and he became a member of the Cambridge Whig Club. Scrope Berdmore Davies and Charles Skinner Matthews were both scholars and wits, the one devoted to gambling, the other to the lewder classics, while the pious and poetical Francis Hodgson, unlike Becher, became a perfect foil for Byron's daring.

Fortified by this intellectual circle, Byron could better bear the unjustifiably cruel attack upon *Hours of Idleness* by the *Edinburgh Review*. Its anonymous reviewer, Henry Brougham, had dismissed his "effusions" as "so much stagnant water." On the contrary, several features of the poet's maturity could be discerned in these juvenilia, if only as wavering images beneath the surface. There was the "roving" theme, a key to Byron's whole life. There were good imitative passages, though the best, which smacked of John Donne, had been banned. There were lines and rhythms which were to be recycled in later poems. Now it was "A Lady" to whom he protested, "I would not lose you for a world"; in due course it would be "Sweet Florence" of Malta.

With the new year of 1808 Byron was to plunge back for another eighteen months into the maelstrom of London or the nostalgia of Newstead, before his true "roving" began.

Without Byron's marvelously versatile prose his next period in London would sound what it was — depressing and repetitive. But his letters to friends redeem it from banality. "I am buried in an abyss of sensuality," he informed Hobhouse, his company the night before having been "seven whores, a *Bawd* and a *Ballet-master.*" Two days later he was suffering from "literary abuse, pecuniary embarrassment, and total enervation."

Byron's gift for compiling lists undoubtedly produced exaggerations. Southwell had been all "cards and old Maids," "parsons and Methodists"; Cambridge nothing but gaming and drinking, "Hazard and Burgundy, Hunting, Mathematics and Newmarket, Riots and Racing." He could never resist throwing in another vice or two for the sake of alliteration, as in the notorious summary of his London life which at nineteen he had sent to Elizabeth Pigot: "Routs, Riots, Balls & Boxing matches, Dowagers & demireps . . . Parliamentary Discussion, Political Details, Masquerades, Mechanics, Argyle Street Institution & Aquatic races, Love & Lotteries, Brookes's & Buonaparte, Exhibitions of pictures with Drapery, & *women without,* . . . Opera-singers & Orators, Wine, Women, Wax works & Weathercocks."

The wayward weathercock which was Byron, however, had begun in 1808 to set towards the East. As soon as he was twenty-one he aimed at an Eastern *"pilgrimage,"* the regular European grand tour being ruled out by the Napoleonic wars. Greece got a mention in February and by November he pictured himself in Persia and India, having crossed "Mount Caucasus" — that Promethean region of the world which was to feature so prominently in Byron's imagination.

Newstead had once more become his home that autumn after Lord Grey's tenancy terminated. Byron took back with him a load of debt and a lighter burden of literary work. He would need to raise another £4,000 for his travels. His literary labors had proved as therapeutic already as his travels were intended to be hereafter. The *Edinburgh Review,* he felt, had "knocked me down," but, he added, "I got up again." Got up and hit back, milling around, as Gentleman Jackson had taught him, against all and sundry in a "ferocious rhapsody" entitled *English Bards and Scotch Reviewers.* He was revising it at Newstead for publication in March 1809.

Prepare for rhyme — I'll publish, right or wrong:
Fools are my theme, let satire be my song.

Though Byron's theme was "fools," he did not fail to praise the Augustan poets, especially his lifelong idol, Alexander Pope. And among the "fools" he numbered not only Robert Southey, whose "teeming muse" was to be a perpetual thorn in his flesh, but also many poets whom he was later to admire: for instance, "mournful" Walter Scott, "simple" Wordsworth, "turgid" and "tumid" Coleridge, and his own guardian, Lord Carlisle, a poetaster denounced for "paralytic puling." Matthew Gregory Lewis, whose Gothick personality and novel *Ambrosio, or The Monk* were to influence Byron in the future, now got short shrift. He wrote of "spectre-mongering" Lewis:

Even Satan's self with thee might dread to dwell,
And in thy skull discern a deeper hell.

Skulls were much in Byron's mind at this time. The Newstead gardener had accidentally dug up what Byron took to be the skull of "some jolly friar or a monk of the abbey, about the time it was demonasteried." He had it polished and mounted as a drinking cup. As for his own skull, he felt that he might have to blow his brains out unless his finances improved.

Still on the subject of death, his favorite black-and-white Newfoundland dog, Boatswain, went mad that November and was buried in a garden tomb designed to receive his master also in due course. "I have now lost everything," he wrote pathetically, "except Old Murray," the family major-domo. There was one thing, however, of which he would have welcomed the loss: his obsessive love for Mary Chaworth-Musters.

He had dined with Mary and John Musters in their home that autumn, only to find his passion for her still tormentingly alive. Indeed, his pain almost equaled the agony he had felt at sixteen on hearing that little Mary Duff was married.

On that occasion he had fallen into "convulsions." Now he wrote a poem to Mary Chaworth-Musters describing how he too, like Adam when banished from Paradise, might resort to "wandering on through distant climes." The presence of Mary, he confessed, was to him an unparalleled "temptation."

The question inevitably arises, was it from Mary, from himself, or from some third person that Byron was "escaping" when he expressed an ever fiercer resolve to go abroad? He revealed to Hanson in April 1809 the existence of "circumstances" that rendered it "absolutely indispensable" for him to quit the country immediately. And writing from Greece seven months later he was to tell Hanson, "I never will live in England if I can avoid it, *why* must remain a secret." He added that the "secret" reason was not a wish to escape from his creditors or literary critics.

The key to Byron's "secret" may well be his passion for Mary Chaworth-Musters. His sister Augusta did not underestimate its dangerous strength. When he eventually returned to England from abroad Augusta dissuaded him from meeting Mary again. "For," said she, "if you do so you will fall in love again, and there will be a scene." Byron's thoughts are often impenetrable, interwoven as they were with historical and family memories, traditions, taboos, superstitions, and all kinds of strange imaginings. Who knows but that he sometimes dreamed of yielding to the "temptation" to possess Mary by force, of fighting a duel with her husband (Byron was more than once to contemplate dueling), of firing a fatal pistol shot, of being tried for murder by his peers and receiving a sentence, unlike his ancestor the "Wicked Lord," of death or transportation?

It is suggested by Professor Marchand that Byron "had a wish to escape his own proclivities toward attachment to boys, or perhaps that he feared a closer connection with the Cambridge choirboy Edleston, who had wanted to live with him in London." On the first point, Byron can hardly have wished to escape his own homosexual tendencies by going to the East, where such things were countenanced; indeed, he made several jokes about "Paederasty" in farewell letters, which seemed to indicate that he was looking forward to homosexual adventures. But by leaving England he would escape the risk of the law and the death penalty. If Edleston was the key to the "secret," Byron may have wished to escape from the boy's excessive devotion to himself, and not his to Edleston. His Cambridge friend was a consumptive, already "very thin" in 1807, and possibly consumed as much by typical jealousy and possessiveness as by his disease.

Whatever the exact ingredients of his "secret" reason for escape, Byron's resolution of 1809 stood firm: "England is not for me" — neither its people nor its customs. He had even fled temporarily from home to avoid the traditional junketings for his coming-of-age on 22 January 1809: ale and punch for the tenants; "an Ox and two Sheep to tear in pieces, with *Ale,* and *Uproar*" for the "rabble."

On 13 March he took his seat in the House of Lords, a convinced supporter of Catholic Emancipation or the right of Roman Catholics to sit in Parliament, a tenet of Whig and Radical faith. In other ways he was to preserve his independence from both political parties. "I shall stand aloof," he said, still feeling as during his minority, "a Citizen of the World." In April he gave a farewell party at Newstead for his particular friends, which was to become a legend of orgiastic drinking, masquerading as monks, romping with his tame bear brought from Cambridge ("he should *sit* for a *Fellowship*") or entertaining his "Paphian girls," whom Thomas Moore astutely guessed were in reality the Newstead housemaids. (Byron had already got a son by "Lucinda," and had provided her with £100 a year.)

Soon afterwards Scrope Davies raised a loan for him on a gambling win. Travel money at last! Byron in turn lent enough to the impecunious Hobhouse for him to come too. The pair sailed from Falmouth in Cornwall on 2 July 1809. Byron's somber mood may be gauged from his farewell letter to Francis Hodgson, in which he again compared himself with the character to whom he felt increasingly akin: "I am like Adam, the first convict sentenced to transportation . . . and thus ends my first chapter. Adieu."

TWO

"The Air of Greece"
(1809–1811)

SHELLEY was to call Byron the "Pilgrim of Eternity." In his first pilgrimage to the East, however, Byron was very much a genius of time and space, of the here and now. Avid of new sensations, he reacted to good and bad alike with brilliant spontaneity rather than deep reflection.

Once aboard the Lisbon packet his mournful mood changed into a rollicking "Huzza," despite the seasickness of his three servants, Hobhouse and himself:

> Fletcher! Murray! Bob! where are you?
>   Stretch'd along the deck like logs — . .
> Hobhouse muttering fearful curses,
>   As the hatchway down he rolls,
> Now his breakfast, now his verses
>   Vomits forth — and damns our souls.

Fletcher was his valet, to whom foreigners were anathema and his master always a hero; Joe Murray was his major-domo; and Bob, the fifteen-year-old son of a Newstead tenant, was Robert Rushton, the "little page" of *Childe Harold*. They were speedily in Lisbon, where Byron found many pleasures — luscious fruit, monkish conversation, the need to carry arms and use foreign oaths, and a testing swim. "I am very happy here," he told Hodgson, "because I loves oranges and talks bad latin to the monks . . . and I goes into society (with my pocket pistols), and I swims in the Tagus all across at once . . . and swears Portuguese." Mastering the tidal Tagus from Old Lisbon to Fort Belem was no small feat; even on a calm day the currents splash and suck around the ancient walls. His monks were at baroque Mafra, a palace containing one of the great libraries of Europe.

In Cintra, the celebrated beauty spot above Lisbon which reminded him of the West Highlands, Byron felt he had now seen all that nature and man could offer: the crags and cork trees shaggy with mountain moss, the leaping torrents and remote unruffled sea, the "toppling convent," the lines of Moorish battlements threading the forests, and, most Gothick and thrilling of all, the Quinta do Ramalhão where once had dwelt William Beckford, author of *Vathek* and notorious creator of the accursed pre-Adamite sultan of that name. The sight of Beckford's abandoned home struck an immediate chord in Byron:

> But now, as if a thing unblest by Man,
> Thy Fairy dwelling is as lone as thou!

Here were several Byronic ingredients for the Gothick cauldron, especially the poignancy of "deserted halls" and the sense of having once been blessed but now being cursed and alone.

The travelers decided to make what Byron called "a gentle Gallop of four hundred miles without intermission through Portugal & Spain," before picking up a ship at Cádiz. They covered seventy miles a day in the scorching sun, a most creditable performance and indeed Wellington's own much-admired regular score during the Peninsular War, which he was then fighting. If the village of Cintra was "perhaps the most delightful in Europe" (the "perhaps" was wise in view of Byron's limited experience) Seville was fine despite its being crammed with a wartime population, while Cádiz was "the prettiest and cleanest town in Europe" and its women the most seductively yet decently dressed "in the world." Byron left Seville on 28 July, the day of the Battle of Talavera. For a moment he was tempted to drop in on Wellington, but he felt he must hurry on, reserving till a later date his grim lines on the three armies which combined "to feed the crow on Talavera's plain."

Doña Josepha Beltram of Seville and her sister had kindly shared their accommodation with the travelers — all four in one small room — Josepha inviting Byron in the middle of the night to share her bed also. While he declined this honor, he exchanged one of his curls for a thick tress of her dark hair, "about three feet in length." Josepha had addressed him as "*tu hermoso*" (you pretty fellow), and the Spanish admiral's daughter in Cádiz audaciously seated him in her chaperon's chair at the opera. Like Miss Hanson long ago in Kensington, they all fell for the "pretty Boy."

From Gibraltar Murray and Rushton were sent home, as being unfitted by age and youth for the anticipated "fatigues" of the pilgrimage. Byron loved his page. He deducted £25 a year from his father's rent for the boy's education. Judging by his underlinings in a letter to Mrs. Byron, his real reason for sending Robert home was fear lest the Turks should love him too: "you *know boys* are not *safe* among the Turks."

While waiting for the packet to carry him from Gibraltar to Malta, he proposed to take in another continent, Africa, whose coastline he had seen from the sea. But the winds proved contrary. Each evening he and Hobhouse would climb the Rock to watch the sunset, Byron gradually sinking, like the sun, into one of his periodic glooms. When they sailed he was observed somewhat caustically by a fellow traveler and writer, John Galt, to spend his time alone on deck in a "rapt mood" — except while smashing empty bottles with his pistols.

Malta roused him once more from "poetical sympathy" (Galt again) to human passion. In British hands since 1799, Malta had been reduced according to Hobhouse by this nation of shopkeepers to "a large warehouse." Byron saw it simply as a setting for the lovely Constance Spencer Smith. (His reception by the governor, though courteous, had disappointed him, for in his juvenile naivety he had expected the *Lord* Byron to be welcomed with a salute of guns.)

Mrs. Spencer Smith was a strapping cosmopolitan beauty, daughter of Baron Herbert, the Austrian ambassador in Constantinople, and now at twenty-four unhappily married to an English diplomat. She had plotted against Napoleon but escaped his "vengeance" by flight. When the governor's aide-de-camp made some "grinning" insinuations about her new romance, Byron courageously proposed a duel. Fortunately his own "vengeance" faded out like Napoleon's and the affair was settled amicably, chiefly because his ship for Greece was about to sail: "& so I escaped murder and adultery."

On 21 September he and Hobhouse left Malta in the brig-of-war *Spider* for western Greece. At this point their "grand tour" proper began. Byron and Constance had arranged a tryst at Malta in a year's time, for this was to be his *"everlasting* passion." As we shall see, however, Byron had no everlasting passion but the freedom of mountains and waters, and the liberation of men and nations.

What signs were there of Byron's development during these first eleven weeks abroad? There were obeisances to ideas of "honor" (the duel) and exhibitions of physical courage and endurance. There were also abstinence (meatless meals) and an increasing astringency in his prose, with a withdrawal from the romantic convention of purple passages: "but damn description," he wrote in Spain, "it is always disgusting."

He was already miscalculating the importance of romantic love to his own life, but showing his loyalty to old and

deep affections. The series of dutiful, frank, and witty letters to his mother seem to obliterate the period of his intense aversion. Finally there was emerging the contrast between his two personalities, already noted with surprise by
John Galt: the "forbidding" introvert, soon to become
Childe Harold; and the "playful" companion "sparkling
with quaint sentences," eventually to become Don Juan.

Two days after leaving Malta the pilgrims caught sight of
their holy land — Greece. It was a mountain range of the
Morea (Peloponnesus) towering above Patras, the *Spider*'s
first port of call. Passing between the Ionian islands of
Cephalonia and Zante, they anchored on the morning of 26
September in the Gulf of Patras, the captain kindly landing
Byron and Hobhouse in a currant ground outside the town,
so that they might spend the inside of that first day on the
sacred soil of classical Greece. Hobhouse recorded: "on the
right, the North, saw the town of Mesaloge." Missolonghi
was the last town Byron saw before he died.

In the currant ground the pilgrims immediately fell to
target shooting. Then they met Mr. Strané, the British vice-
consul and a Greek by nationality, with whom Byron did
business. Hobhouse was delighted with Strané personally —
"a good kind man very ugly" — but as an embryo politician
Hobhouse deplored the British custom of employing native
Greeks as vice-consuls instead of strengthening their position
in these Turkish dominions, as the French did, by sending
out their own nationals. All the "Eastern" lands which Byron visited between 1809 and 1811 lay within the ever-totter-
ing Ottoman Empire — Greece proper, Albania, Turkey in
Europe, and Asia Minor. Only the Ionian Islands were an
exception; until recently French, they were in process of being taken over by the British.

That evening the *Spider* carried Byron and Hobhouse
northwards towards Prevesa on the coast of Epirus in north-
western Greece. As they sailed past two more of the Ionian
Islands, Byron listened to Hobhouse reading aloud from the

Odyssey and enjoyed melancholy thoughts of Penelope's lonely vigil on Ithaca and of Sappho's death leap from the cliff of Levkas. Greece in legend enchanted him; Greece in archaeology was a bore and a reproach. Why did the land of his dreams lie desolate and half buried? At Nicopolis he was more beguiled by the sound of frogs and sheep bells than by the sight of Augustus Caesar's "Victory City" in ruins. As for the victory over Antony and Cleopatra which that city had commemorated, again Byron found the moonlight over Actium Bay far lovelier than any vision of the fleeing Cleopatra — "a queen of forty."

Ioannina was now the travelers' goal. After sleeping rough, twice in a barrack and once in a customhouse, they descended on 5 October through the mountains of Epirus to the beautiful town, glittering among its olive groves and minarets on the shores of Lake Pambotis. Even the sight of a Greek patriot's arm dangling from a plane tree outside a butcher's shop could not entirely destroy their exhilaration.

The arm was the work of Ali Pasha, "Lion of Ioannina," the Turkish despot of all Albania and western Greece as far south as the Peloponnesus. In thirteen years' time Ali himself would be liquidated in Ioannina by the sultan's soldiers. When Byron arrived the Lion of Ioannina had just left his capital to make "a little war" from Tepelenë, his Albanian base. Byron and Hobhouse were ceremoniously received by his ten-year-old grandson, who inquired, his huge black eyes round with astonishment, how one so young as Byron could travel without a "Lala" (tutor or guardian). A shrewd question. Hobhouse was in fact to become Byron's Lala, and like all such, occasionally to prove irksome.

After purchasing two "magnifique" Albanian suits and a *capote* or cloak worn by the neighboring Suliot tribe of rugged mountaineers, Byron decided to visit Ali at Tepelenë. He had already seen and heard much which was later to garnish his Oriental poems: celebrations of Ramadan and Bairam, yataghans and turbans, daggers and pistols crammed into belts and the story of the Greek girl Euphrosyne "sacked" (sewn in a sack) at Ali's command and drowned in Lake Pambotis.

The first lap on Byron's journey to Tepelenë should have taken four hours. His goal was the monastery of Zitza, clinging to a mountaintop in the Pindus range — a prospect, as Byron wrote in *Childe Harold,* "to shock and please the soul." On that evening, however, it was all shock. A violent thunderstorm caught him lingering and caused his guide to panic and lose the way. Near a Turkish burial ground Byron proceeded to compose a lyric to "Florence" — Mrs. Spencer Smith. It was 3 A.M. before he reached Zitza, still in the highest spirits; and a week before the party scrambled out of the crags and gorges, the huts and cowhouses infested by Albanian lice, "the biggest in the world," into Ali's sumptuous headquarters.

The tyrant, posing as a white-bearded patriarch, plied the handsome young aristocrat with sherbet and fruit and paid him absurd compliments in Latin as they sat side by side in the marble hall. Those curls, those "small ears and little white hands," were sure signs of high birth. Would Byron visit him at night "when he was at leisure"? But the role of the pursued by either sex was never acceptable to Byron. He and his party returned unscathed to "Monastic Zitza." Here he spent a chaste night. So pleasant was his company to the monks and his kindness to the peasants that the monks' successors placed a plaque on their outside wall on 19 April 1924, the centenary of the death of their friend "Lordos Byronos."

Back in Ioannina the travelers' sightseeing included another black-eyed grandson of Ali and a vast unidentified amphitheatre. If Hobhouse, the antiquarian of the party, had spotted this as ancient Dodona, Byron might have forgiven him much. For it was one of his deepest reproaches that sacred Dodona had been "all, all forgotten."

In a mood of melancholy to which many things contributed — inherited temperament, aimlessness, the fate of ancient and modern Greece — Byron sat down in Ioannina on

31 October 1809 to tell the story of his own pilgrimage in poetry, before that too, like Dodona, was forgotten. He chose the Spenserian stanza, a lingering rather than a marching meter. To emphasize the Gothick element, the poem was called "A Romaunt," and its hero "Childe Burun" — Burun being an ancient version of the name Byron. In the end Burun was dropped and the poem which was to make him famous became *Childe Harold's Pilgrimage.* "If I am a poet . . ." he was to say, "the air of Greece has made me one."

It was now time to return to Patras and from there head for Athens. Warning the travelers against bandits, Ali had lent them a Turkish vessel with four guns and, luckily, four Greeks among the crew. During a gale the Turkish captain lost control but handed over the helm to the maritime-minded Greeks, who saved them all from shipwreck by running into a rocky bay near Parga. Byron had remained snug in his Suliot capote during the night's hubbub, enjoying it quite as much as the Zitza thunderstorm. On landing they were rescued by a band of Suliots — "robbers" to the world but saviors to them. When Byron offered them a reward their chief replied, "No, I wish you to love me, not to pay me." As they passed Actium again, where Antony had lost the world for love, Byron addressed to "Florence" the line which had already done service to another — "But would not lose thee for a world." Both ladies were to be lost to Byron without a tear.

From Prevesa they hired a bodyguard of fifty Suliots to escort them through the Acarnanian hinterland to Missolonghi, and so by sea to Patras. The best things in marshy Missolonghi were its tiny fish rolls, though only Hobhouse praised them. Byron had nothing whatever to say about this fateful town.

Eager as Byron was to reach Athens, he could not resist going the long way round, over the Parnassus massif instead of by Corinth, in order to see Delphi. Sacred Delphi was as much a disappointment as sacred Dodona, for though its site was well known, scarcely any of its antiquities were above-ground. A fallen pillar of the gymnasium bore the name of Aberdeen, the future prime minister. Byron and Hobhouse inscribed their own names, drank the waters of the Castalian spring without relish, and set off again, up and over Parnassus, for the Boeotian plain. They had seen, recorded Byron mistakenly, "all that Delphi contained."* Parnassus itself had given Byron the most pleasure: its "wild pomp of mountain majesty" and the flight of "twelve Eagles" above it, which he took to be a sign that Apollo accepted his offering of *Childe Harold* — until his irritating Lala pointed out that they were only Egyptian vultures.

The pilgrims passed many ancient shrines on their way southwards. Near Livadia was the alleged Cave of Tryphonius, which had sheltered an oracle, and in Thebes was St. Luke's tomb, some of whose crumbling stones Byron's Albanian servant Vasilly reverently scraped into his tobacco box. Byron had met in Livadia a free-thinking Greek bishop who denounced the Mass as cant. "It is impossible to think better of him for this." If Byron had had to choose between the bishop and Vasilly, he would have been on the side of superstition.

On Christmas Eve they spent the night if not in a stable at any rate in a wretched hut next door to one. In sublime contrast, they had their first breathtaking vision of Athens on Christmas Day. "The plain of Athens," wrote Byron later, "Pentelicus, Hymettus, the Aegean, and the Acropolis, burst upon the eye at once" — framed by the pine trees on Fort Phyle. Byron was well aware that in ancient, heroic times the Greek patriot Thrasybulus had marched out from this same fort to rescue Athens from the rule of tyrants.

They rode into the walled city at eight-thirty that evening and lodged with Mrs. Tarsia Macri, widow of the former "British" vice-consul. Byron was immediately very happy, falling in love with all her three daughters but especially the youngest, Theresa, who was to become his "Maid of Athens."

* Delphi was not excavated until the end of the century.

None of the three was yet fifteen, Theresa only twelve.

At first it was pleasure enough to ride out each day, either down to the peaceful harbor of Piraeus or up one or other of the immemorial mountains, Pentelicus, Hymettus, and Parnes, which encircled Athens. The town was poor and relatively small (ten thousand inhabitants), having long ago lost the dynamism of classical times. Under the Acropolis Greek women would gather wild salads for their many fast days, while parties of Turks sat quietly on their carpets in the shade of ruined columns. Unlike Hobhouse, Byron did not need to step out the distance around the walls (a mere forty-seven minutes' walk) or "potter with map and compass at the foot of Pindus, Parnes, and Parnassus" to find the site of a temple or an ancient city. "I rode my mule up them," said Byron simply. "They had haunted my dreams from boyhood; the pines, the eagles, vultures, and owls were descended from those Themistocles and Alexander had seen."

But soon Byron could not escape the fact that all was far from well with the land of Themistocles. Venetian and Turkish cannon had reduced the gleaming Acropolis to a mass of broken marble, among which several wretched hovels and goat sheds huddled against such pillars of the Propylaea, Parthenon and Erechtheum as were still standing. Byron's Scottish compatriot, Lord Elgin, was busily bringing back to England shiploads of sculptures, and Napoleon had also seized his portion. Worse still in Byron's opinion, many penurious and "degenerate" Greeks thought it was a good thing, since Lord Elgin paid handsomely.

Of course his Lala did not agree with him, and declared that modern architects and sculptors would learn more from the Greek friezes if they were in a British or French museum than if they languished on the Acropolis, to be "ground to powder" by the Turks. Byron retorted that the British were as likely to become artists as the Egyptians to become skaters. In 1815 French workmen were to sob as they carried statues from the Louvre for restoration to Italy. In 1810 Hobhouse saw Greek workmen refusing to carry a statue to Lord Elgin's ship because they thought they heard the statue itself sobbing at the prospect of exile.

Byron's indignation was fueled by his knowledge that not all Greeks accepted the enslavement of their country and the spoliation of their treasures. It was true that the ablest of them held minor office as *codja-bashis* or civil governors under the Turks. Though they kept their religion they had adopted many Turkish customs. For instance, while Byron and Hobhouse stayed with Andreas Londos, the young Greek codja-bashi of Vostitza, they never once set eyes on his family. Nevertheless they soon discovered that the flame of liberty was only waiting to be ignited. Stirred by some political reference, Londos had suddenly sprung to his feet and burst into the Greek war song *"Deute paides ton Hellenon,"* set to the tune of the Marseillaise and later translated by Byron as "Sons of the Greeks, arise!" Londos was to be a leader in the War of Independence which first broke out at Patras, and Byron knew there were others with the same aspirations in Athens.

Two visits to Sounion and one to Marathon in 1810 concentrated Byron's feelings of shame at the degradation of modern Greece. Sounion or Colonni, the romantic Attic cape overlooking the lovely isles of the Cyclades, was the site of a ruined temple. Here Byron did little more than carve his name on an already much-inscribed fallen pillar (now re-erected) and narrowly escaped the attentions of some pirates. But his indignation at Greece's plight was to crystallize in *Don Juan* as his greatest lyric:

> *The isles of Greece, the isles of Greece!*
>   *Where burning Sappho loved and sung,*
> *Where grew the arts of war and peace,*
>   *Where Delos rose, and Phoebus sprung!*
> *Eternal summer gilds them yet,*
> *But all, except their sun, is set.*

Marathon, the historic field of victory over the Persians, was also celebrated in "The Isles of Greece":

> *The mountains look on Marathon —*
>   *And Marathon looks on the sea;*
> *And musing there an hour alone,*
>   *I dream'd that Greece might still be free;*
> *For standing on the Persians' grave,*
>   *I could not deem myself a slave.*

During the first half of February Byron was working at *Childe Harold* in the Macris' home, while Hobhouse did some more "pottering" with map and compass in Euboea. Suddenly a message was brought to them on 4 March by Dr. Francis Darwin, uncle of the great Charles, from the sloop-of-war *Pylades,* offering them an immediate passage to Smyrna. Byron tore himself away the very next afternoon but not without a "tear," as Hobhouse noted, at quitting "his beloved Athens."

Apart from the tear, Byron's emotions, as always, went into his poetry. A few weeks ago his idealized love for Theresa Macri had caused him to break off in imagination his affair with "Sweet Florence": "The spell is broke, the charm is flown!" Now it was Theresa's spell which had to be broken:

> *Maid of Athens, ere we part,*
> *Give, oh give me back my heart!*

Byron had "topographized" Attica, as he put it, in a matter of ten weeks. He intended to topographize those parts of Turkey to which an obliging warship and his own inclination would carry him. Afterwards he was to call this tour "My Grand Giro."

Asia Minor did not at first impress. On an excursion to Ephesus they had to sleep once more in a stable to avoid the overcrowded company of humans, but next morning they could not escape the performance of a Dervish who interspersed his monotonous prayers with sly "indecencies." Byron much preferred the howling of the jackals. In Ephesus Hobhouse found some bricks and granite which he took to be the far-famed Temple of Diana. Byron absolved himself from any participation. "I smoke and stare at mountains, and twirl my mustachios very independently." He was becoming quite Turkish, what with his long pipe, his one "horrible oath" and his masterly inactivity. He had finished his second canto on 28 March and was not to add to *Childe Harold* for six years.

After transferring to the frigate *Salsette,* he permitted Hobhouse to read aloud to him from Homer's *Iliad,* preparatory to exploring the plain of Troy for signs of ancient Ilium. Byron professed to have seen nothing but three huge barrows, supposedly the tombs of heroes, though Hobhouse managed to fill five whole chapters of his travelogue with descriptions and arguments against the theories of previous travelers. When they reached the Hellespont, however, Byron astonished his party, and later the world, by becoming what he ironically called a *"celebrated aquatic genius."* On 16 April he and Lieutenant William Eckenhead of the *Salsette* attempted to swim the channel from Sestos to Abydos, but were defeated by the cold. They tried again on 3 May and succeeded, Byron crossing in one hour and ten minutes, Eckenhead in five minutes less.

In a sense this was the proudest moment of Byron's life. As he said, there was no lovely Hero, no mistress on the other side to encourage him, though the ever-faithful Hobhouse read Ovid's *Hero and Leander* while his comrade was in the water. Friends at home who had hitherto received few or no letters from Byron suddenly got glowing accounts of his "feat," laced with saucy reflections. Surely Leander's "conjugal powers" must have been impaired by his nightly "journeys to Paradise"? After due reflection Byron was able to write to Hodgson two months later: "I plume myself on this achievement more than I could possibly do on any kind of glory, political, poetical or rhetorical." On the day of the swim he had declared, "I have renounced scribbling." Perhaps he would not have been displeased to learn that, in the future, thousands of people who had never read a line of *Childe Harold* would know about Byron swimming the Hellespont.

His burst of euphoria carried him into an ebullient schoolboyish appreciation of the Turks (he was writing to Henry Drury, son of his Harrow headmaster) : "I see not much difference between ourselves & the Turks, save that we have foreskins and they none, that they have long dresses and we short, and that we talk much and they little.* In England the vices in fashion are whoreing & drinking, in Turkey, Sodomy & smoking, we prefer a girl and a bottle, they a pipe and pathic [catamite]. . . . I like the Greeks, who are plausible rascals, with all the Turkish vices [but] without their courage. — However some are brave and all are beautiful."

Swimming the Hellespont seems to have temporarily convinced Byron that after all he was a virile Englishman with duties and ambitions. He informed two friends that on returning home he intended to cut all boon companions, wine, and "carnal company," and "betake myself to politics and Decorum." A third friend was asked to send him English political news. "Have the military murdered any more mechanics?" Was the Radical leader Sir Francis Burdett released from prison? Then the "quicksilver" would dart in another direction, Byron loftily calling himself "a citizen of the world." In any case, there was still Constantinople to be seen.

Not even Cintra or Athens could equal the prospect of Constantinople between the frowning prison of the Seven Towers and the end of the Golden Horn. He reveled in his rides along the Valley of Sweet Waters and around the huge triple walls, covered with ivy and flanked by Turkish burial grounds, "the loveliest spots on earth." (Hobhouse's approach to the famous wall was also characteristic. "I was induced to time myself, in passing under the wall from one point to another, and found the walk to have lasted one hour and seventeen minutes.") They were both lukewarm about Hagia Sophia, though Hobhouse had to admit the dome was fifteen feet wider than St. Paul's. Byron felt what he called a *"cockney"* prejudice in favor of the latter, but — "I prefer the

---

* Byron's phraseology echoes Dr. John Moore's *Zeluco* (1789), on the difference between blacks and whites.

Gothic Cathedral of Seville to St. P's, St. Sophia's and any religious building I have ever seen."

There were also things each of them disliked. Both were repelled by a dog gnawing a dead body and other dogs wolfing the heaps of garbage which stood at every street corner. These "lean dogs" were to find a place in Byron's *Siege of Corinth*. The dancing boys of Galata revolted Hobhouse, and he was saddened by the total absence of street names, lamps and a post office. Byron's chief complaint was less worthy. He and Hobhouse were invited to the palace of the sultan on the morning of the British ambassador's official farewell. In a fit of youthful arrogance, Byron had expected that his rank would entitle him to a higher place in the procession than the ambassador's secretary, Mr. Stratford Canning, whose first cousin, incidentally, was the British foreign secretary and had stamped Byron's passport before he left England. Turkish protocol, however, thought otherwise. Byron sulked for several days but eventually rode behind Mr. Canning.* The occasion hardly rewarded him.

They had to get up before 4:30 A.M. and by choice Byron was a very late riser. Over the outer gates were niches for criminals' heads and a rubbish dump at the side for the bodies. On the way in they were mercilessly squeezed and their toes trodden on, not an agreeable experience for Byron's lame foot. In the presence of the twenty-four-year-old sultan, Mahmoud II, two eunuchs held Byron and Hobhouse tightly by the arm. And it was five and a half hours, most of them spent standing, before they got anything to eat. If Byron remembered these things when he was defying the sultan from Missolonghi it would have added zest to his war.

His love life had come to an end, for relations with women were impossible in Turkey and with his Lala around the al-

* Born two years before Byron, Stratford Canning became Lord Stratford de Redcliffe, living well into his nineties. In 1880 he met the English poet Wilfrid Scawen Blunt and talked of Byron, saying that he had played against Byron in the famous Harrow-Eton cricket match, and in Constantinople had ridden with Byron every day, finding him "very agreeable" and nothing "*scabreux*" in his conversation.

ternative was barred. More distressing, a letter arrived from Hodgson which Hobhouse summarized in his diary: "Tales spread — the *Edleston* is accused of indecency." (Not, presumably, with Byron, whose passion for Edleston we have seen was "violent" but *"pure."*)

His financial affairs were so much embroiled that a continuation of the pilgrimage into Persia and India seemed hopeless. Since he was paying for Hobhouse also, his friend decided to return home. For Byron, a more consoling future beckoned. A return to Greece.

The *Salsette* dropped Byron off at the island of Keos in the Cyclades on 17 July, whence he quickly made his way to Athens, after a sentimental parting from Hobhouse. The friends divided a bunch of wild flowers between them, and Hobhouse said good-bye "not without tears." The absence of Hobhouse meant changes in Byron's habits. Without a Lala, ever informative and efficient (Hobhouse had always done the packing and organized the tours), Byron had to make his own intellectual friends. And with the watchful British eye removed he could live if he wished according to the fashion of the Turks — or of the Greeks, for that matter, who possessed "all the Turkish vices."

First, however, he must avoid a certain fashion at the Villa Macri: the maternal right to push a daughter into wedlock or to take money in lieu of marriage. Unwilling either to marry or to buy the Maid of Athens, Byron rapidly moved his lodgings to the Capuchin Convent (monastery) under the Acropolis, before escaping for a flying tour of the Morea.

Beneath the surface of his "girating" life he was constructing, like an exotic coral reef, the material for his future Levantine tales — the *Siege of Corinth, The Giaour, The Corsair,* and *Lara.* On the surface, he was having an affair with a young Greek named Eustathius Georgiou, who accompanied him on horseback from Vostitza to Patras and back to Tripolitza, "clothed very sprucely in Greek Garments, with those ambrosial curls hanging down his amiable back, and to my utter astonishment and the great abomination of Fletcher, a *parasol* in his hand to shade his complexion from the heat."

Eustathius proved too temperamental a companion even for Byron, with his quarrels, kissing, and tumblings on the sofa, besides being an epileptic. He was sent home from Tripolitza, where Ali Pasha's son Veli held sway. Hardly had Byron dealt with his "amiable boy" before he was faced by the embarrassing attentions of Veli Pasha himself: "He has an awkward manner of throwing his arm round one's waist, and squeezing one's hand in *public*." The temptation to tease Hobhouse with accounts of the double saga was irresistible. His deliberate use of the Greek word for boy, together with his request that Hobhouse should tell their friend "Citoyen" Matthews, known for his revolutionary views and expertise in classical sex, about Eustathius, could mean only one thing to scholars of ancient Greece.*

"You cannot conceive what a delightful companion you are," Byron continued to tease Hobhouse, "now you are gone." And in a later letter: "After all I do love thee, Hobby, thou hast so many good qualities and so many bad ones it is impossible to live with or without thee."

Life in the Capuchin Convent directed Byron's homosexual feelings into more playful channels. The convent was a school for Frankish (Western) boys as well as a hostel for travelers. There were six boarders, and with these "ragazzi" there would be great "scamperings and eating fruit and peltings and playing and I am in fact at school again." Even the convent washerwomen joined in the fun, sticking laundry pins into Fletcher's backside. "We have nothing but riots," wrote Byron, "from noon till night." His affair with a black-eyed beauty, possibly a Turkish girl, was matched by the "fooling" of his Greek interpreter with Dudu Roque, a cousin of the three Macri girls, and of Vasilly with Marianna

---

* Another message to Matthews was that Byron had had "above two hundred pl & opt CS —" (*plenum et optabilem coitum*), which is dog Latin for full sexual satisfaction.

Macri, while the rest of his staff, including Fletcher, had their mistresses. "Vive l'Amour!"

Byron's especial favorite among the "ragazzi" was Nicolo Giraud. He had first taken up with Nicolo while Hobhouse was away in Euboea the year before, but there is no evidence that his feelings for Nicolo were anything but romantic and protective. He was to leave a substantial sum of money for Nicolo's education. This charming sixteen-year-old was the brother-in-law of Lord Elgin's agent, Giovanni Lusieri, and linked Byron with a vastly more talented circle in Athens than any he had yet known, including Danish and German archaeologists. The only distinguished visitor he took against was Lady Hester Stanhope, niece of the Younger Pitt — but then, Byron never liked "that dangerous thing a female wit." Seated in the octagonal Monument of Lysicrates, a classical building incorporated into the convent, he would study Italian and modern Greek, just as he was to learn Armenian in a Venetian monastery six years hence.

With Nicolo, Byron would do the twenty minutes' ride every day to Piraeus and then swim for an hour in the bay. Afterwards they would sit on some promontory overlooking the blue Aegean and isles of Greece, Nicolo silent and attentive, Byron brooding over the stuff of his tales. As he wrote to his mother, "My nature leads me to solitude."

On one of these return rides from Piraeus an incident occurred which burned itself into Byron's memory. Some soldiers and officials passed him on their way to the harbor. His suspicions aroused, he inquired what was afoot. To his horror he was told that a Turkish girl had lived with a *giaour** during a fast. Here she was, sewn in a sack and about to be thrown into the sea. Byron interceded with the authorities and saved her life, sending her to a convent in Boeotia; but she died soon afterwards. If this was the black-eyed beauty whose imminent seduction he had notified to Hobhouse,

---

* *Giaour* ("that unpronounceable name," as Byron wrote) rhymed with *hour,* and was the Eastern word for any infidel. A Christian was a giaour and so was an Indian, as in Beckford's *Vathek.*

Byron may have believed that he caused her death. In which case he would have added this "crime" to his vicarious ancestral guilt and felt doubly justified in telling his wife he was a murderer. Among many nightmares in 1815, the worst was of a dead woman pursuing him. The story of a drowned Turkish girl such as Byron rescued, and of her haunted lover, is told with creepy conviction in his poem *The Giaour*.

Nicolo accompanied Byron on a second "giro" of the Morea that autumn. It was lucky that Nicolo was with him, for his devoted nursing brought Byron through a "malignant fever." He drew from this experience the erroneous conclusion that no fever, however serious, would carry him off.

As usual, in February the brief Athenian winter began, a little snow fell in the plains, flights of wild turkey and woodcock (Byron's favorite dish) came in from the mountains, and his cosmopolitan friends moved out. His own restlessness — "a Gipsy-like wandering disposition" — was always apt to reassert itself; and with money so preposterously tight, it might be as well to wander home. At the same time, the indolent or contented side of his nature urged him to stay.

It was April before he finally made the move. Mrs. Macri's positively last offer of 30,000 piastres for Theresa was rejected and Byron set sail for Malta on the twenty-second with a distinctly Gothick collection of diseases and trophies: "an *Ague,* & a *Clap,* and the *Piles,* all at once," four Athenian skulls, four live tortoises, a serpent-ring carrying a drop of poison in the golden jaws, and a draft of the Attic type of hemlock which had killed Socrates.

The intense heat of Malta together with persistent ill health must have made it easier to intimate to Mrs. Spencer Smith that "the spell was broke, the charm flown." (The faithful lady had arrived punctually at the trysting place and waited for him another half year.) After a tedious voyage — "I yawn and swear to myself" — the frigate *Volage* cast anchor at Sheerness in Kent on 14 July 1811. Byron had been abroad for two years and twelve days. Ever since November 1809 he had begun pointedly to call England "your country," "your Island," when writing home. Greece was his country, as he wrote to his mother at the beginning of his second visit: "the greater part of Greece is already my own, so that I shall only go over my old ground, and look upon my old seas and mountains."

What would he now make of the traditions and prejudices of Old England?

THREE

"Byr'n . . . Byr'n . . . Byr'n . . ."
(1811–1813)

"MY PROSPECTS are not very promising, but I suppose we shall wrestle through life like our Neighbours." Thus Byron to his mother while still at sea. His prospects were in fact full of dazzling promise while his "neighbours," in the sense of his nearest and dearest, wrestled with death and succumbed. He was returning to an England which he called in the words of a popular song, "this tight little island"; it was soon to feel as tight as a noose.

"Some curse hangs over me and mine," he wrote to Scrope Davies on 7 August from Newstead. His mother had died on the first before he could get to her, and at intervals of a few days he heard that the jaunty "Citoyen" Matthews had been drowned in the Cam and Long drowned at sea. Edleston had died of consumption that May. "There is to me something so incomprehensible in death," Byron wrote to Hobhouse, "that I can neither speak or think on the subject." The Reverend Francis Hodgson, however, forced him to do both.

Byron always proved unexpectedly adroit in religious argument. As a student of Voltaire he was quick to occupy picturesque vantage points. "I will bring you ten Mussulmans," he told Hodgson, "shall shame you in all good will towards men, prayer to God, and duty to their neighbours. And is there a Talapoin [Buddhist monk] or a Bonze, who is not superior to a fox-hunting curate?" He saw death as the end, confessing to Hodgson, "there is something Pagan in me that I cannot shake off." He mocked the idea of Christian immortality: "And our carcases, which are to rise again, are they worth raising? I hope, if mine is, that I shall have a better *pair of legs* than I have moved on these two-and-twenty years, or I shall be sadly behind in the squeeze into paradise."

It is probable that Byron's deformity loomed larger than usual during these gloomy months of 1811. When evil struck, his deformity deepened the wound. The defection of a pretty Newstead servant girl named Susan Vaughan from his arms to those of Robert Rushton caused a typically bitter reflection: "I do not blame her, but my own vanity in fancying that such a thing as I am could ever be beloved." Heartless Susan was followed by a stone in his kidney. "If the stone had got into my heart instead of my kidneys," he told Hodgson, "it would have been all the better."

The stone *was* in his heart, as shown by his reaction to Edleston's death. "I have not a tear left for an event," he wrote, "which five years ago would have bowed me to the dust; still it sits heavy on my heart." The poet in him, however, could remove stones from the heart. In his poems to "Thyrza" (Edleston) Byron's heart beat again. But he used the girl's name Thyrza to conceal his love for a boy. When Thomas Moore came to write Byron's biography he asserted that the Thyrza poems were an amalgam of all Byron's lost loves (though not including his bear, as one wit suggested). Moore was here, as elsewhere, exhibiting both tact and subtlety, since in a sense the poet never focuses upon a single limited object or draws inspiration from only one layer of feeling.

Poetry exorcised the grief for Edleston; Augusta Leigh softened the sorrow — and guilt — over his mother. His half

sister was unexpectedly sympathetic. They had not cor-
responded during his two years abroad, Augusta having
taken umbrage at the words "paralytic puling" as applied to
Lord Carlisle, her kinsman. Now it was a puling "baby
Byron" who needed comforting. The loving and lively correspondence of 1806 was renewed. Byron gave Augusta a
moonstone mourning ring in memory of his mother and invited her to stay with him at Newstead. The thought of her
being married made him suggest cynically that marriage
might be his own solution also. "By the bye *I* shall marry if
I can find any thing inclined to barter money for rank." In
the same spirit he had written to congratulate James Wedderburn Webster, a Cambridge friend: "I shall follow your
example when I can get a sufficient price for my Coronet."
But then, as he remarked to Hodgson, "a wife makes such
a damp."

Boredom enveloped him. His letters are gusty with "yawning," while "Heigho ho!" has become a recurrent sigh. The
visit of a Cambridge friend only exacerbated his ennui: "we
have nothing *new* to say on any subject, and yawn at each
other in a sort of *quiet inquietude.*" A jaunt to Harrow
brought no relief. "I am superannuated there too, and, in
short, as old at twenty-three as many men at seventy."

If not marriage, was another Eastern journey the way to
laughter and a renewal of youth? — "Sometimes I think of
the East again, and dearly beloved Greece." While still
smarting under the Susan Vaughan humiliation, he announced to the patient Hodgson: "In the spring of 1813 I
shall leave England for ever."

Yet he had in fact become aware of two new worlds to con-
quer in England. He could enter the world of politics — "and
a session of parliament would suit me well, — any thing to
cure me of conjugating the accursed verb 'ennuyer.'" And
the world of letters lay wide open to him.

It was while preparing *Childe Harold* for publication that
Byron got his toe inside the literary establishment. Appro-

priately enough, his sponsor was Thomas Moore, the popular lyricist and Byron's future biographer. Some rude remark
in *English Bards* had at first persuaded Moore to chal-
lenge Byron to a duel. But — "Tommy loves a lord"; and
after suitable explanations, "Tommy" arranged that the
young lord should dine with his close friend Samuel Rogers,
the banker-poet. A fourth poet, Thomas Campbell, made up
the quartet. The dinner, which took place on 4 November
1811, was something of a landmark for Byron. His behavior
and appearance aroused favorable comment. Delighted to be
present, he was nevertheless a "melancholy Dane," dressed in
elegant black for his mother and eating nothing but potatoes
drenched in vinegar, since his usual biscuits and soda water
were not available. If the new foursome was never to
achieve the coherence of his old Cambridge quartet, it gave
him opportunities to listen to lectures by Coleridge in
Rogers's prestigious company, and to meet Wordsworth.
Poor Hobhouse, away soldiering in Ireland, became jealous
of "the Irish melodist," as Byron affectionately called his
new friend Moore.

These corridors of literary power were directly connected
with the Whig establishment — Holland House in Kensington, where Rogers and Moore were familiars. Here was
Byron's entrée to Opposition politics. Lady Holland, handsome and forceful, was known as the "Sovereign Lady," and
Lord Holland put his political experience at Byron's dis-
posal. The young Opposition peer decided to speak on 27
February 1812 against a government bill to punish machine
breaking with death. That this was no sudden good cause
adopted for the occasion is shown by Byron's lines in his
Curse of Minerva written in Greece:

> *The starved mechanic breaks his rusting loom,*
> *And desperate mans him 'gainst the coming doom.*

As the Industrial Revolution advanced full steam ahead,
a few of its worker-victims refused to die quietly. "Luddite"

riots had broken out among the Nottingham stocking weavers in 1811. Byron, the Nottingham boy, emphasized to Lord Holland, the recorder (judge) of Nottingham, that each new broadloom threw six men out of work, reducing them and their families to starvation. Byron's hot blood boiled at these crimes against humanity but he remembered that the grand Whiggery had never relished "entusymusy" — an expressive version of "enthusiasm" used by a contemporary German singer. "I am a little apprehensive," he wrote to Holland, "that your Lordship will think me too lenient towards these men, and half a *frame-breaker* myself." His maiden speech was nonetheless violently delivered, as he told Hobhouse, "with a kind of modest impudence" that won Opposition applause and Tory abuse. He denounced the use of soldiers against workers, dubbed the new death-tribunals "butchers" presided over by a modern Judge Jeffreys, and brilliantly described the machine breakers as "famished into guilt."

Hobhouse was not there to follow this swim across the political Hellespont, but Dallas, Byron's literary adviser, shook his hand afterwards and noted the poet's glow of exaltation and excitement. As Byron himself recognized, "I was born for opposition."

For his next speech Byron chose the most controversial and equally fought issue of the day, Catholic Emancipation. This was the demand, primarily by Catholic Ireland, that men of the Catholic religion should not be debarred from sitting as members of Parliament. The motion was lost by only one vote, Byron having contributed to the debate in a speech which "kept the House in a roar" (Hobhouse) but was less successful than his first speech in proportion to its greater vehemence against Tory tyranny. "It is on the basis of your tyranny," he intoned in his theatrical singsong, "Napoleon hoped to build his own."

His third and most uncompromising speech was delivered on 1 June 1813 in defense of "the liberty of the subject." A much-respected, elderly M.P. named Major John Cartwright,

father of the Hampden Clubs which were founded to pro-
mote the reform of Parliament, had fallen foul of the military and magistrates at Huddersfield in Yorkshire. He and
six others were arrested while collecting signatures to a pe-
tition for reform. Here was a clear denial of free speech. But
also a slapdown for dangerous democracy. While the House
might theoretically deplore the former, it all but unani-
mously applauded the latter. Since the French Revolution
of 1789, "democracy" had come to mean what "communism"
was to mean after the Russian Revolution of 1917. Byron
later commented upon this, his last speech ever, in the ironical tone of a soldier who has handed in his papers: "Stanhope and I stood against the whole House, and mouthed it
valiantly — and had some fun and a little abuse for our opposition." Why did he withdraw from the parliamentary battle scarcely sixteen months after he had plunged in?

The answer to why a poet does anything cannot be dogmatic. Byron probably felt caught in the crossfire between
human rights, which he cared for passionately, and aristocratic standards, which he valued excessively. He shrank
from contact with the "rabble." When personified, his taste
was for the Holland House set rather than for tankards and
pipes in a smoke-laden Hampden Club. At the same time he
could not endure a future of "politics and Decorum." During
a Whig parliamentary committee meeting he had asked the
Duke of Grafton what they could do next. "Wake up the
Duke of Norfolk," replied Grafton, with a gesture towards
Byron's snoring neighbor. This kind of thing he called "Parliamentary mummeries."

Perhaps Byron was born just too soon. At a slightly later
date his overtheatrical oratory might have developed into
the political style which became so successful with Prime
Minister Canning, whom Byron admired. George Canning,
however, was a talented rhymester not a poet. Is there such
an animal as a politician-poet?

Yes or no was immaterial to Byron. For his embryonic political career had been suddenly superseded by his poetical
pilgrimage.

Nothing is so famous as fame. "I awoke one morning and found myself famous" is Byron's most famous saying. The morning in question was 10 March 1812. On this day his astute publisher, John Murray II, launched *Childe Harold's Pilgrimage*, having given the most important literary critics a preview. Advance interest was high. But nothing to the soaring hysteria that greeted publication. The sales reached 500 in the first three days and about 4,500 in under six months.* Byron was later to hear that his "rhymes" were very popular in the United States — "a rising and far country." He commented with gusto: "These are the first tidings that ever sounded like *Fame* to my ears — to be redde [*sic*] on the banks of the Ohio!" He suddenly felt "posthumous," the romantic's state of seventh heaven.

An analogy might be found in the reception given to Rousseau's *Confessions* when first published in England. Everyone read them, said Georgiana Duchess of Devonshire, for their "romantic candour" in revealing the author's sins. But there was this difference between the *Confessions* and the *Pilgrimage*: the pilgrim was there among them, in and out of every great house, attending theatres, concerts, lectures, and the zoo in Exeter 'Change, where, seeing Chunee the Indian elephant, he wished this deft beast could be his butler The traffic in St. James's Street was held up by carriages trying to deliver invitations to Number 8, Lord Byron's lodgings. He himself was to remember his "*reign* in the spring of 1812" as an orgy of "fete-ing, buzzing and partying compliments of the well-dressed multitude." It was said that you could not sit down at a dining table without hearing the susurration of his name: "Byr'n . . . Byr'n . . . Byr'n. . . ."

* The first edition of *Childe Harold* was 500 copies of quarto size, priced at 30 shillings. A reprint of 3,000 in octavo size was on the market within a day or two, priced at 12 shillings. "How wonderful to wake up and find yourself famous," writes the present John Murray, who most kindly gave me these figures, "on a first edition of 500!" By way of comparison, though not a close one, in 1813 Murray published Southey's *Life of Lord Nelson*. The 3,000 copies in two volumes, priced at 10 shillings, sold slowly.

There was one married woman of twenty-six who did not intend to be a mere voice in a buzzing crowd. Lady Caroline Lamb, born Ponsonby, was the wife of William Lamb, eldest surviving son of Lord Melbourne and earmarked to be a Whig prime minister; her mother was the Countess of Bessborough, sister of the ravishing but now dead Georgiana Duchess of Devonshire. Caroline's background has been described by Peter Quennell, Byron's most evocative biographer, as the "aristocratic bohemianism" of the Devonshire House set. An elfin tomboy, she reproduced this essential contradiction in all her manifestations. Fragile as a rose leaf, she had a voice that raucously dominated dinner tables. She was as brittle as porcelain but tough as fiber glass, to choose a modern analogy; although uneducated, she could draw and paint, write poetry and prose; like a true Romantic she was passionately absorbed in Caroline Lamb. Her nicknames included Young Savage, Devil, Squirrel, Cherubina, Ariel, Fairy Queen. Towards Byron she was to prove predominantly a Young Savage, though the Ariel in her matched the "young Puck" in him (he was described thus as a child), and her short "fawn-flaxen" curls nodded to his dark ringlets. Each was subject to sudden uncontrollable jets of emotion. They were made to meet but not to mingle.

At her first sight of him she had ostentatiously turned on her heel. This was a bait which the spoiled Childe could not resist. "Mad — bad — and dangerous to know," she wrote avidly in her journal. They were introduced soon afterwards at Lady Holland's. Byron pursued her to Melbourne House with the first rose of summer and an exotic carnation in his hand; on his lips the words, "Your Ladyship, I am told, likes all that is new and rare — for a moment."

But the novelty and rarity of *Childe Harold* and its author were not to fade for her like the flowers. Titania gave herself in a spellbound moment; and then the Young Savage emerged to plague him for the rest of the season, and after. If not invited to a party where he was present, she would lurk outside disguised in the livery of one of her pages and thrust her head and shoulders into his carriage. Well might she say, "That beautiful pale face is my fate."

Beauty and pallor in plenty were to be found in the poem, as well as in the poet's face, and Caroline, as one of the first to read *Childe Harold,* was also among the first to identify Byron with his hero. To the pallor of fateful beauty had to be added the darkness and mystery of suspected evil. Whether or not this was the real man — and the question must be discussed — it was irrevocably and ineluctably the Byronic image, to be indelibly stamped upon Western European culture. Byron's contribution to that culture did not stop at *Childe Harold.* Nevertheless, this was the original mold from which much was cast. As such, the Childe and his next of kin, the Giaour, Conrad the Corsair, and Conrad's reincarnation as Lara deserve at least one searching look.

An outcast from society — that is the essential nature of the Byronic hero and lover. Childe Harold is self-outcast, having drugged himself into world-weariness through the "concubines and carnal company" kept at his ancestral abbey. The Giaour has banished himself to a monastery both for causing the death of his lover, Leila, and for slaying her murderer, the Pasha. Conrad once possessed an ancestral castle but he chose to become an outlaw, a corsair; under the name Lara he returns to his castle in a sequel to *The Corsair,* to find that the hidden past has put the old feudal life beyond his reach. In the sense that all four of them, the Childe, the Giaour, the Corsair, and Lara are self-exiled, the Byronic hero is a beacon to every subversive leader and enemy of society.

Beacon, however, will not quite do. For the Byronic hero is a creature of gloom, his appearance conforming to the same dark pattern. Here is Conrad:

> *Sun-burnt his cheek, his forehead high and pale*
> *The sable curls in wild profusion veil;*
> *And oft perforce his rising lip reveals*
> *The haughtier thought it curbs, but scarce conceals.*

Childe Harold's "writhing lip" matches Conrad's. We can be sure that the Childe also had sable curls and that Lara's forehead was pale. We need take only one look at the Giaour:

> See — by the half-illumined wall
> His hood fly back, his dark hair fall,
> That pale brow wildly wreathing round . . . .

At this period Napoleon himself got a lick of the Byronic brush, the poet describing him as "dark & diabolical."

Darker than the sneers and curls was the mystery which shrouded every Byronic hero. Childe Harold was the first exemplar:

> Yet oft-times in his maddest mirthful mood
> Strange pangs would flash along Childe Harold's brow
> As if the memory of some deadly feud
> Or disappointed passion lurk'd below:
> But this none knew, nor haply cared to know . . . .

With the Giaour expiating some "dark deed he will not name," Lara exhibiting "that chilling mystery of mien" and Conrad altogether a "man of loneliness and mystery," it is not surprising that the poet himself was credited in his own person with diabolical secrets. Ladies almost fainted at "the sort of *under* look he used to give."

The mystery attached to the Byronic hero often had a supernatural tinge. The Giaour gallops past like a "demon of the night" and later, in his cell,

> Dark and unearthly is the scowl
> That glares beneath his dusky cowl.

Ultimately the Giaour lays claim to supernatural wickedness:

> But look — 'tis written on my brow!
> There read of Cain the curse and crime . . .

— while Childe Harold, in probing his own "secret woe," dis-
covers the same clue:

> *It is that settled, ceaseless gloom*
> *The fabled Hebrew wanderer bore*   .

In Lara's unconcealed affinity with Lucifer we move on
to a new Byronic plane which will be of increasing significance in the future:

> *There was in him a vital scorn of all:*
> *As if the worst had fall'n which could befall,*
> *He stood a stranger in this breathing world,*
> *An erring spirit from another hurled . . . .*

The Lucifer or "fallen angel" element is present in every
Byronic hero. In Lara:

> *Yet there was softness too in his regard,*
> *At times, a heart as not by nature hard . . . .*

In the Corsair:

> *Yet was not Conrad thus by Nature sent*
> *To lead the guilty — guilt's worst instrument . . . .*
> *Warp'd by the world in Disappointment's school . . . .*
> *Too firm to yield, and far too proud to stoop . . . .*

In the Giaour:

> *The close observer can espy*
> *A noble soul, and lineage high.*

Childe Harold, too, has "lineage long" which had once been
"glorious."

These fallen angels, with their secret sense of being both
more glorious and more villainous than ordinary mortals,
must of necessity be presented as creatures apart. Loneliness

is the beginning and end of youthful Byronism. The Childe feels himself "at length alone" when he reaches the wilds of Albania, and Byron, whirling from Holland House in Kensington to Melbourne House in Whitehall (both Whig salons), from Rogers's house to Sheridan's to Mme de Staël's, would reflect in his journal, "I only go out to get me a fresh appetite for being alone."

If in the end the whole Byronic thing did not quite add up, Byron would be the first to repudiate it. What sort of an outcast was he whom all society lionized? But for a time he was willing to play, while smarting under the paradox.

Byron's passion for Caroline burned itself out between the spring and summer of 1812. "Then your heart — my poor Caro, what a little volcano! that pours *lava* through your veins, & yet I cannot wish it a bit colder," he had written to her in April. "I have always thought you the cleverest most agreeable, absurd, amiable, perplexing, dangerous fascinating little being." But on 19 May he was writing, "This dream, this delirium of two months must pass away." The truth was that while Byron might create his own scandals, he did not care to have Caro's lunacies thrust upon him. He would merely bite his nails and jealously threaten to wring her "obstinate little neck"; she bit through her glass at dinner when she saw him leaning towards another woman. She sent him some of her pubic hair asking for his in return; none of his ideal women, Turkish or Greek heroines of romance, would have dreamed of being so immodest.

She tried at least twice to make him elope with her, first by arriving in disguise at his rooms, second by hiding in a surgeon's house where Byron, having been appealed to by her frantic mother, located Caroline by bribing a coachman who had brought him a message from her. Even her father-in-law's patience had become exhausted and he said that she might "go and be damned!" Lady Bessborough, however, eventually got Caroline off to Ireland, though "little mania" was to return and wreak sporadic vengeance. Byron's effigy was burned on a bonfire and his family motto parodied on her pages' buttons — *Ne Crede Byron*.

While the affair with "little mania" was in its early stages, Byron met William Lamb's first cousin Annabella Milbanke. This clever but naive girl of twenty had come up from her Durham home, Seaham, for the season. Byron ought to have known that Annabella was not for him. She was a bluestocking and on the whole he did not like "blues," though Mme de Staël was an exception, "for *she is sane*." Annabella's specialty was mathematics and her systematic approach to life's problems was not suited to the volatile Childe. However, the circumstances of their first meeting temporarily blinded him to their incompatibility.

He first saw her at a morning party organized by Caroline on 25 March 1812 to practice the steps of a dizzy new dance imported from Germany. An introduction was effected on 14 April. Unable to perform himself, the lame poet was disgusted at having to watch this "Voluptuous Waltz," in which for the first time dancing partners found themselves in each other's arms. His mood of the moment predisposed him in favor of Miss Milbanke and her "retired modesty" as against those whose diaphanous garments seemed an invitation to more than the waltz:

> *Round all the confines of the yielded waist,*
> *The stranger's hand may wander undisplac'd . . . .*

Byron found Miss Milbanke's figure "perfect for her height," and her brown hair, broad brow, apple cheeks, pointed chin and serious expression altogether "piquant." That she was an heiress and would be a peeress in her own right also pricked his curiosity. "She interested me exceedingly."

For her part Annabella was quietly bowled over by the famous charm. "Lord Byron is without exception . . . more agreeable in conversation than any person I ever knew." She had devoured *Childe Harold* and assumed that Byron *was* the Childe. He had "a *noble* heart" but "perverted by un-kindness"; he repented "the evil he has done, though he has not resolution (without aid) to adopt a new course of con-duct and feeling." To win her heart, she decided, he lacked only "calm benevolence" — but calm benevolence was pre-cisely the quality in which she herself excelled and which she would bring to the Childe's aid. When she overheard him ask someone at a party, "Do you think there is one person here who dares to look into himself?" she too was *"bound"* to him, as only those soaked in the yearnings of the Romantic movement could be. She would cleanse his heart, so that he would dare at last to look into it. She heard him say, "I have not a friend in the world!" and her dedication was complete. "I vowed in secret to be a devoted friend to this lone being."

Lone being? In order to understand Annabella's disaster, it is necessary to ask how far Byron should be identified with Childe Harold. For in using the words "lone being" Anna-bella was subscribing unreservedly to the Childe Harold myth.

Byron like everyone else had his mysterious recesses, his inner regions of loneliness, his guilty secrets real or imag-inary. No doubt, being a poet, all his sensations were heightened. He was shyer, more aloof than most. But in another sense he was emphatically not Childe Harold. "I would not be such a fellow," he wrote, "as I have made my hero for all the world." Many of his qualities were very unChilde-like indeed. Far from being habitually secretive, he could be totally uninhibited. His friends reveled in him as a boon companion, spirited, playful, mischievous, witty, often convulsed not with "strange pangs" but uproarious laughter. We cannot imagine the Childe rolling about on his chair as Byron did when Mme de Staël, at a dinner party, wrestled with a protruding whalebone in her corset.

Midway between Byron's Childe-like gloom and unChilde-like gaiety gleamed his satirical genius. From Mme de Staël downwards — "her pen behind her ear and her mouth full of ink" — no one escaped his satire. To him ridicule was "the only weapon which the English climate cannot rust." Life was absurd, impossible. Like "those theorems," as he explained to Annabella, "in which, after ringing the changes upon AB and CD, etc., I at last came to which is absurd — which is impossible, and at this point I have always arrived and I fear always shall through life."

Annabella on the contrary would always arrive through life at the deadly serious. If her cousin Caroline Lamb showed her Byron's comment on their incipient friendship, Annabella would have missed the note of flippancy. "I have no desire to be better acquainted with Miss Millbank [sic]," he wrote to appease Caro; "she is too good for a fallen spirit to know, and I should like her more if she were less perfect." There was no flippancy in Miss Milbanke and no fun in *Childe Harold*. Byron's genius was not meant to be circumscribed either by the woman or the poem.

At the end of the season he drifted to Cheltenham, where he took the medicinal waters "because they were sufficiently disgusting." Liberated from Caroline, whom he could now neither endure nor resist, he again saw a possible alternative in that "extraordinary" girl, her cousin, with the scientific brain, pretty figure and "placid countenance." Fortunately — or so he thought — fate had given him the perfect intermediary.

Elizabeth Lady Melbourne was the sister of Annabella's father, Sir Ralph Milbanke. She had been a lovely and subtle brunette, and though now sixty-two she was still the epitome of eighteenth-century chic. In the past she had conducted an amour with Lord Egremont of such finesse that nobody knew for certain whether Egremont or Melbourne was the father of her second son, William. Byron was immediately entranced by this ultrafeminine "sort of modern Aspasia." He wrote of her: "If she had been younger, I might have lost my head." While he and Caroline lost their heads interminably, Lady Melbourne was the arch-exponent of discretion. She if anyone could save Byron from himself.

Lady Melbourne agreed that Annabella might be the way out for him. She broached the subject ingeniously with her niece. What sort of man did Annabella desire for a husband? Annabella's sententious reply, in which she described an ideal man whose strong feelings were governed by duty and reason, provoked her aunt into commenting that she was "on stilts"; to which Annabella neatly riposted that she was "only *on tip-toe.*" But not, apparently, on tiptoe for Byron. For when the poet sent a rather prosaic proposal of marriage via Lady Melbourne, Annabella conscientiously analyzed his character in her diary on 8 October and on the twelfth turned him down. She still saw him as pure Childe Harold, swinging between evil and good, disguising his goodness out of perverse pride. Despite his being "extremely humble towards persons whose character he respects" and to whom "he would probably confess his errors," Annabella decided not to give him the opportunity. She could never feel for him "that strong affection" which would make her "happy in domestic life."

Her refusal was as stiff as his proposal. Nevertheless he wrote with apparent equanimity to Lady Melbourne: "I thank you again for your efforts with my Princess of Parallelograms." She was as puzzling as the hypotenuse but had behaved with perfect rectitude. "Her proceedings are quite rectangular, or rather we are two parallel lines prolonged to infinity side by side but never to meet." In any case, the greatest attraction of marriage with Annabella had been to have Lady Melbourne as his aunt. By November he was writing to Lady Melbourne: "I congratulate Annabella and myself on our mutual escape. That would have been but a *cold collation,* and I prefer hot suppers." The hot supper had in fact already been provided by a new mistress, and Byron was tucking in.

She was the Countess of Oxford. He had met her often during the previous summer at parties frequented by Whigs, ranging from aristocratic supporters of the London Hampden Club for reform, of which he was a member, to sup-

porters of Princess Caroline, the Prince Regent's hated wife.
A specialist in Radical lovers, Lady Oxford was to be Byron's
only politically minded mistress until he went to Italy. Born
Jane Scott in a country rectory, Lady Oxford had used her
considerable brains to study free thought and free love. The
radical leader Sir Francis Burdett had been among her lovers; and her children, each as beautiful as herself, were
known as the Harleian Miscellany, from the famous collection of manuscripts, which in this case had undoubtedly
been fathered by her husband, Edward Harley Earl of Oxford. She first invited Byron to stay with her in September.
Autumn was the season for "autumnal charms." Though
Lady Oxford, now to become Byron's charming mistress, was,
like Cleopatra, "a queen of forty," each one of his visits to
her home at Eywood in Herefordshire proved to be a romantic island in a sea of troubles.

On 9 November he managed at last to repudiate Caroline
completely, after she had sent "a long *German* tirade" of
furious suspicion to Lady Oxford. (The adjective "German"
probably referred to the German literary fashion called
Sturm und Drang — storm and stress — of the 1760's, on
which Caroline appropriately enough had been brought up.
Until Byron met Matthew Gregory Lewis and Shelley in
Switzerland, he was allergic to German romanticism, especially when expounded by Caroline Lamb or Mme de Staël.)
"Lady Caroline —" he wrote back himself, "our affections
are not our own — mine are engaged. I love another . . . I
am no longer yr. lover."* Having once pronounced her an
"absurd" but fascinating little being, she was still "absurd"
but now the most "contemptibly wicked of human produc-
tions." When she dared to demand a lock of his hair he sent
her one of Lady Oxford's instead.

The "yawning" which had subsided during the autumn of
1812 assailed him again with full force in the following

---

* Caroline was to print a version of that letter in her romantic, preposterous and sometimes witty novel about Byron called *Glenarvon*.

year. He must travel, either with the Oxfords who were leaving for the Mediterranean in June 1813, or to Persia with Lord Sligo, who had been his companion when "girating" the Morea, or to Russia with Hobhouse. None of these prospects materialized. Would he go no more a-roving? Suddenly his half sister Augusta descended on him in London. Like every Byron she was in financial straits. Her home at Six Mile Bottom near Newmarket and her three small daughters did not compensate for the bankrupt horsey colonel, her husband, who appeared in Newmarket mostly for the races. Within some six or eight weeks Byron was proposing to go a-roving with Augusta, in a manner which shocked himself and shattered his friends.

Augusta in June 1813 was still only twenty-nine. Her gentle sensuality, dark hair, beautiful eyes, and Grecian mouth could have come out of his Eastern romances. Docile and devoted, she went about with him like Leila following her Giaour. But it was her being a Byron that drew him closest: her having his shyness, his laughter. "Do you think there is one person here who dares to look into himself?" he had once asked. Now he dared to look into Augusta and saw — himself. That alone would have been enough happiness for any Narcissus of the Romantic era. But for Byron there was the added sensation of forbidden love. He was soon to tell Annabella: "The great object of life is sensation."

Gradually, however, there was another sensation not so pleasant as the first — sexual guilt. Ill-treated by her husband, Augusta would do anything her "baby Byron" wanted. It is as certain as these things can be that she was his lover. Her unthinking acquiescence in his crime must have increased his guilty torment. Whither was he leading his "Guss," his "Goose"? The very innocence of her pet names was a reproach. On 18 August he tried to unburden himself to his confidante, Lady Melbourne, but could not write the words: "I will tell —" he began but ended abruptly, "no I won't." Four days later he broke to Moore the news of "an entirely new scrape," far more serious than any of the past year. "It is unlucky we can neither live with nor without these women."

Byron had not been able to "live with or without" Hobhouse in 1810. Now it was women. His whole existence on one level was a double negative. He could not live with or without politics and action. The Greek national war of liberation was at last to solve his dilemma.

On the same day that Byron was confessing to Moore, Annabella tacitly confessed to Byron the mistake she had made in rejecting his offer. She wrote him a long letter on 22 August of friendship and advice, but concealed her motive by making a declaration of imaginary, unrequited love for another: "the strongest affections of my heart are without hope." Her advice was ironically apposite. "Have an object that will permanently occupy your feelings & exercise your reason."

Augusta did indeed permanently occupy his feelings and he exercised his reason at last by making the situation clear to Lady Melbourne. His Aspasia, "modern" though she might be, was horrified. Finding that Byron contemplated an elopement, she implored him to go abroad, if go he must, without Augusta. But he would not promise; indeed he asked Murray to let him know of a ship sailing for Gibraltar — Minorca — Zante — *any* ship taking passengers — "I have a friend . . ."

Luckily Augusta was not his only one. At the critical moment his old Cambridge friend James Wedderburn Webster invited Byron to stay with him and his wife, Lady Frances, at Aston Hall in Yorkshire. This was the very house to which his father, "Mad Jack" Byron, had taken Augusta's mother, once another man's wife. Now the son needed some other man's wife to break the spiraling affair with the wife of Colonel Leigh.

Wedderburn Webster was a fool and Frances his wife foolish; nevertheless Byron's two visits to Aston, in late September and early October 1813, served to postpone the Augusta denouement.

"Bold Webster" was Byron's present nickname for his host. Webster's unfaithfulness had long since lost him his wife's affection. This insipidly pious young woman whose beauty was as pallid as her moral sense had not seemed to Byron the type to attract him, though she might well appeal to dragoons. In fact like most pretty things she appealed to him strongly.

Byron's visit began quietly, a relief after weeks of hectic obsession with Augusta. The Webster children, he wrote, "only scream in a low voice," and Lady Frances seemed all but impervious to his automatic advances. Then the tempo quickened. He found that "Fanny" was attracted to him after all. She passed him notes in her music book. But would she fall? Was it for nothing that she was "measured for a new Bible every month"? The test came before the party moved on to Newstead in mid-October. Webster must have allowed Byron to be alone with her in the billiard room. Here Byron put the question. She gave him encouragement, though like Drake they finished the game. Once at Newstead, they met at 2 A.M. for the final round of the other game. She admitted her love but threw herself on his mercy, with a suppliant "No." His report to Lady Melbourne on the result was half-chivalrous, half-comical: "I spared her." But in his continuing account of the affair to Lady Melbourne, written as a sparkling serial, he showed that the struggle was not quite over. Elopement was still running in his head and Lady Frances might after all be "the friend" with whom he eloped to Gibraltar — Minorca — Zante. All was *Sturm und Drang.*

In November 1813 he was in London again, as famous and sought after as ever but inwardly distraught. Suddenly he found relief in pouring out *The Bride of Abydos,* night after night, when the day's "fete-ings and buzzings" were done. It took him one week.

In this Turkish tale, as Byron called it, the beautiful Zuleika, daughter of a pasha, is content to marry Osman Bey —
until her half brother Selim declares for her a love which
is more than that of a brother for a sister. They make a dash
for liberty but Selim is shot dead beside the Hellespont and
Zuleika dies brokenhearted. Zuleika was three-quarters Augusta and one-quarter Frances; her father was wholly Ali
Pasha. When the cathartic week was completed and Byron
was polishing *The Bride* for John Murray, he changed Selim
and Zuleika into cousins. The poem appeared on 2 December 1813 and sold six thousand copies immediately.

After this burst of poetic activity the trivial round began
again. He described it on 7 December in the journal he had
kept since 13 November 1813: "sleep, eating, and swilling —
buttoning and unbuttoning — how much remains of down-
right existence? The summer of a dormouse." But existence
was prolonged by another tempest of creation. Byron laid
aside his guilt-ridden, dejected journal on 18 December and
began *The Corsair*. The gale blew itself out in ten days and
the poem was finished. Meanwhile he had created for a
thirsty public, who lacked today's stream of romantic thrill-
ers, a verse-story of compelling fascination.

Leaving behind his lovely Medora, Conrad the Corsair has
quitted his piratical lair for a foray on Seyd Pasha's kingdom.
Conrad is captured by Seyd but rescued by the treachery of
the slave Gulnare, who murders her master in his sleep for
love of Conrad. He flees home with Gulnare, only to find
that Medora has mysteriously died of grief.

We now have two Byronic slave women, Leila in *The
Giaour* and Gulnare in *The Corsair*, both betraying their
masters for a Selim or a Conrad. In each case the hero half
regrets the slave's infatuation for him: "Yet sometimes, with
remorse, in vain," says Selim, "I wish she had not loved
again"; Conrad feels "the bodings of his breast" as he allows
Gulnare's lips to meet his "with broken sigh." Each is Byron
tormented by his own situation. With Medora dead, Conrad
and Gulnare disappear also — but not as happy lovers. For

Conrad's one virtue has been his sense of honor and this is indelibly stained by Gulnare's crime, committed on his behalf. And so in the last couplet of the poem Conrad vanishes into the void:

> *He left a Corsair's name to other times,*
> *Link'd with one virtue, and a thousand crimes.**

It was not so easy for Byron to solve his problem by vanishing into the void. He had in his own words rung "the changes upon AB and CD," upon Caroline-Annabella and Lady Oxford–Lady Frances, yet the result was still the Euclidean "absurd" or "impossible." There was always one insistent chime which he could not get out of his head — Augusta.

* The likeness between this couplet and the last lines of Beckford's *Vathek* is striking: "Thus the Caliph Vathek, who for the sake of . . . hidden power had sullied himself with a thousand crimes, became a prey to . . . remorse without mitigation" — remorse being his one virtue.

FOUR

Courtship and Marriage
(1814–1815)

"THE Year of Revelry" was to be Byron's title for 1814 after Napoleon's banishment to Elba, a half-ironic view of Europe's festive future — and his own. He and Augusta spent a bitterly cold three weeks from 17 January to 6 February "snowbound and thaw-swamped" at Newstead. On 22 January, his twenty-sixth birthday, he ordered the customary flags to be hung out on the Abbey walls, and stared at the four Athenian skulls lying in their coffin until they seemed animated.

Augusta was heavily pregnant, having conceived at the height of that first season with Byron. Before taking her to Newstead he had confessed to Lady Melbourne that this love of theirs, because forbidden, made other loves seem "insipid," but "it had a mixture of the terrible." Their intentions, however, had been "very different"; and when they failed to adhere to them the fault in her had been due to mere "weakness," but in him to "folly" — or worse. "Pray do not speak so harshly of her to me — the cause of all." If even Lady Melbourne spoke harshly, what would the conventional world say when it found out?

For the moment, however, the world was busy execrating

Byron on political grounds. The European sovereigns were closing in on Napoleon. The Tories scented victory. This was the moment Byron chose to republish under his own name his bitter *Lines to a Lady Weeping*, the "Lady" being Princess Charlotte of Wales, who had wept in 1812 at her father's desertion of the Whigs on becoming Prince Regent.

In the face of press "hysterics," when he was called a deformed Richard III, an atheist, a rebel and a devil, Byron showed combative resilience. He wrote to Lady Melbourne, "I have that within me that bounds against opposition" — words which were to echo in his head and to emerge at length in the last canto of *Childe Harold:*

> *But there is that within me which shall tire*
> *Torture and Time, and breathe when I expire . . . .*

He kept up his spirits by maintaining an outsider's point of view throughout the stirring events of the spring of 1814. "My politics are to me like a young mistress to an old man," he wrote, "— the worse they grow the fonder I become of them." When fate was rushing down upon Napoleon, Byron wrote defiantly in his journal, "I believe and hope he will win"; when news arrived on 6 April that the "sad whining" Napoleon had ingloriously abdicated, Byron dashed off an *Ode to Napoleon Buonaparte* in which he trounced the fallen idol for failing to defy the Allies to the end, like Prometheus on his rock; when gouty Louis XVIII was paraded through London "in all the pomp and rabblement of royalty," prior to his restoration by the Allies, Byron refused Murray's offer of a seat overlooking the procession: "You know I am a Jacobin." He could not help suspecting that Napoleon would "play them some trick still."

At Six Mile Bottom on 14 April 1814, eight days after the news of Napoleon's abdication arrived, his sister had given birth to a daughter, Elizabeth Medora Leigh. Was Byron the father?

There are arguments for and against his paternity. He had

been painfully anxious about the confinement but when Lady Melbourne asked whether his involvement with Augusta was worthwhile, he replied, "Oh! but it [the affair] is 'worth while,' I can't tell you why, and it [the baby] is *not* an 'Ape,' and if it is, that must be my fault."

Byron may have been referring to the medieval superstition that the child of incest was a monster. Or to the more common belief that the child of a woman who was shocked during pregnancy would be adversely affected. That Byron believed in this old wives' tale is shown by his violent reaction when his parrot bit Annabella's toe during *her* pregnancy. Terrified lest his wife should produce a "winged child," he hurled parrot and cage out of the window. The bird survived and, more philosophical than its master, merely ejaculated "Johnny!"

Despite Byron's anxiety over Medora's birth, this child never supplanted her eldest sister Georgiana, undoubtedly Leigh's child, in Byron's affections. He called her "*my* Georgiana" and "a Beauty." The rest were "fine ⊹ but damnable Squallers." Nor did he ever make plans for Medora as he did for his illegitimate daughter Allegra, or write a poem to Medora as he did to his illegitimate son. As for the argument that the dates precluded Colonel Leigh from being the father, he could have seen Augusta in London, or at Six Mile Bottom during the Newmarket meeting of July.

No dogmatic answer can be given. Byron himself probably had doubts. The doubts remain.

What Byron had called in the spring "the rabblement of royalty" blossomed into revelry as the summer advanced. "The summer of the sovereigns" was another of his evocative phrases. In June and July the Prince Regent entertained the sovereigns and their victorious generals with a series of magnificent festivities. London went mad over Wellington and Blücher, the British and Prussian commanders, and Tsar Alexander. Byron's health was not at first festive after the prolonged winter. But by dint of renewed dieting and boxing, he recovered sufficiently to enjoy the celebrations, if not their cause. Sometimes he would drink fifteen bottles of soda water in a night, knocking off their tops with a poker to quench his raging thirst more quickly. Tom Moore remembered one meal when Byron considered his only safe fare to be lobsters washed down with alternate draughts of neat brandy and hot water.

Another of his Eastern tales, *Lara,* proved even more effective than boxing and brandy as a relief from his love affair.* Like Conrad (and Byron) Lara found that to have been "Lord of himself" since earliest youth was but a "heritage of woe," a "fearful empire" bestowing only opportunities for sin: "the thousand paths that slope the way to crime." Lara indeed had learned nothing from Conrad's "thousand crimes." Neither had succeeded in reaching a Rousseau-like, natural freedom. They both remained slaves of their own passions. As who was not?

> *Behold — but who hath seen, or e'er shall see,*
> *Man as himself — the secret spirit free?*

Byron's difficulties still revolved around Augusta, again his partner during the 1814 season. On 28 March he had moved to a ground-floor flat in Albany, Piccadilly. Lord Althorp had vacated these rooms on his marriage, and Byron wrote, "I have gotten his spacious bachelor apartments" — as if life were now at last to be spaciousness and calm. But the disadvantages were soon all too palpable. Caroline Lamb began haunting him again, with her insectlike figure and huge wild eyes in bony sockets, waiting outside his door until a servant opened it and then darting in. One day in his absence she saw *Vathek* lying on his table and inscribed in it, "Remember me." When Byron returned he dashed off be-

---

* It was also the first poem for which he agreed to accept money for himself from his publisher — £700. Pride had hitherto forbidden him. In the same year, 1814, the publisher Longman paid Thomas Moore, his "favorite" poet, £3,000 for *Lalla Rookh* without having seen a line of it. Two years later Byron was to receive £2,000 from Murray for *Childe Harold,* Canto III, and *The Prisoner of Chillon* together.

neath Caroline's salutation two stanzas which Vathek himself, expert hater though he was, would have envied for their
expression of sheer loathing. The second verse ran:

> *Remember thee! Ay, doubt it not;*
> *Thy husband too shall think of thee;*
> *By neither shall thou be forgot,*
> *Thou false to him, thou fiend to me!*

Caroline, however, recalled (or invented) a day when he
had kissed her tenderly on the lips and said, "Poor Caro, if
every one hates me, you, I see, will never change" — and
then had shown her part of his incriminating correspondence
with Lady Melbourne about Augusta. (It is equally probable, or perhaps even more so, that she had read the letters
after rifling her mother-in-law's desk. Caroline would stop
at nothing, and indeed once forged a letter from Byron to
Murray in order to obtain Byron's portrait.)

Byron's vitriol was poured out on himself as much as on
the "mad or bad" Caro, as *he* now called *her*. To whom had
he been "false" and a "fiend" but his sister? As he had written to Lady Melbourne, his love for Augusta was partly
"diabolical." But the old method was still open to him of
exorcising his demon. He could do as Lord Althorp had
done. Vacate his "spacious bachelor apartments" and marry.

There was no lack of unsuitable candidates. His friend
Tom Moore canvassed in vain the charms of Lady Adelaide
Forbes, whose profile was pure Apollo Belvedere. Byron was
less than enthusiastic about Lady Frances Webster's younger
sisters, both exquisitely pretty and silly. Mary Chaworth,
having separated from Mr. Musters, conceived the desperate
idea of again becoming Byron's *femme fatale;* she tried to
trap him at Hastings where he was holidaying with Augusta,
but he fled just before she arrived, answering none of her
frantic letters; whereat poor Mary went mad. Augusta ran a
more successful candidate for longer: her young friend Lady
Charlotte Leveson-Gower was as shy and pretty as an antelope — Byron's favorite analogy for lovely women. But

Lady Charlotte had the antelope's gift for flight. In response to Mrs. Leigh's approaches on Byron's behalf she sent a refusal on 9 September. Lady Melbourne, meanwhile, knew that her own previous candidate was still in the cards. Annabella, in fact, had for months been conducting her own candidature far more efficiently than ever her aunt had done it for her.

Annabella Milbanke suddenly opened fire again, as we have seen, on 22 August 1813. She wrote Byron the first of many letters, but concealed her purpose by inventing an unrequited love for another. Her motive was presented as Platonic friendship, which, "though it can never change to love, deserves to be considered as more than worldly friendship."

Byron replied on 28 August accepting her friendship and adding: "It is a feeling towards you with which I cannot trust myself. I doubt whether I could help loving you."

The affair had thus progressed in one bound further than Annabella can have dared to hope, considering her rejection of his proposal in 1812. Many years later Byron commented on this new stage in their relations: "Friendship is a dangerous word for young ladies; it is Love full-fledged, and waiting for a fine day to fly."

The fine day was over a year in coming. Meanwhile Annabella trembled on the edge of her nest at Seaham, seldom venturing southwards for the Year of Revelry, but supplying Byron with immensely verbose and often obscure counsel. She had begged him not to reveal the correspondence to her aunt, but he soon discovered that Lady Melbourne favored it. Anything seemed better than Augusta. He himself remained clear-eyed while keeping the fledgling happy with occasional love calls. "Yesterday a very pretty letter from Annabella, which I answered," he confided to his journal towards the end of 1813. "What an odd situation and friendship is ours! — without one spark of love on either side."

In March 1814 Byron warned Annabella about a rumor

that he had made her a second proposal and been again refused; to which she replied by implication she could not
refuse a new offer which had not been made. This time he
noted: "I shall be in love with her again if I don't take
care." She had just read *The Corsair,* which she thought disclosed a Shakespearean knowledge of the human heart's
"secret workings." No doubt she hoped he guessed her own
heart's secret. Next month Annabella's father invited him to
stay at Seaham. "I am not now in love with her," he informed his *Tante* Lady Melbourne; "but I can't at all foresee that I should not be, if it came a warm June (as Falstaff
observes)." Seriously, he admired her "as a very superior
woman" — but, again the qualification — she was "a little en-
cumbered with Virtue." Lady Melbourne, still alarmed
about Augusta, urged him to visit Seaham.

Came a warm June, however, and he merely received a
"prim & pretty" letter from Annabella, while it was his
spangled cousin Mrs. Wilmot whom he met at Lady Sitwell's
party and celebrated in two of his most entrancing lines,
written the next morning, after a tumbler of brandy on going to bed and a consequent bad night:

> *She walks in beauty, like the night*
> *Of cloudless climes and starry skies . . . .*

Came a warm July and it was Caroline, not Annabella, who
flirted with him at a masquerade in honor of Wellington,
where Byron, disguised as a monk and discussing Platonism
with a friend, scolded Caroline for showing him her green
pantaloons.

That month the Seaham visit was postponed because of
the illness of Annabella's uncle Lord Wentworth. In apolo-
gizing to Byron for this delay, Annabella added an apology
for her own "involuntary constraint" in his presence last
year, making her "repulsively cold." Byron sent no reply,
since his "A †" (as he often wrote Augusta's name) was
now occupying his mind at that not very "fashashashionable
watering place," Hastings, rather than his plain "A" at Sea-

ham. The plain "A" thereupon advanced another pace, re-iterating her attachment to him which, however, remained "imperfect." Byron replied that of course he had not forgotten her attachment to his rival, so what was she trying to say? "Pray write to me openly and *harshly.*"

Annabella came into the open at last and confessed that she had been "deceived" all along in imagining a rival attachment; "nothing could now induce me to marry him." What were Byron's own feelings? Was he "in *any* danger of that attachment to me which might interfere with your peace of mind"? If so, "I would ask you to consider by what course the danger may be avoided."

"I will answer your question as openly as I can," he wrote on 10 August. "I did — do — and always shall love you."

Such openness merely provoked the tortuous Annabella into taking another sidestep; she still could not select him as her "guide, her support, her example on earth, with a view to Immortality."

He too could be stiff. "Very well," he answered, "— now we can talk of something else."

He was thinking of something else. He took Augusta and her children to stay with him at Newstead. From there she finally proposed on his behalf, as we have seen, to Lady Charlotte Leveson-Gower. An affirmative skip from the lively antelope would put an end to Annabella's playfulness which Caroline, incidentally, was later to describe as the "dance of an elephant."

But when the antelope's answer was no, Byron proposed on the very same day, 9 September, to Annabella. His proposal, however, was tentative: "Are the objections to which you alluded insuperable? or is there any line or change of conduct which could possibly remove them?"

Augusta had tried to stop him, for she and Moore both felt that the "learned lady" was not rich enough and too "straight-laced" for him. Nevertheless Augusta read over her brother's letter and decided it was too "pretty" to be wasted. So many "pretty" letters had passed between Byron and

Annabella since August 1813. And now Annabella must have believed that her life was to be as pretty as the letters. For in Byron's letter of 9 September he offered himself as a reformed or reformable character, and also as one who loved her and always would (10 August). Could he expect any other answer than the one he got?

He spent nine days nonetheless in wondering about the result. If Miss Milbanke insisted there was no *"possibility"* of hope — he did not want a "pledge" — he would go to Italy with Hobhouse and make up for her loss with Venice, the Alps and Parmesan cheeses. Such was the level of his romance.

Her answer arrived on 18 September. He turned so pale that Augusta thought he would faint. He had got the unwanted pledge. "I am and have long been pledged to myself," wrote Annabella, "to make your happiness my first object in life." *Crede Byron.* "I will *trust* to you for all I should look up to — all I can love."

Only a moment before Miss Milbanke's acceptance arrived, the Newstead gardener had brought in to Byron his mother's long-lost wedding ring. "It never rains but it pours," he said to Augusta as he handed her Annabella's letter. He had just decided that his bride should be married with the unearthed ring if she accepted him, and now he read that she not only accepted but had sent a duplicate copy to Albany. This time Augusta found it the "prettiest" letter ever written.

Though Byron denied it, Lady Melbourne sensed that he was lukewarm. "You can't conceive how I long to call you Aunt," he wrote. There was no comparable longing to call Annabella wife.

Among the first ominous signs was his announcement to Annabella that their engagement had come too late: "I yet wish to be good — with you I cannot but be happy; but I never shall be what I would have been." He meant that by her refusal of two years ago she had missed the chance to reform him, while giving him the fatal opportunity to ruin himself with Augusta. This "too late" theme was to be repeated many times, to Lady Melbourne and Lady Jersey as well as Annabella.

Another anxiety was lest Annabella should not be able to control his vagaries: "I fear she won't govern me — & if she don't it will not do at all." Nevertheless he referred to himself, hopefully, as Lord Annabella.

His invitation to Hobhouse to be best man included the wish that his friend might take a wife at the same time. Then they would all four be coupled "like people electrified in company through the same chain."

Procrastination over the Seaham visit was a further danger signal. He had not seen Annabella for ten months, he told Moore in September, but what with Hanson's delay over getting Byron's property into "matrimonial array,"* and his own nerves, it was 2 November before he arrived. In the five weeks between 20 September and 27 October he had three times referred to his bride as Desdemona in *Othello*.

Nor was the reunion propitious. Annabella proved so silent and overwrought that Byron feared she did not love him, while she formed the same impression of him, and indeed offered to release him from the engagement; at which he promptly fainted. *"Then* I was *sure* he must love me," recalled Annabella many years later. "And did he not?" asked her interlocutor, Mrs. Harriet Beecher Stowe. Looking enormously sad, Annabella replied that Byron's faint was caused by *"fear of detection"* — of the Augusta affair.

After a bare fortnight at Seaham, Annabella decided that he had better go home until the actual wedding. She had not reckoned with his seductive lovemaking. He in turn already detected incompatibilities, though not sexual ones. Instead of "governing" him as he had hoped, so that he became "very docile with a gentle guide," she herself indulged in

---

* The marriage settlement was £60,000, "secured on mortgage of the estate."

"feelings" and was taken ill every three days. "Sometimes we are too much alike," he told Lady Melbourne, "and then again too unlike." The disparity was due to her "system, and squaring her notions to the devil knows what." In fact, she could not play him by ear, like a mother, as did Augusta, though he found her susceptible to the "eloquence of *action*" and "quite *caressable* into kindness."

As soon as his disturbing presence was removed, all her confidence in him, herself and the marriage returned. He, on the contrary, felt his resolution ebbing. Up to the last moment he made desperate attempts to extricate himself. Could not the marriage be postponed until his estates were sold and they had enough to live on? — "perhaps the clouds may disperse in a month or two — do as you please." The Milbanke parents were pleased to go ahead. On the way to Seaham the reluctant bridegroom broke his journey at Six Mile Bottom for Christmas and tried to break the engagement by letter. Augusta stopped him. His best man, Hobhouse, noted Byron's "indifference, almost aversion" to the bride.

The pair arrived at Seaham late and unannounced on 30 December. Hobhouse at first marked down "Miss" as dowdy. But by the second day he was drawn by her curious magnetism. She seemed "most attractive" to him, especially after a jolly New Year's Eve, when he impersonated her in a mock marriage ceremony. But the tempo declined through Sunday, 1 January, and Byron awoke on the second, his wedding day, in melancholy mood. He dipped into an Ovid (was it Ovid in love or Ovid in exile?) and mooned about the grounds until called to the drawing room at 11 A.M. There the bridal pair knelt on cushions "stuffed with Peach-stones," according to Byron, they were so hard. The bride said "I Anne Isabella," firm as a rock, but the bridegroom "hitched" over "I George Gordon." Hobhouse considered the bride's muslin dress and jacket "very plain indeed," though he approved of the way she gazed at Byron throughout. For his part, Byron recalled his sensations in *The Dream*:

and he spoke
The fitting vows, but heard not his own words,
And all things reel'd around him . . . .

Hobhouse, however, remembered how Byron had looked at him with a half-smile when he came to "with all my worldly goods I thee endow." Lady Byron's going-away dress, recorded the best man, was "slate coloured."

"*Miss Milbanke,* are you ready?" said Byron to his bride, and, superstitious as ever, recognized the evil omen. Next moment they were both in the traveling carriage, Byron clinging to Hobhouse's hand through the window as if he could never let go.

There was a desperate beginning to the honeymoon, or "treaclemoon" as Byron called it, though vitriol would have been a better word. Driving through the icy afternoon, Annabella trembled while Byron sang Albanian war songs or vented his personal spleen. "It *must* come to a separation!" They reached the Milbankes' Yorkshire seat of Halnaby, forty miles away, in the dark. Still in the dark, presumably, he "*had* Lady B on the sofa before dinner" (Moore's recollection from Byron's burned memoirs). But a lurid glow suffused the first night. He awoke suddenly to see the flames of the sea-coal fire reflected on the red curtains of their marriage bed. Where was he but "fairly in hell," with Proserpine lying beside him? Next morning he met his wife in the library with a wintry greeting: "It is too late now. It is done, and cannot be undone."

From then on, things occasionally brightened. Despite midnight wanderings with dagger and pistol in search of imaginary avengers, and hints at being insane, satanic, murderous, incestuous, suicidal, a Cain, and the would-be seducer of children (Lady Charlotte Harley), he gave Annabella some agreeable times. She enjoyed copying the *Hebrew Melodies* for him as he composed them. Copying Augusta was even more rewarding. When Annabella managed to laugh like Augusta and address him playfully as Duck, he would respond with the pet name of Pippin, for her apple cheeks. Sometimes he would revert to the "child-side" which Augusta brought out in him, calling himself "poor B — *poor* B." Even at bad moments there could be compensations. He held a knife over her when he found her supposedly studying incest in Dryden's *Don Sebastian*. It is probable that Annabella did indeed read *Don Sebastian* with her husband's incest in mind, since in July 1816 she wrote to Augusta that the thought of it had nearly driven her to madness *"from the first week of my marriage."* Nevertheless she now looked up at him so innocently that he melted: "If anything could make me believe in heaven," he said, "it is the expression of your countenance at this moment." Once he nearly suffocated himself with carbon fumes by throwing water on the fire. It was she who saved him, as he thought, from death and Old Nick. "Perhaps I shall go to Heaven," he said softly, "holding by the hem of your garment." This was precisely Annabella's idea.

They moved back to Seaham towards the end of January, and then Annabella would walk with him beside the wild waves putting her hand on his arm and feeling that the sky had a soul when those eyes looked upon it. But Seaham by March had become to him "a yawn." It was almost a replica of Southwell in his boyhood, all cards, old parsons and old maids. On the twelfth Byron and Annabella arrived at Six Mile Bottom on their way to London. This seemed like a deliberate step into the abyss.

Annabella had insisted on accompanying Byron against his wishes. He had begun to love her and realized that only his "diabolical" side would flourish in a triangular situation. But Annabella had never met Augusta. She had her hopes as well as her suspicions. Could not both brother and sister cling to her garment and be carried to heaven?

Six Mile Bottom was sheer hell. A letter awaiting him about Newstead with the usual blank prospects started

Byron off in a temper. Annabella was the first to be humiliated. He sent her to bed early. "We don't want *you* my charmer." He ordered himself and Augusta a brooch each, engraved with crosses — "If she knew what these mean! do you remember our signs at Newstead?" He perpetrated the "gross indelicacy" of telling Augusta in front of Annabella that he knew she, Augusta, favored the new fashion of wearing knickers. "There have been moments," wrote Annabella later, "when I could have plunged a dagger into her heart."

Gradually his fury and frustration poured itself out over both women, so that they drew together against him. Byron drowned his indigestion in magnesia and his remorse in wine. Half his cruelties were drunken. To cap all, Annabella found she was pregnant and Napoleon escaped from Elba. There was need for a general escape from Six Mile Bottom. Particularly for the sake of the expected child. Annabella could hardly have forgotten what Byron had told her at Halnaby: that he was a Zeluco, the villain of Dr. John Moore's Gothick novel who strangled his baby because he believed it to be the child of incest.

At last the scene changed for the better. Unable to bear more horrors, Augusta sent her brother and sister-in-law home on 28 March. "Home" was now 13 Piccadilly Terrace, facing Green Park and backing towards the garden at Hyde Park Corner, where now stands the Byron statue. It was a fine house, though the number 13 was never to Byron's taste and the rent was £700 a year, which would swallow up Annabella's marriage settlement of £20,000.

Byron's mood improved also. "For ten days he was kinder than I have ever seen him," remembered Annabella. Then, with what seemed like a death-wish to her marriage, she invited Augusta to stay. "You are a fool for letting her come to the house," raged Byron; "and you will find it will make a great difference to *you* in all ways." The "lowering looks" with which he received his sister soon turned to ostentatious affection. Why did Annabella commit this folly? She had her reasons. "It was hopeless to keep them apart," she wrote later, "— it was not hopeless, in my opinion, to keep them innocent. I felt myself the guardian of these two beings, *indeed* 'on the brink of a precipice': and in this I sought to forget my own miserable and most humiliating condition."

Annabella's messianic obsession is clear, her passion for offering the hem of her garment. She was prepared to suffer a death-in-life for the sins of Byron and Augusta.

In analyzing the causes of the Byron-Annabella fiasco, the part played by their respective philosophies must not be overlooked. Byron and his wife were both "believers" in a sense. "The worst of it is, I *do believe*," he had told her at Halnaby — but his background was Calvinistic and gloomy. His eighteenth-century skepticism sometimes dispersed the miasma but it always re-formed.

Annabella the clever, "the pattern of the North," the spoiled child of elderly parents, had brought herself up in a very different school. Relentlessly pious, she was a "blue" of the Hannah More type, the lady who preached to titled women and demanded good works in return for their good fortune. This was no travesty of religion. In Annabella it was to produce an affinity with social pioneers like the Methodists, Quakers and Unitarians, and such distinguished nineteenth-century women as Elizabeth Fry, Florence Nightingale and Harriet Beecher Stowe. But the Hannah More mentality could also develop into patronage, self-satisfaction, and generations of Ladies Bountiful. Of this Annabella had her full share — Byron less than none. One can as well imagine a smug Cain, his favorite alter ego.

Nevertheless there was something in him which responded even while he jeered. Byron's attraction to Annabella was the feeling of the eighteenth century for the nineteenth century. Stirred now to admiration now to cynicism, one moment sympathetic the next critical, he illustrated the transition of an era into its successor.

Life in London was by no means intolerable for Byron that spring. He went round most days to John Murray's in

Albemarle Street, where on 7 April he first met Walter Scott. The two lame poets would go "thumping downstairs side by side" at the end of their morning sessions, their intimacy unaffected by Byron's trick of "mischief-making" and "mistifying," or by differences over religion and politics. Scott the romantic Tory could well indulge Lord Byron the Liberal "patrician" — and in any case Byron's politics did not seem "very fixed." Nor for that matter did his religion. When Scott predicted his conversion Byron said sharply: "I suppose you are one of those who prophesy I will turn Methodist." No, replied Scott, something less ordinary. "I would rather look to see you retreat upon the Catholic faith, and distinguish yourself by the austerity of your penances." Byron smiled "gravely" at this sally "and seemed to allow I might be right." They both laughed heartily at the thought of what the public would say about their exchange of ominous gifts: a gold-mounted Turkish dagger from Scott to Byron and a silver urn filled with Athenian bones from Byron to Scott. Sometimes Byron was as gloomy as his gift; in which case his older friend would either wait or somehow lead him back into conversation, "when the shadows almost always left his countenance like the mist rising from a landscape." If Byron showed another weakness — irrational "starts of suspicion" at what he took to be an offensive innuendo — Scott would "let his mind, like a troubled spring, work itself clear, which it did in a minute or two." If only young Lady Byron could have had the same knack. But as the valet Fletcher was to say: "I never yet knew a lady that could not manage my Lord, *except* my Lady."

Another new interest for Byron was the Drury Lane Theatre. It was now under the management of a dashing group of Radicals including Byron himself, Samuel Whitbread M.P., John Cam Hobhouse and the Honorable Douglas Kinnaird. Both Hobhouse and Kinnaird wrote scripts and the latter gave huge parties known as his "mob dinners." Moreover Edmund Kean, the famous tragic actor, had burst upon a somewhat depressed stage as Shylock in 1814, restoring the theatre's fortunes. As a member of the management subcommittee, Byron was provided with fascinating outside duties during a difficult time at home: "the scenes I had to go through! — the authors and the authoresses, and the milliners, and the wild Irishmen . . . who came in upon me! to all of whom it was proper to give a civil answer, and a hearing, and a reading." This self-control among so many "strutters and fretters" (as Byron called the actors), shows that he might have handled Annabella had he wished; and indeed he often confessed that his temper broke the marriage.

He did in fact succeed during the spring and summer in concealing his marital troubles from the world. People would remark upon his attentiveness to his wife when they went out together. This was not simply playacting but an expression of his mercurial temperament. When not irritated he sparkled with playfulness and grace. A young American visitor, the future historian George Ticknor, observed Byron's instincts both to please and to shock. Ticknor was warmly received at Piccadilly Terrace and charmed by Byron's affection for Lady Byron. Suddenly the Waterloo victory of 18 June was announced: "My Lord, my Lord, a great battle . . . Buonaparte is entirely defeated." "I'm d——d sorry for it," said his lordship, adding: "I didn't know but that I might live to see Lord Castlereagh's head on a pole. But I suppose I shan't, now." (He lived to hear of the foreign secretary's suicide — Castlereagh cut his own throat.)

Meanwhile the victory drew many of Byron's circle to Paris, including the Websters and Caroline Lamb. Byron became positively paternal towards "bold Webster," warning him against having a love affair with the "mad & malignant" Caroline ("Keep clear of her"), agreeing to stand godfather to the Websters' new baby, but sagely refusing to discuss Fanny's alleged affair with Wellington.

Towards the end of June it was Annabella's turn to ask Augusta to leave. The wife at once began to enjoy her husband's company: "There was a sort of conventional language of nonsense between us — which relieved his fears of 'Ser-

mons and Sentiment.' . . . In the midst of this childishness
. . . he would deliver the deepest reflections and then shrink
again into frolic and levity." Annabella was especially enchanted by these transitions — "till I learned to consider
those light and brilliant effusions only as the foam that
might float on the waters of bitterness." That was her systematic mistake. The simile which she chose showed that she
believed Byron to be of one piece, like the dark ocean whose
surface alone sometimes sparkled. The true metaphor for
Byron was Walter Scott's "spring," which changed as it
flowed from "clear" to "troubled" and back again forever.

The departure of Augusta did not free Byron and Annabella from their other problem — creditors. The first one had
descended like a wolf on the fold in April, when Byron
brought his heiress to the Duchess of Devonshire's grand
house at 13 Piccadilly. The death of Annabella's uncle, Lord
Wentworth, later that month, convinced a growing horde of
creditors that there was money in 13 Piccadilly Terrace. Far
from it. The Wentworth fortune went first to the Milbankes.
They also received the Wentworth family name, becoming
henceforth the Noels.

Byron could scarcely quit his house without meeting a dun
on the doorstep. Early in August he put up both Newstead
and Rochdale to auction. They did not reach the reserve
price. Frantic with anxiety, he would fly into furies at home
and get drunk as a lord at Kinnaird's where all was "hiccup
and happiness." There was a kind of happiness at the theatre
also, where he took a young mistress, Susan Boyce. Annabella's advancing pregnancy deprived him of her sexual comfort, though he may, according to one rumor, have attempted
sodomy when coming home drunk. Sometimes he would not
speak to her for days. "Am I in the way?" she once asked,
coming into his study. "Damnably," he shouted — an atroc-
ity, however, for which he immediately apologized. At the
end of October he could write to his friend Moore that Lady
Byron was "very ponderous and prosperous."

"I wish to make a few observations respecting the nature

of my greatest fear for B.," Annabella wrote to Augusta early in November "— and I think daily I understand the case better. His misfortune is an habitual *passion for Excitement*, which is always found in ardent temperaments, where the pursuits are not in some degree organised" (he had in fact "organised" himself into writing *The Siege of Corinth*, of which one line ran, "And some are restlessly at home"). "The love of tormenting," Annabella continued, "arises chiefly from this Source. Drinking, Gaming, etc. are all of the same origin."

A few days later she discovered a new origin for Byron's violent passions. For the first time a bailiff entered 13 Piccadilly Terrace and slept there. Byron rushed out of the house threatening a thousand crimes and blaming all on Annabella, who had married him against his will. "Things never were so serious," she told Augusta. "I have thought that since last Saturday (on which he sat drinking with Kinnaird's party till ½ past four in the morning), his *head* had never been right." If only his cousin George Byron would laugh him out of his "excessive horrors" over the bailiff. He behaved "as if no mortal had ever experienced any thing so shocking."

The point Annabella missed was that no mortal ever had. Byron was a poet. As he wrote to Leigh Hunt a month later, "Poets have an uneasy mind in an uneasy body" — Collins, Chatterton and Cowper mad, Pope crooked, Milton blind. Byron was capable of exalting any humiliation whether of debt or deformity into an excessive horror. Then the troubled waters would clear, if left to themselves. But Annabella knew only how to stir them. He would catch her gazing at him in pity and anxiety. Her periods of superhuman calm were even more maddening. In the autumn he recommenced the nightmares and night prowlings, armed against an imaginary assassin, as at Halnaby. Certainly the house was full of people. After the bailiff, Augusta arrived, invited again by the ill-advised Annabella. As might have been expected, Byron railed at them both. Augusta in turn invited George Byron to stay and restore their morale. A bodyguard was organized by the servants to protect their mistress: Mrs. Clermont, the lady's maid who was there at Byron's own suggestion, slept next door to Annabella, while the midwife and Fletcher did alternate sentry-go outside all night.

"I wish a boy of course," Byron had written to Webster in September. Three hours before her labor began Lady Byron remembered — or thought she did — Byron storming into her room and screaming that he hoped she would die. While she lay and grappled with her pains he quelled his indigestion by gulping soda water in the room below. Those who did not understand his method with bottle tops said that he was deliberately hurling them at the ceiling. The same people produced a macabre horror story when on 10 December his baby daughter, Augusta Ada, was born. "The child *was* born dead, wasn't it?" he asked before entering the bedroom. Byron forcibly denied the story to Hobhouse and even Mrs. Clermont testified to his devotion to his daughter. But this apparently did not prevent him from planning to use Ada against her mother. Annabella recollected his standing over the cradle and exulting: "Oh! what an implement of torture have I acquired in you!"

The situation might still have been saved but for the duns. Byron decided the family could no longer afford to live in style at Piccadilly Terrace. He therefore peremptorily ordered Annabella on 3 January 1815 to go and stay with her parents at the Wentworth estate in Leicestershire, Kirkby Mallory, as soon as convenient, taking Ada with her. He would follow when he had wound up Number 13.

This was Annabella's chance. She had long suspected that Byron's debts, drunkenness, and remorse had driven him mad. She feared for her child's life. A conference was held on 8 January at which she consulted Dr. Matthew Baillie (who had examined Byron's lame foot as a boy) about his "case." Had her husband the excuse of insanity? Finding himself unable to pronounce, Baillie left it for Francis Le

Mann, Annabella's physician, to interview Byron personally. Meanwhile Baillie advised Annabella to leave Number 13 and await Le Mann's verdict at her parents' home in Kirkby Mallory..

Byron saw her for the last time on 14 January in his room, where he was sitting with Augusta. He backed away from Annabella's outstretched hand, quoting ironically, "Where shall we three meet again?" She replied, "In heaven, I trust." But he would not get there by the hem of her garment.

Next morning the honeymoon carriage stood ready to take her away forever. She went downstairs before he was up. Sentinels were no longer posted outside her door, but outside his was a mat on which his Newfoundland dog used to lie. "For a moment I was tempted to throw myself on it," she recalled, "and wait at all hazards, but it was only a moment — and I passed on."

Those two scenes, the first in his room and the second outside his door, summed up Byron's dilemma. Poor Annabella swung between heaven and the doormat, uplift and despair. She could offer him her exhortations or her self-abasement. Both were extremes. What Byron needed, as he had said so often, was to be "managed" and "governed" by a "gentle guide."

FIVE

Separation and Exile
(1816)

BYRON'S STORY now enters a period of four months when every letter has been scrutinized, every word meticulously weighed by his or Annabella's partisans. He emerges with his usual clarity. His wife's attitude as always remains partially opaque.

Throughout January 1816 Byron was operating on two levels. The boiling point he had reached over Ada's birth was maintained. Augusta, still at 13 Piccadilly Terrace with him, suspected what would now be called hypermania. "I was struck previously with a wildness in his eyes," she told Annabella; and when he described himself as "the greatest man living" not excepting Napoleon ("God, I don't know that I do except even him") she was convinced. His cousin George Byron, also still around, warned him about the Noels' probable defense of their daughter. "Let them come forward, I'll Glory in it!" he exclaimed, exaggerating his promiscuity at the theatre (Susan Boyce was his only adultery) and boasting that he would marry Miss Margaret Mercer Elphinstone, a sensible heiress who had been interested in him before his marriage, as soon as Annabella divorced him. Even Thomas Moore, who had been away for a year, noticed the change. "Do you know, my dear B," he wrote, "there was something in your last letter — a sort of unquiet mystery, as well as a want of your usual elasticity of spirits — which have hung upon my mind unpleasantly ever since."

Equally unpleasantly did Byron's marriage hang upon his mind — at least on part of it, the part that he deliberately allowed to swing wildly on its hinges in the gusts of his passion. But the other part expected a return in due course to normal life with Annabella and their child. This attitude was encouraged by two letters from Annabella written to him immediately after her departure.

Annabella had left for Kirkby not entirely because Byron "turned her out of the house" (a myth which dies hard) but partly because Dr. Baillie advised an experimental separation. Baillie added that she should write soothingly and lightly so as not to irritate his supposed malady. The result, written on the fifteenth, began "Dearest B" and ended: "Ada's love to you with mine. Pip." And on the sixteenth: "Dearest Duck . . . Love to the good goose and everybody's love to you both from hence. Ever thy most loving Pippin . . . Pip . . . Ip."

But within a day or two something happened to "Pip" which caused her to disclose all Byron's brutalities to her parents, and to postpone his visit to Kirkby, which she had told him on the sixteenth they all eagerly awaited. The Noels made her promise to leave Byron if Le Mann's verdict was "sane." On the twentieth Lady Noel (formerly Milbanke) went to London, armed with an indictment by Annabella against her husband on sixteen counts. Among the drunkenness, adultery, threats* and insults was listed a "con-

---

* One listed threat was to install his mistress at Number 13. Another threat, made in front of Annabella and Augusta, was to corrupt his favorite niece, Georgiana, then aged seven. Each was a case of what Shelley called Byron's "childish love of astonishing people and creating a sensation" — as when he shocked Claire Clairmont with a tale of having had an unfaithful mistress sewn in a sack and drowned. Incidentally Georgiana's life was ruined not by Byron but by her husband (a Trevanion cousin), by her sister Medora, and by her amoral mother Augusta.

vulsive fit" one evening at the Drury Lane Theatre. This had been caused by Edmund Kean's horrific simulation of madness in the part of Sir Giles Overreach, the villain of Massinger's play *A New Way to Pay Old Debts*. Possibly these themes of madness and debt had combined to send Byron off. Incest with Augusta was not on the list. Annabella did not mention her suspicions, having decided that the worst of them were false. "I have *wronged* you," she wrote to Augusta on the sixteenth, presumably meaning that she no longer believed that the brother and sister had had intercourse since his marriage. After her mother had gone Annabella broke down. She longed to be back at Number 13, "if only in the coal-hole."

What had happened to change her mind? Professor Marchand connects Annabella's sudden revulsion with the arrival of the London post. Some remark from Augusta, George Byron or Mrs. Clermont (also still at 13 Piccadilly Terrace) had perhaps told her "in a flash" that Byron was not mad but bad. Her love had created her self-delusion. Now it crumbled.

Moreover on the eighteenth a letter arrived from her friend Selina Doyle, definitely advising her to take "the final step," separation. Since Byron's complaint, wrote Miss Doyle, was "insanity" caused by "Jealous Love," Annabella's presence must always "aggravate the Complaint instead of soothing."

Apart from letters, Annabella had had time to think again about herself and make a shattering discovery. Deeply self-analytical, she had always been absorbed in her own processes and powers. On the honeymoon Byron had complained of her "feelings," scruples and mysterious indispositions. All this adds up to a highly strung, introverted character, potentially as explosive as Byron's but restrained, unlike his, by a rigorous philosophy. The lid blew off at Kirkby, not because Byron might be bad — he had taken good care to tell her this himself — but because *she* had been proved to possess no magic touch, no saving power.

Her messianic obsession has been described. This, her religion, was what mattered to her. While living with Byron she could persuade herself it worked. Was she afraid of his violence? Hanson asked her. Not for herself, she replied; "my eye can always put down his!!!" It was the eye of a lion tamer. But once away from him, the eye turned in on itself. There it saw the terrifying truth. She had failed and must fail in her mission. For she had fallen in love with the irredeemable Lucifer. As she was to write in 1851: "There was a deliberate purpose to set God's will and the human law at defiance." And Byron himself seemed to accept his Satanism, saying bitterly to her: "It is my destiny to ruin all I come near." Not only could she never in this life restore him to heaven, but he might drag her down with him to hell, rendering her own moral sense "worthless and debased." This was why she must never go back. She was in an agony of crushed pride and fear for her soul.

Byron meanwhile was going his casual way as if nothing were at stake. "Pip's" letters went unanswered while he busied himself with charities he could ill afford. Refusing a large sum from Murray, he ordered it to be divided between Coleridge the poet, the dramatist Charles Robert Maturin, great-uncle of Oscar Wilde, and the radical philosopher William Godwin.

But on the enemy's front events were moving purposefully. Le Mann told Lady Noel he would treat Byron for his liver as there was "nothing like settled lunacy." She therefore put her daughter's case for a separation in the hands of a lawyer, Dr. Stephen Lushington. At his suggestion Annabella's father sent Byron on 2 February a letter proposing a quiet separation.

There was no question of Byron's taking it quietly. Hobhouse found him on the fifth "completely knocked up" by this unexpected blow — it was the very day Byron had proposed going to Kirkby — but resolute in defiance. He blamed Lady Noel and Mrs. Clermont for the crisis and wrote an impassioned appeal to Annabella. There had been "errors" in the past year, no doubt, caused by disease and distress over money, "but I loved you . . . and will not give you up."

Annabella had become "almost insensible" when the separation letter was on its way; Byron's reply made her roll on the floor in anguish. Nevertheless she forced herself to reply so coldly that he accused her of being "much changed." She leaped to the defense of her consistency, asserting that she had been a "consistently" dutiful wife and was still consistent. "Now my resolution cannot be changed." She gave a significant reason for her leaving him: not his derangement but *"total* dereliction of principle" in which he "gloried." This of course was the Lucifer theme of "evil be thou my good."

In seeking the reason for the catastrophe, Hobhouse had at first been bewildered. Byron insisted that he himself could not *"guess* at the immediate cause" and assured Hobhouse he had told him *"all."* Rightly deciding that the separation was in that case inexplicable, Hobhouse probed Augusta and George Byron and ultimately got from them a fresh tale of horrors: menaces, furies, neglects, other women, turning Annabella out, locked doors, and pistols. Much the same story was finally wrung from Byron himself, who now oscillated between threats to blow his brains out and an impulse to rush abroad with Hobby once he was "quit of such a woman."

On 22 February Annabella suddenly imparted to Lushington a secret reason for her separating from Byron. It was her growing suspicion of his incest. Up till now Lushington had talked of a possible reconciliation. At once his advice was reversed. Annabella must have no further contact with Byron; and though she would not be able to *prove* the charge of incest, it would be cited as Byron's method of torturing her and a potent reason for her leaving him. A week later (29 February) Hobhouse discovered that "a story has now got abroad against her [Mrs. Leigh] & B!!!" On the same day Byron wrote aggressively to Moore: "I am at war 'with all the world and his wife'; or rather, 'all the world *and my* wife' at war with me." But Hobhouse was now against any war and in favor of a private settlement.

On 5 March Annabella herself disclosed to Hobhouse "*that something had passed which she had as yet told to no one, and which nothing but the absolute necessity of justifying herself in court should wring from her.*" (This is surely still a reference to the incest. Professor G. Wilson Knight, however, takes it as a hint at Byron's alleged sodomy, which he considers to be the main cause of the separation.) On the eighth, one of Annabella's partisans weighed in with a confirmation of horrors. This was George Wilmot, Byron's cousin and husband of the lady who walked in beauty like the night. Wilmot threatened that "something horrid" would be proved against Byron, though it was "no enormity."

Hobhouse was determined, if successful in persuading Byron to settle quietly, to get a quid pro quo from Annabella. He therefore presented a list of infamous charges against Byron for Annabella to deny: "cruelty, systematic unremitted neglect, gross & repeated infidelities — incest & ——." The blank was sodomy.

However, Hobhouse was only partially successful. For Annabella's final statement did not deny the last two, and worst, charges, but denied only that she had *spread them* or would *use them* if forced to contest the separation. Would Byron force her?

His bellicosity had vanished almost at a touch. As usual he proved "manageable" by his friends. To Moore, who condoled with him on his choice of Annabella as a wife, he replied on the eighth that there was no fault in his *choice* "(unless in *choosing at all*)." As in the case of Augusta, he went on to blame himself for the disaster. He admitted his "strange and desultory habits" acquired owing to youthful license, "scrambling about, over and through the world"; disordered health during marriage and a "mind ill at ease," producing "excess" and "temper"; but if he had been in "even a tolerable situation" financially, he might have "gone on fairly."

Next day, 9 March, Byron virtually agreed to a proposed financial settlement. It was the same day on which he accepted Annabella's (partial) denial of the "two reports." Under a separation order he and Annabella would share equally her present fortune of £1,000, and when Lady Noel died the Kirkby estate would also be shared "on fair terms."

Augusta's position was less satisfactory. She was again in an advanced stage of pregnancy and clapping tongues broadcast (with no excuse this time) that Byron was the father. It is true that Colonel Leigh and Annabella proved staunch. Leigh denied the gossip and Annabella refused to abjure Augusta's company while a shred of doubt remained, despite the danger of seeming to condone the incest. As Annabella wrote to Augusta on 1 April, "I never was, nor never can be, so *mercilessly* virtuous as to admit *no* excuses for even the worst of errors." But Augusta's continued presence with Byron at Piccadilly Terrace had become intolerable. She removed herself to — of all places — St. James's Palace. Here she resumed her duties as bedchamber woman to that mercilessly virtuous sovereign, Queen Charlotte.

To forget his grief in the prospect of going abroad was still Byron's plan. On 21 March he wrote to the ever-dilatory Hanson asking him to hasten the overdue interest on Annabella's marriage settlement, "as I can conceive that can have nothing to do with the subject of the present discussion." The present discussion — separation — was to be legally concluded in exactly one month. Yet Byron maintained throughout March and April 1816, and indeed to the end of his life, that he still did not know the "specific" cause of the separation. Biographers must step in where Byron failed to tread.

Sodomy can be ruled out. First, there is no positive evidence. The nearest thing is Hobhouse's comment many years later that Lord Holland heard Byron "had tried to ——— her." This could be mere speculation, part of the price Byron

paid in permitting a quiet settlement. Second, there is negative evidence. George Wilmot, as we have seen, told Hobhouse the cause was "horrid" but not "an enormity." Yet so
great an enormity was sodomy that Hobhouse avoided the
word, putting a dash instead. Third, if Byron only tried it
once, perhaps when drunk, why did Annabella abandon him
— the man she loved? Alternatively, if he made it his practice, why did she submit? To get round this embarrassment,
it has been suggested that Annabella was too innocent to
know what was happening and was enlightened only by Mrs.
Clermont. This is ludicrous. The mathematical Annabella,
a highly educated bluestocking, cannot have been completely
ignorant of human geometry.

Incestuous love is the next possibility. Wilmot's pro-
nouncement of "no enormity" does not exclude incest. The
word was written openly by Hobhouse. Incest was not a civil
crime until the twentieth century. Cases were familiar from
eighteenth-century tales like *Zeluco* and *Vathek*, from Alfieri's play *Myrrha*, from Byron's own poem *Parisina*, and
from the rumored liaison of the Duke of Cumberland and
Princess Sophia. The narcissism of the Romantics made this
form of love especially attractive. And as Byron's grandson,
Lord Lovelace, pointed out in his *Astarte*, love for a half
sister with whom one had not been brought up was scarcely
"an enormity."

On the other hand, both sodomy and incest seem to be
ruled out as causes of the separation by a manuscript in John
Murray's possession, recording a much later conversation
between Hobhouse and a friend. Apparently reminiscing
about the blacklist he had presented to Lady Byron for denial on 8 March 1816, Hobhouse said: "I wrote down every
vice and sin, and crime, and horror in short of which a human being can be capable, and I said, 'Now I shall not stir in
this business till you tell me whether you accuse him of any
of these things, and which of them it is.' And the answer was,
'It is none of these things.' Then I said, 'What is it?' But
they would never say."

This remembered blacklist would have been a formidable one if it included all that Byron had written about in his poetry and quoted in order to chill Annabella's spine — murder, bigamy, piracy, homosexuality, Vathek's devil worship, and Zeluco's strangulation of his child. These particular horrors can of course be ruled out, though his paroxysms at the time of. Ada's birth would have contributed to Annabella's sense of evil.

In Annabella's mind, incest must be ruled out also. It was not Augusta's suspected sin which caused her abruptly to appeal to her parents after 16 January. For Annabella had temporarily ceased to harbor suspicions of Augusta. And once Annabella had revealed these suspicions to Lushington on 22 February and thus scotched his plan for a reconciliation, they could again be dropped — as indeed Annabella did drop them until Caroline Lamb made it her business to resurrect them. (On 27 March Caroline called upon Annabella and told her about Byron's alleged confessions of incest and "worse crimes" with boys.)

With the "two reports" of major vices ruled out, together with the phantom horrors, only one possible conclusion remains. There was no single, immediate cause of separation, and Byron was right. It happened because it happened, as in so many unhappy marriages. But many contributory factors existed, some of which, as we have seen, Byron himself named. Besides these there was his ambivalence about women, except the one woman — Augusta — made in his own image; and the knowledge that he was a hunter by nature and had been pursued.

On Annabella's side, there was the inexorable pursuit, conducted partly by subterfuge (according to Hobhouse she told Byron she had invented the "other man" to "hook" him) ; the extreme anxiousness resulting in delicate health; her "too *high-wrought*" mind like "*Proof* Spirits" as her mother said; her rectangularity which triumphed over her intention not to be "mercilessly virtuous"; above all the collapse of her own powers. What should she have done when

Byron jeeringly advocated a Continental type of marriage in which they both would take lovers — he Augusta? As she wrote to the Reverend Francis Hodgson, "my security depended on the total abandonment of every moral and religious principle against which . . . his hatred and endeavours were uniformly directed."

She had lived with these unspeakable things from 2 January 1815 until 15 January 1816. A day or two away from him opened her eyes. Exhausted human nature did the rest. She could not face it again.

Byron said many farewells during his last month, and many were said to him. His most unforgiving was to Mrs. Clermont in verses which began, "Born in the garret, in the kitchen bred." This caused great offense right down to 1870, when Mrs. Harriet Beecher Stowe, Annabella's champion, lauded Mrs. Clermont to the American public as "a most excellent, respectable, well-behaved Englishwoman." Byron's most forgiving farewell was composed for Annabella: "Even though unforgiving, never / 'Gainst thee shall my heart rebel."

Female society proved the most unforgiving towards him. At a party to which he escorted Augusta only two ladies were polite, whereas four newspapers defended him: the *Examiner, Morning Chronicle, News,* and *Independent Whig*. The two sympathetic ladies were Lady Jersey, the hostess, and Margaret Mercer Elphinstone, who parted from Byron with the words, "You should have married me, and then this would not have happened to you!" Abusive farewells came from other sections of the press, for instance:

> *He goes, in foreign lands prepared to find*
> *A life more suited to his guilty mind.*

The satirical novelist Thomas Love Peacock was to celebrate in his *Nightmare Abbey* the farewell dinner given by Byron's friends to the poet. The melancholy and romantic poet Mr. Cypress (Byron) departs "to rake seas and rivers, lakes and canals, for the moon of ideal beauty." So delighted was Byron when he read this passage in 1818 that he sent Peacock a rosebud. It was framed by the novelist in a gold locket inscribed, "From Byron to T. L. Peacock, 1819."

On 14 April 1816 Byron and Augusta said good-bye to one another in blinding tears, as it turned out, forever.

> *Thou wert the solitary star*
> *Which rose and set not to the last.*

But Augusta was not quite the *solitary star.* Through his usual mixture of kindness and weakness with women, Byron had allowed yet another pursuer to get inside his defenses at the eleventh hour. This was seventeen-year-old Claire (Jane) Clairmont, stepdaughter of William Godwin, the philosopher of free love and other amiable theories.

The libertarian tenets of Godwin's family had been severely tested of late. His daughter Mary Godwin by Mary Wollstonecraft had eloped with the young poet Percy Bysshe Shelley, to Godwin's fury. The publicity over Byron now suggested to Claire that she might have a poet-lover of her own. Letters and a literary composition arrived for Byron from 13 Arabella Row, Pimlico. These were the regular preliminaries of romantic young ladies who beset him. But Claire was prepared to sleep with him as soon as she could arrange a rendezvous. This happened somewhere outside London during his last week in England. The best that can be said is that both their wounded vanities were assuaged. Byron had no intention of maintaining the frail liaison, but his farewell message to Claire was unwise: *Poste Restante, at Geneva.*

The deed of separation was signed on 21 April, with the support of his male friends. By the twenty-third he was ready to leave 13 Piccadilly Terrace — and the duns to move in *en masse.* He and Hobhouse waited in wind-swept Dover through the twenty-fourth, visiting the nearby tomb of Charles Churchill, an eighteenth-century satiric poet. In

Churchill's Grave Byron wrote his farewell to the England where he, like Churchill, seemed to have been "the comet of a season."

A few inquisitive society ladies, disguised as chambermaids, took a final peep at Byron on 25 April. He walked with Hobhouse down towards a rough sea, where he boarded the packet. Hobhouse watched it bounding away towards Ostend: "the dear fellow pulled off his cap & wav'd it to me. . . . God bless him for a gallant spirit and a kind one."

Byron was also a hopeful spirit, or at least not entirely despondent. In conveying congratulations to Thomas Moore that March on an honorary appointment, Byron had written something which may stand for his own valediction: "These be dignities which await only the virtuous. But then recollect you are *six* and *thirty* . . . and I have eight years good to run before I arrive at such hoary perfection; by which time, — if I *am* at all, — it will probably be in a state of great or progressing merits." He had exactly eight years to run and many of them were to be "good."

The inn at Ostend was foreign soil again. Byron celebrated with a predatory spring. His personal physician, Dr. John William Polidori, wrote in his diary, "As soon as he reached his room, Lord Byron fell like a thunderbolt upon the chambermaid." (This "Pollydolly," as Byron called him, was to be the uncle of the three Rossettis, Dante Gabriel, Christina and William Michael.) A Swiss courier had also been hired to accompany Byron, and there was always his valet, "the learned Fletcher," as well as his page, Robert Rushton.

Flanders did not appeal to Byron: neither its voluptuous art nor its flat landscape. "Reubens' women have all red gowns and red shoulders — to say nothing of necks," he wrote to Augusta. ". . . Level roads don't suit me, as thou knowest; it must be up hill or down." The great *pavés* along which Wellington and Blücher had driven Napoleon were merely "an eternity of pavement." But the site of Waterloo struck

Byron dumb. For the first five minutes he did not speak at all. Then he said, "I have seen the plains of Marathon, and these are as fine." He fell into silence again when they drove down to the château of Hougoument, until his mood again veered round and he galloped over the battlefield on horseback shouting wild Albanian songs. As the party drove on towards Germany, Byron's experiences began to form themselves into a new, third canto for the Childe:

> *And Harold stands upon this place of skulls,*
> *The grave of France, the deadly Waterloo!*

He rumbled southeastwards in his great mock Napoleonic coach, painted dark green and costing £500. Memories of earlier carefree travels kept returning. The Rhine offered him its "valley of sweet waters," once his favorite ride at Constantinople, and the shepherds of the Swiss Alps with their peaceful pipes reminded him by contrast of the Greek shepherds, a pipe in one hand but a musket in the other. Violence he could only condone in the cause of national freedom: the dead of Morat near Avenches, for instance, where the Swiss had defeated their Burgundian oppressors in the fifteenth century and a few of whose heaped bones Byron sent to Murray — enough to make "a quarter of a hero," rather than a set of knife handles, as was the custom. This Swiss example of heroic death was celebrated in *Childe Harold,* Canto III: "Morat and Marathon twin names shall stand."

The travelers had crossed the Jura, Byron and Polidori debating whether "clouds were mountains or mountains clouds." Suddenly Byron recognized his love for the next four months, the Lake of Geneva or Lake Leman; a loved one as gentle as Augusta: "Lake Leman woos me with its crystal face."

On 25 May they put up at M. Dejean's Hôtel d'Angleterre just short of the town of Geneva. Feeling little younger than the ancient bones, Byron registered as "Age: 100." M. Dejean made him change it to the correct twenty-eight; but not before Claire Clairmont, who had arrived two weeks earlier with the Shelleys, spotted Byron's name. "I am sorry you are grown so old," she wrote playfully, "— indeed I suspected you were 200, from the slowness of your journey. . . . Well, heaven send you sweet sleep — I am so happy. *Claire.*"

Byron was not so happy. Nevertheless it was his own fault. Why had he given her his address? His heart had "alighted on the nearest perch" during that bare London March, as he once told Lady Melbourne his heart always did; but now he wished to cut away the perch from under it. This was impossible. Shelley had come to Geneva expecting to meet Byron, Mary having been introduced in London. By 10 June Shelley's party were installed in the Villa Montalègre at Cologny above the harbor, and Byron a few hundreds yards higher up at the Villa Diodati. His small bedroom got the morning sun, and from the verandah running around three sides of the villa, supported on slender columns, he could see the crystalline Lake of Geneva.

The thirty-year-old poet John Milton had been a guest at the Villa Diodati some two centuries earlier and had walked by the same romantic shore. A century before Milton, the Swiss religious reformer John Calvin had launched his dour gospel of predestination from a narrow, low-backed chair in Geneva, to Byron's future bane. Exactly one century after Milton, in 1739, the young English poet Thomas Gray announced to all Romantics what the Alps could do for the soul: "Not a torrent, not a cliff but is pregnant with religion and poetry. There are certain scenes that would awe an atheist into disbelief." A year after Byron's death William Hazlitt, the literary critic, was to deride this alpine piety: "The crossing of the Alps has, I believe, given some of our fashionables a shivering-fit of morality." During the eighteenth century Jean-Jacques Rousseau had stamped the lakeside indelibly with the story of Julie and St. Preux, lovers from his *Nouvelle Héloïse;* while Edward Gibbon had once fallen in love with Mme de Staël's mother, Mlle Susanne

Curchod, and when that ended, had written *The History of the Decline and Fall of the Roman Empire*. Voltaire had lived at Ferney; Mme de Staël was still at Coppet. And now Byron and Shelley, two shy poets of the youngest generation, met by this lake for the first time on 27 May 1816.

Shelley's friendship was to influence both the poetry and career of Byron. It was partly under Shelley's stimulus that Byron's agony of mind now expressed itself in a new, Promethean phase of Romantic metaphysics. In later years Shelley's revolutionary ideals were to play a part in drawing Byron back into an active career. Though the younger poet was only twenty-three, Byron already knew Shelley's *Queen Mab* (1813) with its total rejection of kings, priests, and statesmen, culminating in the reiterated assertion, "There is no God!" Shelley's substitute belief in man's perfectability — "Yet every heart contains perfection's germ" — was far from being Byron's creed. But there were to be hours spent sailing on Lake Leman, riding into the mountains, and talking around the open fireplace at the Villa Diodati, when Shelley's intense way of looking at nature and man would for a time almost become Byron's own.

The first excursion was by boat up the lake. Byron and Shelley set sail from Geneva on 22 June, leaving Polidori behind, since he had sprained his ankle jumping off a wall, at Byron's suggestion, to assist Mary. (The young doctor seems to have felt some jealousy of his employer. "What is there excepting writing poetry," he had asked Byron earlier, "that I cannot do better than you?" "First," replied Byron, "I can hit with a pistol the keyhole of that door — Secondly, I can swim across that river [the Rhine] . . . — and thirdly, I can give you a d——d good thrashing." Now poor Pollydolly could not even jump better than Byron.)

Their guiding spirit was to be Rousseau, and their ports of call the villages sanctified by the *Nouvelle Héloïse*. Rousseau in his *Confessions* described how he had selected these scenes for his great love story and earthly paradise: "I chose that lake around which my heart has never ceased to wander

. . . the richness and variety of its landscape, the magnificence and majesty of the whole." After Byron and Shelley had enjoyed mountain honey at Meillerie, the scene of St. Preux's exile, a violent squall arose and tested their courage to the utmost. Each reacted bravely in his own way, Shelley the nonswimmer sitting with arms folded prepared to slip unresistingly to the bottom, Byron stripped and ready to rescue them both.

They limped into St. Gingolph, however, and next day visited the medieval castle of Chillon at the end of the lake, where Julie had sustained her fatal accident. Here the dungeons and torture chambers inspired the two poets with characteristic responses. Recoiling in horrified silence from such bestial ugliness, Shelley wrote a *Hymn to Intellectual Beauty*. He entreated its spirit to calm him, whose fate it was "to fear himself, and love all human kind." Byron, while also fearing himself, did not love *all* human kind, but those who defied their fate in the service of others. At Chillon there had been one such, the Swiss religious reformer and patriot Prior François Bonivard of St. Victor's, Geneva. He had challenged the Duke of Savoy and been supposedly chained below lake level at Chillon to the fifth pillar of a dungeon for four years, until in 1536 the Bernese troops captured the castle and freed him. Byron may have carved his own signature on the third pillar of Bonivard's prison, where it was seen by a visitor in 1821, and is now preserved under glass.* He certainly wrote one of his most popular poems, *The Prisoner of Chillon*, in two days, virtually on the spot.

Byron had improved on the guide's tales, imagining Bonivard forced to watch his brothers die of starvation. On release he finds that life has come full circle, and if home is a prison, prison can be a hermitage and home:

> *My very chains and I grew friends,*
> *So much a long communion tends*

* For a man of Byron's height, 5 feet 8½ inches, it is carved suspiciously high up.

> *To make us what we are: — even I*
> *Regain'd my freedom with a sigh.*

Today we know that Bonivard was not quite the martyr of Byron's poem. He was not chained, nor was his prison below lake level (though an optical illusion may have made it seem so). Enjoying a ripe, even overripe old age, Bonivard married four times and had his young fourth wife drowned for adultery. The idea of his six dead brothers was probably lifted by Byron from Dante's *Inferno,* Canto XXXIII. None of this affects the beauty of Byron's poem, which is timeless. Bonivard remains a Promethean figure, chained to a pillar instead of a rock, and defying "them" for the sake of "us."

From Chillon the two poets sailed to Clarens and there yielded themselves up once more to the spirit of Jean-Jacques. "Thank God, Polidori is not here," said Byron as they walked at evening in "Julie's grove," on the hillside beneath the château. Rousseau had worshipped, if not "intellectual beauty" like Shelley, at least "ideal Beauty," and the influence of Rousseau on the Romantics can scarcely be exaggerated. Through him the glorification of feeling became established. Moreover in his own life he exemplified the Romantic's typical brooding over real or imagined persecution; he was an exile; and he wrote words which may have struck a chord both in Byron and Shelley: "If one wishes to devote one's books to the true benefit of one's country, one must write them abroad."

On 27 June Rousseau's two disciples sailed into Ouchy, the port for Lausanne. This being the anniversary of the day on which Gibbon completed his *Decline and Fall,* they visited the decaying summerhouse in Lausanne where he had worked. Murray received some Gibbonian acacia and rose leaves, together with the news that the third canto of *Childe Harold* was practically finished. In this canto the lake excursion is relived. We hear "the light drip of the suspended oar," we see "stars which are the poetry of heaven," we breath "a living fragrance from the shore." But the moun-

tain range, too, has spoken to Byron and sometimes with the
voice of Wordsworth's pantheism:

> *Are not the mountains, waves, and skies a part*
> *Of me and of my Soul, as I of them?*

Byron was later to remark, "When I was in Switzerland,
Shelley used to dose me with Wordsworth physic even to
nausea" — the nausea perhaps supervening after he had
penned such imitative lines as the following:

> *to me*
> *High mountains are a feeling, but the hum*
> *Of human cities torture* . . . .

Wordsworth had already said in *Tintern Abbey* that mountains were to him "a feeling"; and Byron's rejection of the
cities' hum was not to last. After all, he was preparing to go
to lively Italy as soon as Hobhouse could get a passport and
join him. (Hobhouse's book on the Hundred Days had
aroused official suspicion.) It is possible, of course, that
Byron was thinking primarily of the hum of Geneva.

"Switzerland is a curst selfish, swinish country of brutes
placed in the most romantic region in the world." Thus
Byron in 1821. He was having to leave Ravenna in Italy for
political reasons, and had thought of returning to his
Genevan haunts of five years back. But his inquiries revealed
that "there was a colony of English all over the canton of
Geneva, etc.," presumably causing another rise in house rents
even beyond the expensive Villa Diodati.

There were several reasons in fact why Switzerland, Byron's
"most romantic region in the world," could not be his permanent home. The Genevese were not yet English-speaking,
or for that matter Italian-speaking, Byron's only fluent foreign tongue. He got on well with the local literati — the
Pichets, Sismondi, Schlegel, his young banker M. Hentsch
and old Bonstetten of Berne, who had known Thomas Gray
at Cambridge. But it was not until the great Goethe fell

passionately for Byron that his fame resounded through Germany and Switzerland, *The Prisoner of Chillon* being first translated into German in 1819 by Rudolf Vyss, author of *The Swiss Family Robinson*.

The Swiss whom Byron liked entertained the English whom he did not like. Mme de Staël was a case in point. She defended him valiantly over the separation and even tried, though in vain, to arrange a reconciliation with Annabella. No doubt at fifty she was "Old Mother Stale" to Byron and had "a most unconscionable insatiability of talking and shining"; nevertheless he liked "our lady of Coppet," as he also called her, saluting her as the most brilliant woman of the age, and perhaps of any age. But the English he met in the courtyard, on the steps, on the staircase, in the library and salons of turreted Coppet — !

On his first visit, his very name caused the novelist Elizabeth Hervey, half sister of William Beckford, to faint — "*too much* — at *sixty-five* years of age," commented the Duchesse de Broglie, Mme de Staël's daughter. They stared at him, he said, "as at some outlandish beast in a raree show," or as if "his Satanic Majesty had been among them." His page was rumored to be either Caroline Lamb or Augusta Leigh in disguise. English telescopes would be trained from Geneva upon the Villa Diodati and stories circulated of skirts on the terrace. Soon the stories got back to England, where delicious shudders were aroused at the "bad company" Byron was keeping in Switzerland, so bad that he was "shunned" by all, English and natives. And indeed Byron was having trouble — though not from "all these 'mistresses,'" as Augusta heard. "I have had but one," wrote Byron defensively. That one was Claire Clairmont.

Claire realized she was pregnant by Byron. This did not worry her. Mary had her eighteen-month-old illegitimate baby William by Shelley, and they were not able to marry until after December 1816, when Shelley's wife Harriet drowned herself. It was not marriage that Claire hoped for. She had imbibed the Godwin philosophy to the extent of giving Byron in one of her letters a motto for the married state: *Abandon hope all ye who enter here.* Her hope was for a loving intimacy, strengthened through their child.

She would transcribe *Chillon* for him, and in the evenings all four friends would join in poetical or philosophical discussions, often given a macabre direction by Shelley's imagination. When Byron read aloud his favorite *Christabel* by Coleridge, Shelley had what Byron called "a fit of fantasy," which Polidori successfully treated. The withered breast of the evil lamia or witch, Lady Geraldine, in *Christabel* had reminded Shelley, as he gazed at Mary, of a woman he had heard of with eyes for nipples.

Their speculations also tended towards cosmic profundities, for the century was absorbing earlier discoveries and stood on the edge of vast new ones. Dr. Erasmus Darwin's experiments in animation, as the friends understood them, were to be followed half a century later by Charles Darwin's evolution. Already there was galvanism, moon-magnetism, animal magnetism, and soon there would be spiritualism. The Industrial Revolution had enslaved the ancient Greek "element" of water as steam, and now the "element" of fire was about to be harnessed as electricity. The nature of electricity and its connection with lightning had been known since the great discovery of Benjamin Franklin in the eighteenth century. In *Childe Harold,* Canto III, Byron tried to embody all his most dynamic feelings in the one word — "Lightning"; while in *Manfred* the hero was to speak of "the Promethean spark, / The lightning of my being." Shelley was later to become the poetical high priest of this elemental discovery in his *Prometheus Unbound,* where the immortal bearer of electricity produces an earthly paradise. But Prometheus *bound* — the mythical savior of mankind through fire, who had been exiled to the Caucasus and cruelly punished by Heaven — was already much in the four friends' minds.

Byron's short poem *Prometheus* heralded the triumph of spirit over torture; and indeed all the poetry he wrote in July of 1816 had Promethean touches. (Shelley had translated the *Prometheus Bound* of Aeschylus for Byron before the latter wrote his ode.) Inspired by a Continental collection of horror stories and probably also by Georges Cuvier's researches on extinct animals, Byron wrote his *Darkness*, a ghastly vision of the last men, at the end of the world:

> *I had a dream, which was not all a dream.*
> *The bright sun was extinguish'd, and the stars*
> *Did wander darkling in the eternal space,*
> *Rayless, and pathless, and the icy earth*
> *Swung blind and blackening in the moonless air . . . .*

When all four decided to write a ghost story each, Mary was the only one to succeed; she wrote her *Frankenstein, or the Modern Prometheus,* after an excruciating nightmare somewhat in the style of Shelley's "fit of fantasy." Shelley and Claire dropped out and Byron wrote a mere fragment about the ruins of Ephesus, which Polidori was later thought to have plagiarized as *The Vampyre.* But Byron, too, could curdle the blood when he howled out his Albanian songs over the water. Perhaps for that reason they called him "Albè." The arrival of Matthew Gregory Lewis on 18 August gave a further creative twist to Byron's thought, for the "Monk" had brought with him Goethe's *Faust,* from which he read aloud, translating as he went along.

Albè, however, was determined to bring the idyll to an end. He realized that Claire's child would bind him closer to her unless he severed the connection with her completely. This he did, leaving Shelley to take her and Mary home on 29 August. Byron's only concession was that he would bring up the child and allow Claire to see it as an "aunt" — though not to see him. Byron did not love bluestockings, he did not love intelligent good looks that lacked beauty and voluptuousness, he did not love Claire. Perhaps the cruel hurt he caused would have been even deeper had he behaved more kindly. At any rate he needed some such excuse when he described the end of the affair to Augusta with evident qualms: "Now, dearest . . . Now, don't scold; but what could I do? . . . I was not in love, nor have any love left for any; but I could not exactly play the Stoic with a woman, who had scrambled eight hundred miles to unphilosophise me. Besides, I had been regaled of late with so many 'two courses and a *desert*' (Alas!) of aversion, that I was fain to take a little love." At the close of this lame letter he could only relapse into the old Calvinistic clichés of childhood: "I seem destined to set people by the ears."

Hobhouse arrived, passport and all, just before the Shelleys left. He was able to report to Augusta a great improvement in her brother's health — "no brandy . . . nor deluges of soda water . . . even the scream has died away." But Byron's first excursion with Hobhouse, to Chamonix, was not a great success. The highest point was their discovery of Shelley's entry in the hotel register. Perhaps inspired by Byron's "100" years of age, Shelley had given his destination as Hell and his occupation (in Greek) as "Democratic, Philanthropic, and atheist" — the first two to be later translated by his enemies as "revolutionary" and "pervert." Byron erased the entry for the sake of his friend's reputation, but Shelley had repeated the quip in other hotels. The lowest point was reached when an English lady tourist exclaimed on facing Mont Blanc, "Did you ever see any thing more *rural?*" — as if, wrote Byron, "it was Highgate, or Hampstead, or Brompton or Hayes."

On 17 September the two friends disappeared for thirteen days into the Bernese Oberland. Byron kept a journal of the expedition for Augusta, having written to her on the day he started: "Had you been a Nun — and I a Monk — that we might have talked through a grate instead of across the sea — no matter — my voice and my heart are ever thine — B." Sailing as he was from Rousseau's Ouchy, it was easy to see Augusta as another "Nouvelle Héloïse," and perhaps himself as Abelard.

The tour of the high Alps was Byron's attempt to exorcise his misery by action instead of writing. True, he kept the journal, but his prose was never an anodyne in the same way as his poetry; in prose his sense of reality was too near the surface.

At first the excursion seemed to be succeeding. There was

the exhilaration of climbing and tumbling on the Dent de Jaman, the Wengernalp (now with its "Byron Hill"), and the Scheidegg; viewing the Jungfrau, the wicked Eiger and the Grindelwald Glacier by starlight; visiting remote villages on Lake Thun and Lake Brienz, and watching the peasants waltz — "the dancing much better than in England; the English can't Waltz, never could nor ever will." Byron even managed to reverse the roles of himself and Hobby at Zitza, for at Lauterbrunnen "H." got isolated by a storm and Byron had to send a man, a cloak, and an umbrella to his Lala's rescue. He welcomed fatigue: "so much the better — I shall sleep."

But despite his many striking descriptions — a mountain's "epaulettes of cloud," a river "rapid as anger," a glacier "like *a frozen hurricane,*" a peak "shining like truth," weather "as the day on which Paradise was made" — Paradise inexorably lost out to Hell. Infernal similes leaped naturally to Byron's pen, unlike Gray's. The Staubbach falls were like "the *tail* of a white horse streaming in the wind . . . the '*pale* horse' on which *Death* is mounted in the Apocalypse"; an avalanche was the Devil being pelted into Hell; clouds curling up the precipices were "the foam of the Ocean of Hell . . . white, and sulphury."

Nature, action, and prose were not the instruments to banish Byron's "recollections of bitterness" — his loss of both Augusta and Annabella. The memorial tablet to General Ludlow in St. Martin's Church, Vevey, merely reminded him that even a regicide's wife, Lady Ludlow, had followed *her* husband into exile, and maintained her love for him "unshaken" though "tried." When they passed "*whole woods of withered pines — all withered*" he seemed to see himself and his family. On the last day he confessed his failure: "neither the music of the Shepherd, the crashing of the Avalanche, nor the torrent, the mountain, the Glacier, the Forest, nor the Clouds, have for one moment lightened the weight upon my heart, nor enabled me to lose my own wretched identity in the majesty, and the power, and the Glory, around, above, and beneath me."

Had he but known Augusta's fate, the boiling clouds would have seemed more sulfurous still. Annabella had forgiven her. And in this formidable process was included Augusta's re-education in morality. There were new rules about showing Annabella her brother's letters, and not replying intimately to him, especially avoiding all *"marks* which may recall wrong ideas to his mind." Augusta must *"rectify* instead of *soothing* or *indulging* his feelings."

He was uneasily aware of Augusta's attempted rectifications, though he went on ending his letters with the *mark* now forbidden to her: +. Meanwhile he had written the first two acts of *Manfred,* a poetic drama described as *A Mystery,* which was partially to succeed where his excursions and journal failed.

Count Manfred is the Byronic hero of a fatal love affair carried forward into a new dimension. Instead of Childe Harold's vaguely sinister "apartness," the count is spiritually alone in his Gothic alpine castle, where he has achieved a Faustian knowledge of good and evil which fans his "Promethean spark." He realizes he is "half dust half deity," and is totally frustrated by the limitations of mortality. At the same time "some half-maddening sin" in his past has added to the unbearable misery of the present, while fear of death has hitherto stood between him and "self-oblivion" through suicide. His destiny is apparently to "wither" like the blasted pine wood, unless he can summon the courage — or is it cowardice? — to destroy himself. This he at length attempts to do by hurling himself from a crag of the Jungfrau (Byron had once felt suicidal in the high Alps) but a chamois hunter pulls him back. Beside a cataract he reveals his past sin to the Witch of the Alps: how the heart of his sister Astarte, his beloved, "gaz'd on mine, and wither'd." Astarte is now in the underworld or Hall of Arimanes, spirit of evil. Though Manfred descends into the underworld and meets her phantom, she will not say she loves or even forgives him. All she can promise is an end to his wretched existence on the morrow.

So ends *Manfred,* Act II. Byron could not see the way to

Act III, any more than he could see an escape from his own "wretched identity." On 8 September he had written to Augusta about Annabella: "she — or rather the Separation — has broken my heart. I feel as if an Elephant had trodden on it, — but I try. . . . I breathe lead." Caroline Lamb had once spoken of her cousin's having the playfulness of an elephant. Now the metaphor had come true and Annabella was dancing on Byron's heart.

His stay of over four months in Switzerland had not cured the misery he had brought with him from England. Indeed, the stupendous impression of tempest and avalanche (it had been an exceptionally stormy summer) had in some ways made it worse. In his own words written of *Childe Harold,* Canto III: "I was half mad during the time of its composition, between metaphysics, mountains, lakes, love unextinguishable, thoughts unutterable, and the nightmare of my own delinquencies."

Nevertheless Switzerland was not a miasmic or stagnant experience, but in Professor Clubbe's words, "a watershed." Byron had descended to the underworld of Arimanes because he realized that only through death could life be renewed. The "July 1816" poems were shot through with the new Promethean fire: *Prometheus* itself and the "Godlike crime"; *Lake Leman* and "the heirs of immortality"; Chillon's "Eternal Spirit of the chainless Mind"; *Monody on Sheridan* and his "fire from Heaven"; *A Fragment* on the "breathless being" of death; *The Dream* and the "Quick Spirit of the Universe"; *Darkness* and the "prayer for light"; and finally the Promethean cry in *Stanzas to Augusta:* "They may torture, but shall not subdue me —."

Like the hero of *Manfred,* with his exhilarating and immortal "Promethean spark" but his grim and mortal loneliness — "The lion is alone, and so am I" — Byron knew that he himself must live on and meet his fate on the morrow; but how?

SIX

Abandonment to Venice
(1816–1819)

"THE GREENEST ISLAND of my imagination." Always excepting Greece, Venice had won this supreme place in Byron's
heart long before he set eyes on its palaces and churches, its
bridges and canals. It was this "greenest island" which lured
him into Italy. He and Hobhouse passed one night at the
monastery of St. Maurice, crossed the magnificent Simplon
— "quite out of all mortal computation" — and entered
Milan on 12 October.

Milan solved nothing. Its cathedral was not quite up to
Seville's, and Byron's visits to the famous Ambrosian Library
were used by him to underline his deep discontent with the
established order of things. When the librarian tried to interest him in pious manuscripts, he preferred to study the love
letters of a pope's daughter to a cardinal,* and to dream over
a lock of her fair hair. Being forbidden to copy the letters, he
learned them by heart. "And pray what do you think is one
of her *signatures?*" he wrote to Augusta; "— why this + a
Cross — which she says 'is to stand for her name &c.' Is not
this amusing?" To Byron it was also poignant, for he was

* Lucrezia Borgia, daughter of Pope Alexander VI, to Cardinal Bembo.

losing touch with his own ✝, he did not know precisely why. On the twenty-eighth he confided to Augusta that his good health was marred by fits of giddiness and deafness, his hair was graying and his teeth were sometimes "looseish" — which made him think he would be like Swift "& the *withered* tree he saw." Byron had seen a whole forest of *withered* trees in the high Alps, and had not yet got them out of his system.

The French writer Stendhal (at present still using his real name of M. Beyle) was in Milan at the time, and later wrote up a long and sometimes fabricated account of Byron. His description of Byron's "excellent pimp, an Italian doctor," was an immense libel on Polidori. His story, however, of a political row in which Polidori involved Byron rings true. Byron had given the young doctor his congé before the final expedition into the Bernese Oberland because "he had an alacrity of getting into scrapes." The doctor preceded Byron to Milan, where sure enough he demonstrated his "alacrity" by picking a quarrel with an odious Austrian officer who had refused to remove his military hat at the opera. Though Byron's intervention rescued Pollydolly from the guard-house where he had been locked up, it could not save him from banishment to Florence. He now went out of Byron's life and out of the world five years later, when he committed suicide after gambling losses.

The Milan incident only confirmed what Byron had already heard about Austrian bullying from his friends the Italian literati, all of them nationalists. Since the Congress of Vienna in 1815, Italy had been subject to Austrian, papal and Bourbon domination. Among the Italian nationalists were two Greeks, the brothers Karvellas; freedom was indivisible and the Italian freedom movement could now be linked with what Byron had learned five or six years earlier in Athens. "Sons of the Greeks, arise!" had been the cry then. "Italia! Oh, Italia" would be the theme when Canto IV of *Childe Harold* came to be written.

What with the Austrians and the local banditti, Byron and his party were thankful to be leaving Milan on 3 November

ABANDONMENT TO VENICE ⁊ 113

in one piece. An attempt by the Austrians to requisition his horses produced the retort that rather than relinquish them he would shoot them through the head in the middle of the road. As for the robbers, "it is something like poor dear Turkey in that respect," he wrote, "but not so good, for there you have as great a body of rogues to watch the regular banditti." Other lapses in Milanese morals were reported by Byron with sly gravity. A mother and son were pointed out to him at the opera who lived together unnaturally like "the Theban dynasty" of Jocasta and Oedipus.

Verona pleased him, though he could hardly bring himself to write about it. Description was still a bore to him if not "disgusting." He singled out the vast amphitheatre of Augustus — "beats even Greece" — the rampant Gothic ornaments of the Scaliger tombs and Juliet's granite sarcophagus "with withered leaves in it, in a wild and desolate conventual garden . . . blighted as their love." It is perhaps surprising that anything of the sarcophagus remains, since Byron like other tourists sent home pieces of its stone to his family. (Ada and the Leigh children had already received some crystals from Mont Blanc.)

Byron had nothing to say of Verona's sinister medieval prison tower, which would have struck horror into Shelley; and he completely missed the Montecchi (Montague) castle of Romeo in the hills between Verona and Vicenza, though the governor's wife in Venice told him about them afterwards. As he said, "a poor virtuoso am I." It is only from Hobhouse that we know they inspected Andrea Palladio's architectural masterpieces in Vicenza. Byron was not even tempted to mention the fantastic *trompe l'oeil* of Palladio's Olympic Theatre, whose repertoire had opened in 1585 with the *Oedipus.* Virtuosity in visual design left him cold. Virtuosity in poetry was more and more to his taste.

At last on 10 November the two friends were rowed across the dark, rain-swept lagoon and into Venice. On this first mysterious voyage in a gondola Byron had only Hobhouse by his side. Soon, however, his gondola's purposes were expanded:

> *It glides along the water looking blackly,*
> *Just like a coffin clapt in a canoe,*
> *Where none can make out what you say or do . . . .*

For the sake of Shylock, Byron gazed at the steep, covered-in bridge which the boatman told them was the Rialto. But he had no intention of staying permanently on the Grand Canal in a hotel that had been a palace in Venice's great days. For Venice was decaying under the Austrian heel.

He swiftly shut out this picture of faded glory by moving into a narrow street off the Piazza San Marco called the Frezzeria, which still hummed with commerce and animal spirits. Below were shops, some with goods on the pavement; above, windows which could look into those opposite unless the shutters were closed. Byron's lodgings were over a linen draper's. Here he fell, once more like a thunderbolt, upon the draper's wife.

Marianna Segati, the wife, was something of a thunderbolt herself, as were all red-blooded Venetian women of this class. Prosperous, with servants and one child, Marianna nevertheless cared, as Byron said, for nothing but passion. These Venetian children of nature had few scruples beyond their simple code. They saw no impropriety in a married woman's accepting an *amoroso* provided she limited herself to one affair, did not conceal it, and got the approval of "the prior claimant." Signor Segati, approving of the English milord, paid his own addresses to another signora, while Byron remained in "fathomless love": love for Marianna's Venetian dialect, soft as Somersetshire, her black oriental eyes, curls of a gloss as dark as Lady Jersey's, and appearance "altogether like an antelope." But an antelope who did not flee or tell mama. Marianna's ferocity showed when an interloping antelope tried to usurp her position. One evening her sister-in-law visited Byron uninvited. Marianna marched in and curtsied. Then she suddenly seized her relative by the hair and administered sixteen boxes on the ear. The visitor fled, leaving Marianna swooning in Byron's arms, to be restored eventually by Signor Segati and the servants. The story flew all over Venice. "But, here, nobody minds such trifles," wrote Byron to Moore, "except to be amused by them." English visitors, however, throughout Italy were beginning to hear with shock and relish of the wicked lord's doings.

The contented sensuality of life with Marianna did not extinguish Byron's angry feelings about Annabella and society as a whole. In writing to Augusta he now referred to his wife openly as "that virtuous monster Miss Milbanke." His fury would rise to fever pitch whenever some misleading rumor reached him about Ada: that Lady Byron was taking her abroad; that Lady Byron was attacking his legal rights as father. Wealthy English travelers he increasingly detested. What a relief that they preferred Florence and Naples to the silent canals of Venice, where they missed "the rattle of hackney coaches, without which they can't sleep." His prejudices encompassed the Venetian nobility also, who were "a sad-looking race — the gentry rather better." And the peasants and shopkeepers were best of all.

It is true that he still clung to the idea of returning to England in 1817. But only two things in England really engaged his interest: the possibility of leading a social revolution and the literary life at John Murray's. Otherwise he still felt that the separation had made him "as much an object of proscription as any political plot could have done."

"Are you not near the Luddites?" he asked Moore who had moved to the North. "By the Lord! if there's a row, but I'll be among ye! How go on the weavers — the breakers of frames — the Lutherans of politics — the reformers?" And he burst into extempore rhymes in which, however, a Luddite rising proved less attractive than the forthcoming Venetian carnival:

> *But the Carnival's coming*
> *Oh Thomas Moore . . .*
> *Masking and mumming*
> *Fifing and drumming*

>   *Guitarring and strumming*
>   *Oh Thomas Moore.*

There was still in the poet a vein of something — perhaps, he often thought, of his fighting Norman blood — which rejected the secondhand inspiration of books. "If I live ten years longer," he wrote to Moore a few weeks later, "you will see, however, that it is not over with me — I don't mean in literature, for that is nothing; and it may seem odd enough to say, I do not think it my vocation." (Shelley also was soon to write: "I consider Poetry very subordinate to moral & political science, & if I were well, certainly I should aspire to the latter.") Part of Byron had agreed with Annabella when she wrote in her last-but-one affectionate letter "Dearest B . . . . Don't give yourself up to the abominable trade of versifying."

If he liked "the abominable trade" at all, it was for the camaraderie of Albemarle Street. Having found out that Murray was reading aloud his letters to the assembled company, Byron made a point of sending something worth reading, either in the way of wickedness or wit. "My Adriatic nymph [Marianna]," he wrote to Murray in a postscript, "is this moment here, and I must therefore repose from this letter, rocked by the beating of her heart." Later on he offered Murray some sample lines with which to refuse a medical tragedy which Polidori had submitted to him for publication:

>   *Dear Doctor, — I have read your play*
>   *Which is a good one in its way, —*
>   *Purges the eyes and moves the bowels,*
>   *And drenches handkerchiefs like towels . . . .*
>   *But — and I grieve to speak it — plays*
>   *Are drugs — mere drugs, Sir, nowadays. . . .*
>   *There's Byron too, who once did better, . . .*
>   *So alter'd since last year his pen is,*
>   *I think he's lost his wits at Venice.*

But literary frolicking with his English friends was minor sport compared with the carnival. "The day after to-morrow (to-morrow being Christmas-day)," he wrote to Moore excitedly, "the Carnival begins. I dine with the Countess Albrizzi and a party, and go to the opera. On that day the Phenix, (not the Insurance Office, but the theatre of that name), opens: I have got me a box there for the season." Byron was in his element as he entered between the Fenice Theatre's classical pillars and under the masks of comedy and tragedy. The season of 1817 began with a piece based on Livy's classical *History* which greatly pleased Byron: how one hundred and fifty Roman matrons poisoned one hundred and fifty husbands "in the good old time."

The Countess Albrizzi, his hostess, represented those rare members of the Venetian nobility who were not "sad-looking." A Corfiot by birth, she was "a very learned, unaffected, good-natured woman, very polite to strangers, and, I believe, not at all dissolute, as most of the women are." He nominated her "the De Staël of Venice," for she had written with distinction on the work of Canova, and it was here in the exquisite setting of the Albrizzi Palace that he first saw beauty in contemporary sculpture. Canova's bust of Helen of Troy seemed to him beyond man's thought or nature's achievement: "Behold the *Helen* of the *heart!*" Above and around this poem in marble were the long painted ceilings by Veronese with life-size flying cupids and wreaths in stucco, the Longhi room, the ballroom surmounted by molded golden pleats to look like a tent, the Louis XVI room with silk chairs and matching curtains patterned in sprigs and ribbons, gilt mirrors and tall windows whose irregular glass gave a faint ripple to the view of canal and garden outside. A portrait of the Archduke Charles and the King of Naples visiting this palazzo testified to the grandeur of the Albrizzi family.

The carnival, however, quickly swept Byron into wilder currents. Every night for six weeks there was a display of "All the Virtue and Vice in Venice" — balls, operas, ridottos, routs, parties, "and the Devil knows what." On 18 February when the carnival closed, Byron stayed up all night at the famous Fenice masked ball, where crowds of merrymakers pranced about on the covered-in pit, protected by their masks from any need of restraint.

The mask, indeed, was an appropriate symbol throughout Byron's life, and particularly during this period, for the two sides of his nature. While in London during 1815 he had amused himself by consulting a celebrated craniologist from Germany named Spurzheim. Though Spurzheim was not above making a fool of himself (he pronounced Coleridge to be lacking in "the organ of imagination") he gave a convincing picture of Byron's "very antithetical" bumps: "for every thing developed in & on this same skull of mine," quoted Byron, "has its *opposite* in great force, so that to believe him [Spurzheim] my good & evil are at perpetual war." The story of Byron's first months in Venice did nothing to discredit this thesis. While the masked figure was that of an *amoroso* entirely abandoned to revelry, the eyes that glittered behind the mask had spent most of the daytime fixed upon things very different from the lithe figures of Venetian nymphs.

During their first week in Venice Byron and Hobhouse visited by gondola the Armenian convent on the island of San Lazzaro. Skimming over the "tranquil lake," past a few sandbanks and the isle reserved for the city's madhouse, they landed on a stone quay in front of long buildings with regular square windows and a campanile behind. A dozen bearded monks in long black habits with leather belts received them. The order had been founded by Abbot Mechitar in 1717, "to improve the language of the Armenian Nation for the glory of J.C. Our Lord." The two friends were led through the cloisters with their plain white arches and subtropical garden into the fine library, where Byron found "some very curious Mss," and so down to the huge pillared printing room which housed the presses.

Monks and monasteries had always appealed to Byron since

the old days of Zitza and the Capuchin convent in Athens. There were also childhood memories of Newstead mingling with the Gothick craze for church bells and graves, not to mention a deeper vein of mysticism. "Besides, when I turn thirty," he wrote to Murray, "I will turn devout; I feel a great devotion that way in catholic churches, and when I hear the organ."

He heard the organ in the painted chapel of San Lazzaro but heard little else. The peace was profound and peculiarly grateful to Byron in his present state of tension. He found himself arranging to return to the Armenian fathers and assist them in their language mission. He would study Armenian, helping Father Paschal, "a learned and pious soul," in his production of an Armenian-English grammar and dictionary. Father Paschal responded with warmth to this "young man, quick, sociable, with burning eyes." Soon Byron was visiting daily. The grammar was published early in 1817, but he did not relinquish his new way of life, which was to last for nearly six months.

At first the strenuous studies distracted his mind from the bewildering ambiguities of Augusta's letters (her "damned crinkum crankum"), and also from the fact that he had been "tuneless" since crossing the Alps. "I found that my mind wanted something craggy to break upon," he told Moore, and this craggy thing he found in the Armenian alphabet with its thirty-eight letters. The good abbot-general, who had "a beard like a meteor," allotted him a small room of his own with a view of the sea, a table and two carved cane chairs. As his nightly roisterings in Venice got more frantic his daily retreat became more precious. After his lessons with Father Paschal he would sit on the terrace talking to the monks, a large dog lying at his feet and the City of the Doges flaming in sunset clouds behind them. At last his muse returned.

It was while sitting alone on a little hill in the monks' olive garden that he found he could finish his poetic drama *Manfred*. Act III opens with a lonely tower in Manfred's castle where a room is being prepared for his death. The abbot of St. Maurice enters and entreats him to repent. He replies proudly that he cannot. Time was when he hoped to be a statesman, an "enlightener of nations," but in order to lead "the herd" a man must mingle with it. "The lion is alone," says Manfred, "and so am I."

This is a pride from which the whole Byron-Shelley circle tended to suffer, because the herd had misunderstood and persecuted them. Like Frankenstein's monster, they were unloved and therefore antisocial.

In *Manfred* the hero's possession of superhuman powers and forbidden knowledge enabled Byron to introduce what was to become a favorite theme of his: that superhumanity, far from being a sin, was a legitimate throwback to a third race of giants or supermen, halfway between gods and mortals. This race had been created before the Flood, according to the Book of Genesis, by a union of angels and human beings. (The peris of Eastern mythology were similarly a third or halfway race, which Byron had met in *Vathek.*) Byron may have been remembering mysterious passages in his early Bible reading, upon which were superimposed his knowledge of the "ante-Flood" period, acquired through Cuvier's discoveries of prehistoric remains. And so in the drama, when Satan comes for Manfred's soul, Manfred is able to defy him. For it was not through a pact with the Devil (like Faust's) that Manfred conducted his experiments in his tower, but by studying the

> *knowledge of our Fathers — when the earth*
> *Saw men and spirits walking side by side* . . . .

Manfred's famous farewell to the setting sun is made in the same spirit of sun worship as that of

> *the vigorous race*
> *Of undiseased mankind, the giant sons*
> *Of the embrace of Angels, with a sex*
> *More beautiful than they* . . . .

Byron, like so many writers before and since, hankered after
a new race of "undiseased mankind." Manfred's inexpiable
sin — his forbidden love for his sister — would surely have
been no more a sin among "undiseased mankind" than was
forbidden knowledge. Indeed Byron was to point out in *Cain*
that Adam populated the earth only through his children's
love for one another. But in his own world Manfred has
sinned by breaking Astarte's heart. Again, however, Satan
cannot punish him, for he will punish himself:

> *I have not been thy dupe, nor am thy prey —*
> *But was my own destroyer, and will be*
> *My own hereafter.*

Manfred contained Byron's most profound and poignant
thoughts, so far, about man's aspirations and fate. Because
of this, he was deeply dissatisfied with it, especially the recal-
citrant last act. This he rewrote in the summer of 1817, making the abbot a sympathetic instead of a harsh character —
perhaps an unconscious tribute to the monks of San Lazzaro.
The published drama was ecstatically praised for its poetry,
violently denounced for its impiety and laughed at (by Peacock) for its fashionable effects. Mr. Glowry's tower in
Nightmare Abbey represents a skit on Castle Manfred, and
Peacock wonders where the "heterogeneous mythological
company" in *Manfred*, comprising the Persian Arimanes,
Greek Nemesis, Scandinavian Valkyre-Destinies, astrological
spirits of medieval alchemists, elemental Danish witch and
chorus of Dr. Faustus's devils, could ever have met, except
at a table d'hôte like the kings in Voltaire's *Candide*.

Byron himself was concerned at taunts of plagiarism. He
denied ever having read Marlowe's *Doctor Faustus*, and at
this stage minimized Goethe's influence. One thing he
thought he had made sure of: his poetical drama could never
be submitted to the perils of a stage performance. Nevertheless, such was its grip on the nineteenth century that *Manfred* was acted in 1834, 1863, 1864, 1867, and 1873. There had

been Schumann's overture in 1850, and its apotheosis came in 1885 with Tchaikovsky's symphony.

The dissolute night-life of carnival time ended too late to save Byron from high fever followed by extreme listlessness. The end of *Manfred,* he said, "has the dregs of my fever," and indeed Manfred's very last words to the abbot reflected Byron's own world-weariness: "Old man, 'tis not so difficult to die." The moral of *Manfred,* however, was that dying was too easy. Byron must struggle on; indeed his physical exhaustion could coexist, paradoxically, with a glorious burst of lyrical genius:

> *So we'll go no more a roving*
> *So late into the night,*
> *Though the heart be still as loving,*
> *And the moon be still as bright.*
>
> *For the sword outwears its sheath,*
> *And the soul wears out the breast,*
> *And the heart must pause to breathe,*
> *And love itself have rest.*

By mid-April Byron was fit enough to join Hobhouse in Rome. As luck would have it, his new experiences were such as to intensify his returning creativeness. On his way to Rome he passed through Ferrara, where the dukes of Este had given hospitality to his evil genius Calvin. Skirting Ferrara's tremendous prison-fortress, he found in its shadow the tiny prison cell of the sixteenth-century poet Tasso. Through one grating the staring passers-by had seen the allegedly mad poet writing his *Jerusalem;* through a second "abhorred grate" his food was thrust into a pitch-dark cell. In his *Lament of Tasso* Byron makes the Italian poet say, "I loved all Solitude" — but had not thought to be incarcerated for seven years as a maniac. So also Byron: after "imputed madness," relegated to "prison'd solitude" imposed by his wife and society.

In Rome he moved from the ridiculous to the abhorrent,

to the flattering, to the sublime. On the roof of St. Peter's there was a ludicrous scene when Lady Liddell recognized the Gorgon curls of Lord Byron and hissed to her young daughter, "Don't look at him, he is dangerous to look at." A public execution horrified him. He had attended on the principle that everything should be seen once; and the hanging of Bellingham, the assassin of Prime Minister Perceval, which he had witnessed in 1812, had been "vulgar" compared with the blood, screams and prayers of this Italian guillotining. Rome's art convinced him that sublimity could be attained by man as well as by nature. Hitherto Byron had seen perfection only in mountains, seas, rivers, "two or three women . . . some horses; and a lion (at Veli Pasha's) in the Morea; and a tiger at supper in Exeter 'Change." Now he could fully understand the enthusiasm for Art which previously he had thought *"cant."*

Hobhouse had persuaded him to sit to the highly regarded sculptor Bertel Thorwaldsen for a magnificent bust — though Byron refused the final flattery of a marble wreath for fear of looking "a mountebank." (Today the bust, on the staircase at 50 Albemarle Street, is crowned with laurel.)

It was the total glory of Rome, however, in history and myth which bowled him over: "As a *whole, ancient* and *modern,* it beats Greece, Constantinople, every thing." While ill in Venice he had written to his literary agent, Kinnaird, "having just turned nine & twenty I seriously think of giving up altogether — unless Rome should madden me into a fourth Canto — which it may or may not." After three weeks of riding over the Seven Hills he had completely recovered his health and was inspired to write, eventually, 186 stanzas of the fourth and last canto of *Childe Harold,* beginning with a prison and ending with the free ocean, that "dark-heaving," "boundless, endless, and sublime" image of eternity:

> *I stood in Venice, on the Bridge of Sighs;*
> *A palace and a prison on each hand . . . .*

. . . .

> *There is society, where none intrudes,*
> *By the deep Sea, and music in its roar:*
> *I love not Man the less, but Nature more* . . . .

Again Byron's pilgrimage was satirized as well as idolized. Mr. Cypress in *Nightmare Abbey* makes an after-dinner speech on the desperate "upas tree" theory of life, basing himself on Byron's 122nd and 126th stanzas. Here Byron's Calvinistic upbringing has tortured him into the belief that man is in every sense a "false creation":

> *Of its own beauty is the mind diseased,*
> *And fevers into false creation* . . . .
> *The unreach'd Paradise of our despair* . . . .

All we retain, as men, is "our right of thought."

This was genuine suffering expressed in moving and often beautiful language. But was it the best Byron could do? He himself had criticized *Manfred* for being "too much in my old style," and *Childe Harold*, Canto IV, was the same. He was in fact returning to Venice ripe for something quite new.

His first act on arrival was to lease a summer villa at La Mira on the river Brenta, some seven miles from Venice, where he could keep horses and gallop over the flat parched fields. This Palladian palace had belonged to the Foscarini family but did not boast the splendor of more famous villas: Zelottese frescoes, Veronese paintings and sly masks and lamias copied from the pagan art newly discovered at Pompeii. Nonetheless, Byron quickly imported a racy element of comedy into his own holiday villa. A beautiful peasant girl named Margarita Cogni, married to a baker and therefore known as La Fornarina, became a rival to Marianna and soon ousted her amid tumult. Margarita was twenty-two like Marianna and had everything that Marianna possessed and more: she was taller, stronger, wilder; more beautiful, animal, and fierce. Byron found in her "a Pantaloon humour" and the boon of illiteracy, so that she could not "plague me with letters." (However, she secretly taught herself to distinguish from the handwriting whether Byron's private letters were written to him by men or women.) England and indeed the civilized world was becoming ever remoter. A bond was broken when "the very kind" Mme de Staël died in 1817 and Lady Melbourne, "the best, and kindest, and ablest female I ever knew — old or young," in the following year.

Venetian life, with all its comical sexuality, was suddenly concentrated for him into potential verse in September 1817. Signor Segati had told him some up-to-date gossip about the return of a "dead" husband to a Venetian woman who had meanwhile taken an *amoroso*. At the same time Byron was unexpectedly presented with the verse form in which to embody his interpretation of this tale. It was John Hookham Frere's mock-heroic romance, written under the pen name of Whistlecraft, and composed in the meter of Pulci's medieval *Morgante Maggiore* about giants and monks — a subject and manner so congenial to Byron that he later translated the poem himself. In Frere's ironic tone and confidentially talkative style Byron found exactly what he needed for his new poem. *Beppo* ("Joe") was born: the popular comedy of a husband, a lover and a hardheaded lady who neither dealt in "Mathematics" like an English bluestocking, nor smelled of bread and butter like the nursery-reared English "Miss."

In November Byron and Hobhouse were back in Venice, both staying in the Frezzeria. They developed a routine of work, entertainments and gallops along the Lido. But Hobhouse returned to England early in January; whereupon Byron, liberated as at Athens in 1811, plunged remorselessly into the maelstrom of another carnival. On 2 February he was again confessing to Moore, "I have hardly had a wink of sleep this week past. We are in the agonies of the Carnival's last days. . . . I have had some curious masking adventures this Carnival." Once the furious Fornarina snatched off the mask of a lady who had dared to take *her* Byron's arm. "I will work the mine of my youth," he continued, "to the last veins of the ore, and then — good night. I have lived, and am content."

Byron was no doubt thinking of the fact that on 22 January 1818 he had celebrated his thirtieth birthday. A fact to which he did not give another thought was that on the very same evening, at the Countess Albrizzi's, he had met a bride of three days, the seventeen-year-old Countess Guiccioli. This meeting was to be a curious false dawn, for Byron did not see Teresa Guiccioli again for nearly fifteen months. Meanwhile the year 1818 was to be an important one in his life.

Having heard that Newstead had been sold during the previous November to his Harrow friend Thomas Wildman for £94,500, Byron was relatively free for the first time in his life from financial anxiety.

At the beginning of the summer he left the somewhat squalid Frezzeria for a splendid mansion on the Grand Canal. This was the Palazzo Mocenigo, property of a Venetian family who had given the city seven doges. Byron paid 200 gold louis a year for the center block. There were the usual steps for gondolas and square, grated windows on water level, two stories above, each with an immense triple window and stone balcony, and many smaller rooms under a red tiled roof. Rich plasterwork and a mosaic floor among the best in Italy adorned his main salon. One legend credited him with a high dive from his balcony into the Grand Canal, but he had no wish to impale himself on the chevaux-de-frise of gondola stakes below. The story was probably an amalgam of several other events. He would often swim home from a party in a neighboring palazzo carrying a torch in his left hand to warn gondoliers; he raced and beat both an Italian named Angelo Mengaldo and a Scot from the Lido to the Grand Canal; and La Fornarina threw herself into the canal as a demonstration against the end of her affair with Byron and was fished out half-drowned.

Instead of suiting his new life to the dignity of a Mocenigo prince, Byron only increased the fantastic scale and furious pace of his activities, physical and intellectual. He acquired what Moore apologetically calls "an unworthy Harem" headed by Elena da Mosta who, according to Byron, "clapt" him — "some noble, some middling, some low, & all whores." Byron put them at two hundred strong; but as this was the same figure he had given at Athens it may be reckoned as symbolic. To this "world of harlotry," which cost him some £3,000, was added a staff of fourteen servants, including his renowned gondolier "Tita" Falcieri of the ferocious black beard but gentle heart, and a growing menagerie of monkeys, a fox, mastiffs and a sheep dog named Mutz from Switzerland.

With self-indulgence of every kind had returned in full force his old enemy, portliness. A friend of Annabella's in Venice reported that Apollo was bloated, his face far more like a full moon than ever hers was, while Hanson, who visited him on business and probably handed him a pen to sign with, noticed that his knuckles were lost in fat. It is both comical and sad to picture this puffy Romeo in March 1819 heaving himself onto the balcony of eighteen-year-old Angelina, daughter of a Venetian noble; though after an intervention by the police and a priest, he "spared her."

This was all physical, partly revenge on the Princess of Parallelograms, partly a genuine appetite. There had also been a new development in his emotional life that he was ill-equipped to cope with.

Clara Allegra, Byron's daugter by Claire Clairmont, had been born in Bath on 12 January 1817. He received the news while in Rome and during the next year began to dream fondly of his "*il*-legitimate" as well as his "little legitimate" Ada, in both of whom he was "quite wrapt up." This was to Moore, who had just lost a daughter. To Hobhouse he was as usual chary of showing emotion when requesting him in February 1818 to have Allegra sent out. "A clerk can bring the [Newstead] papers (and, by-the-bye, my *shild* by Clare, at the same time. Pray desire Shelley to pack it carefully), with *tooth-powder, red only;* magnesia, soda-powders, tooth-brushes, diachylon plaster, and any new novels good for anything."

Shelley, instead of packing "it," himself brought Allegra from England as far as Bagni di Lucca near Pisa, together with Claire, Mary and their own two babies, William and Clara. Unshakably resolved never to see Claire again, Byron received his daughter and her nurse at the Palazzo Mocenigo. Allegra at first delighted him, especially her blue eyes and fair curls, which in no way reminded him of her dark mother. But she had Papa's "devil of a Spirit," and it was hardly surprising that she showed it, considering her experiences. Apart from the rackety zoo-life all around her, she was cared for by the Shelleys' Swiss nurse, thirty-year-old Elise, who was probably pregnant by Shelley and had already given birth to an illegitimate child when in her twenties.

In August the Shelleys and Claire heard from Elise that Byron had handed over Allegra to Mrs. Richard Hoppner, wife of the pleasant, erudite English consul-general in Venice. Shelley decided to take Claire to see Allegra at the Hoppners and afterwards to beard Byron in his den, despite the lurid stories from gondoliers and innkeepers. He arrived unannounced at 3 P.M. on 23 August 1818. The interview, which lasted for fourteen hours, was a unique success. It was to result in Shelley's later composing *Julian and Maddalo* (Shelley and Byron), one of his greatest poems; in Byron's generously offering Shelley the loan of the Villa d'Este in the Euganean hills (rented by Byron from the Hoppners), where Claire could see Allegra; and in Shelley's discovering that Byron had almost finished Canto 1 of a supremely important new work — *Don Juan*.

The two poets glided over the lagoon, where they saw the madhouse which was to figure so prominently in *Julian and Maddalo*, galloped on the Lido and argued till 5 A.M. in a charmed atmosphere reminiscent of the old Diodati days. Shelley wrote of Byron as Count Maddalo, "His more serious conversation is a sort of *intoxication.*" Alas, it was delicious intoxication in a growing desert for both of them.

While bringing Mary and their two children from Lucca to Venice in September, preparatory to visiting the Villa d'Este, Shelley failed to take in that Clara, "little Ca," was dangerously ill with fever. Her death in convulsions was as sad a comment on Shelley's callousness as Allegra's death four years later was to be on Byron's. Mary Shelley did not recover for a year, if then; meanwhile Shelley registered at Naples in December 1818 an illegitimate daughter named Elena, who was boarded with a Neapolitan family but died of fever in 1820. For various reasons, including the fact that Elise was married a month after Elena's birth to an Italian servant named Paolo Foggi, who afterwards blackmailed Shelley, it seems likely that Elise was the mother. Self-criticism and dejection were to be Shelley's mood for many months.*

Dejection and self-criticism were to be Byron's mood also. By September 1818 he had completed the first canto of *Don Juan* and begun the second. But despite this testimony to the liberation and expansion of his genius (he had earlier composed a lively Cossack tale called *Mazeppa*) Byron's future was dismal indeed. Would *Don Juan* ever see the light of day?

There was a whole string of reasons why Byron's publisher Murray thought the poem must be drastically cut, while his friend Hobhouse wanted to suppress it altogether. A desperate picture of Byron emerges in March 1819: physically the swollen Romeo, intellectually the frantic author driven into a corner but insisting on publication even if anonymously. Yet such was the force of his vitality that within two months the whole "200 whores" had been banished, and within four months *Don Juan* was launched on a gasping world.

* See *Shelley: The Pursuit* by Richard Holmes (1974). Elise spread a story through the Hoppners that Claire was Elena's mother, which Byron was inclined to believe.

SEVEN

Don Juan's Last Attachment
(1819–1821)

Well — well; the world must turn upon its axis,
*   And all mankind turn with it, heads or tails,*
And live and die, make love and pay our taxes,
*   And as the veering wind shifts, shift our sails;*
The king commands us, and the doctor quacks us,
*   The priest instructs, and so our life exhales*
A little breath, love, wine, ambition, fame,
Fighting, devotion, dust, — perhaps a name.

THIS NEATLY summed up Byron's physically exhausted state
as he began the second canto of *Don Juan*. Then the "veering wind" of which he spoke shifted at the beginning of
April 1819; it was "heads" instead of "tails," and his life suddenly began to exhale love and devotion in vast quantities.

Two cynical old people were accidentally responsible for
the startling shift. One was the raddled but still amorous
Countess Benzoni, his hostess at a reception or *conversa-
zione*. She wheedled her reluctant guest into meeting a nine-
teen-year-old contessa, Teresa Guiccioli, who had arrived
late and tired. The other was a red-haired, bewhiskered, sex-
ually eccentric nobleman of fifty-eight, Count Alessandro
Guiccioli, Teresa's husband. He had insisted upon the equally
reluctant Teresa's accompanying him to the party.

It was not love at first sight, for Teresa and Byron had together inspected Canova's Helen of Troy at the Palazzo Albrizzi a year earlier. On that occasion there had been no reaction. Now Byron realized that he had found his own Helen who, in the words of Marlowe's *Doctor Faustus,* which Byron swore he had never read, would make him "immortal with a kiss."

The kiss followed next night, when he invited Teresa into his gondola and conducted her to the rented room where he was accustomed to take his whores, according to what his Italian friend Mendalgo called *"son orrible systhème";* the night after, in the same hideout, she was seduced. For another week or so delirious passion swept them to and fro among the pleasures of Venice, until Count Guiccioli took her off on a tour of his country estates round Bologna, and so to the Palazzo Guiccioli in Ravenna.

Byron's Helen had red-gold Titian curls, a brilliantly fair skin, dazzling teeth, blue eyes and a full, voluptuous figure. She was indeed somewhat top-heavy, not possessing the elegant long legs which her fine arms and bust seemed to require; but Byron had already forgotten his words in *Don Juan,* Canto 1, "I do not like a dumpy woman" — and anyway he had then been thinking of Lady Byron. Teresa was convent-educated in a then-modern style that laid stress on European culture and enabled her to discuss Dante with her lover. Those short, shapely legs, however, were in no danger of sporting blue stockings. She was like Augusta rather than Annabella in her love of laughter and engaging touches of silliness. Her marriage had been one of convenience. Her father, Count Ruggero Gamba, who had a huge family (his wife was soon to die in giving birth to her twentieth child), needed a very rich husband for Teresa. Count Guiccioli was very rich indeed. One evening at the Palazzo Gamba in Ravenna he had inspected Teresa, walking around her candle in hand like a prospective buyer in a slave market. All Italian girls were used to the idea of a loveless marriage and Teresa's first experience of passion was as unexpected as it was overwhelming. She fell head over heels in love with Byron's beauty — so unlike the ancient red whiskers — and "the thousand enchantments that surrounded him." She would have understood the dictum of Juan's lover, Julia:

> *Man's love is of man's life a thing apart,*
> *'Tis woman's whole existence* . . . .

Love was soon to be for Byron also a large part of his existence. It is true that Teresa's departure from Venice was the signal for slight backsliding with Angelina, when incidentally he literally slipped into the Grand Canal from the gondola steps and arrived dripping at his assignation. He did not as yet foresee the depth of his devotion to Teresa.

There was, moreover, an element in his new relationship which reintroduced the thing he had hated most about England and had fondly hoped was absent from Italy — cant. Cant was of the essence of *serventismo,* the status which innocent Teresa had in ten ecstatic days clamped upon him. According to Italian mores, every wife was entitled to her cavalier *servente, amico,* or *cicisbeo,* who was officially her husband's friend and the bearer of her fan and shawl but in fact her lover. The rules which governed *serventismo* were even stricter than those of marriage. The headstrong Teresa had already flouted them by calling her cavalier "mio Byron" in public and marching alone into his box at the opera. In this she resembled Caroline Lamb. Unconventionality always made Byron ill at ease; in this case, fear for Teresa's reputation was added. Deeper still was a personal distaste for the whole concept of a cavalier *servente.* In *Don Juan* he was to speak contemptuously of the marriage state as "that moral centaur, man and wife." But what sort of mythical animal was the *dama* and her *amico?* A moral chimera, perhaps, with the three heads of husband, wife, and lover.

Despite these reservations, Byron was preparing to follow Teresa to Ravenna. "You have been mine — and, whatever the outcome — I am, and eternally shall be, entirely yours," he wrote to her towards the end of April. In May he heard that she had had a miscarriage: "certes I am not the father of the foetus," he hastily assured Douglas Kinnaird, "for she was three months advanced before our first passade." Teresa's illness was a new factor in delaying his departure from Venice. It was now that his frustrated heart alighted once more upon the nearest perch, which happened to be the young Angelina. A few hours before this comical casual escapade he had plunged in memory and imagination into the love which for him was not a perch but a cage. He wrote a letter to Augusta. This famous letter of 17 May 1819 — Annabella's birthday — was so impassioned in tone, so verbally explicit, that it is generally cited as Exhibit Number 1 on the question of their incest. His "perfect & boundless attachment," he wrote to his sister, "renders me utterly incapable of *real* love for any other human being — for what could they be to me after *you?* My own ╪ ╪ ╪ ╪ we may have been very wrong — but I repent of nothing except that first marriage. . . . and whenever I love anything it is because it reminds me in some way or other of yourself."

This was not the frame of mind in which a cavalier generally approached his lady. Nevertheless, Byron's faithfulness to Augusta genuinely reproduced itself in loyalty to Teresa. To drag himself away from watery Venice on 29 May, as he did, for a scorching cross-country journey to Ravenna, argued commitment rather than ambivalence.

In again passing through Ferrara he drifted into romantic melancholy, indulging it by a visit to the city's cemetery. The simple epitaphs, especially *"Implora pace,"* seemed to him "absolute music." He told Murray that his own resting-place should be the foreigners' burying ground at the Lido, with "those two words, and no more, put over me. I trust they won't think of pickling, and bringing me home to Clod or Blunderbuss Hall." Later he met a man who asked him if he knew Lord Byron. "I told him *no* (no one knows himself, *you* know) ." He wrote this also to Murray, who well understood the Romantics' creed of the unfathomable ego.

Almost suffocated with heat, Byron reached the Pellegrino

Inn at Bologna — only to find that the expected letter from
Teresa had not arrived. Should he turn round and go back?
But Ravenna had been Dante's retreat in exile. Here was his
tomb and the Convent of St. Joseph, where he had written
part of the *Divine Comedy*. Byron must go forward.

As it turned out Teresa had not written because she had
had a relapse and was at death's door. But her health,
though still precarious, responded to her lover's presence.
This was the moment for Byron to break the strings of *serventismo* by suggesting that they should run away together
— "and for this a great Love is necessary — and some courage," he wrote to her. "Have you enough? I can anticipate
your answer. It will be long and divinely written but it will
end in a negative." It did. Remembering his last proposal
to elope, and Fanny Webster's answer, Byron may not have
expected — or deeply desired — anything else. The strings of
serventismo would have been gossamer to the chains of
elopement.

As Teresa grew stronger she entered an earthly paradise
and he a state of qualified bliss. They rode together beneath
the massive umbrella pines along the coast — "Evergreen
forest! . . . / How have I loved the twilight hour and thee!"
— listening to the nightingales and cicadas. She showed her
laughable side by wearing a spectacular sky-blue riding habit
but failing entirely to control her horse, which bit his, and
her poetic side by quoting Dante in her musical Italian voice.
It was at her suggestion that he wrote his *Prophecy of Dante*.
The poem echoed many of Byron's feelings about his own
exile, and his "ineffable" love for his own Beatrice. Osten-
sibly it was the Florentine exile's lament over fourteenth-
century factions, and his prediction of "evil days" to come if
faction persisted. Thanks to the Gambas and Guicciolis, he
now found himself involved in nineteenth-century Italian
politics. Like Dante, Byron was to be "the new Prometheus
of new men."

Ravenna, as part of the Romagna, was ruled by the papal
government working under and with the foreign despotism

of Austria. But a spirit of independence was abroad in the Romagna very different from Venice's decadent frivolity. Since the Congress of Aix-la-Chapelle in 1818, it had been clear that subject peoples could expect nothing from the new European concert. Castlereagh for Britain and Metternich for Austria had agreed that any signs of independence must immediately be suppressed. To them, such movements could only presage a revival of the dreaded French Revolution which in turn had produced the Terror and the Napoleonic wars of aggression. They forgot that the great Revolution had once stood for liberty. It was for liberty that the Italian cities were now beginning to conspire.

Byron found himself operating among many shades of nationalist opinion, ranging from the dedicated libertarian to the double-crosser. Representing the concentrated spirit of patriotism was the Gamba family, especially Teresa's brother Pietro. Byron loved this twenty-year-old boy for his enthusiasm, high spirits and humor, and was to call him "a very fine, brave fellow . . . and wild about liberty." Old Guiccioli's loyalties, however, were ambiguous. More significant than the aristocracy, apart from its provision of leadership, were the secret centers of popular agitation, especially the Carbonari. They got their name from the charcoal burners, whose deep forests, hidden huts and blackened faces made them ideal symbols of conspiracy.

It has been shrewdly remarked by Iris Origo, Teresa Guiccioli's biographer, that Byron's part in all this ferment was not that of a professional whose first step in a planned political campaign was taken in Milan, his second in Ravenna and his last in Greece. Far less was he the instrument of English liberalism. "He was in politics a dilettante," she writes, "an aristocrat at odds with society, an intellectual with a strong partiality for liberty."

True, Byron was a political dilettante; but only in the same sense that *Don Juan* can be described as the expression of poetical dilettantism raised to a degree of genius. Byron's politics were no more planned than his *Don Juan*. And of this, his greatest poem, he wrote impatiently to Murray in 1819: "I *have* no plan — I *had* no plan. . . . Why, Man, the Soul of such writing is its licence; at least the *liberty* of that *licence,* if one likes, — *not* that one should abuse it." Systematic poetry like systematic politics or indeed a systematic life-style irked him. He derided Leigh Hunt's "system" of style in poetry, and Wordsworth's "system" of Lake philosophy and Coleridge's metaphysics. "When a man talks of his system it is like a woman talking of her *virtue,*" he wrote. "I let them talk on." In politics Byron might have been happy with some version of modern anarchism — *"not* that one should abuse it." He would strike in politics as in poetry wherever and whenever the iron was hot. Meanwhile, *Don Juan,* however inchoate, was intended to have two definite characteristics. *"Human"* was to be its key word; and it must also appear "a little quietly facetious upon every thing."

On 15 July 1819 John Murray published the first two cantos and Byron waited anxiously to hear how his little bit of quiet facetiousness would be received.

The poet's friends and publisher, whom Byron lumped together as his "damned puritanical committee," had forced him to accept an anonymous first edition and the total exclusion of his savage dedication to the poet laureate Robert Southey, who had associated him with a "Satanic school" of poetry. Byron himself had proposed to omit an indecent couplet on "dry-Bob," and also to cut the ferocious stanzas on Castlereagh which labeled him an "intellectual eunuch . . . / Cobbling at manacles for all mankind." Byron's naive reason for this latter cut was that he could not at present offer Castlereagh the pleasure of a duel in retaliation — which goes to show how much Byron's three-year exile had cut him off from postwar England. It was no longer 1809, when Castlereagh and Canning had shot pieces out of each other's clothing with dueling pistols. England had begun moving into the age of morality, which was to culminate in Victorianism.

Nevertheless it was early days yet, and Byron was able to

act the "Porcupine" (his metaphor) on many contested
points in *Don Juan*, resisting criticism or pricking his "committee" into reluctant acquiescence. His friend Douglas Kinnaird, for instance, had written that though the poem was
"exquisite," it "must be *cut* for the *Syphilis*." Byron rightly
believed that the pains and penalties of vice were not in
themselves immoral, and therefore should not be regarded
as unmentionable in a satire on the human condition. He
won; and so we have intact the poet's satirical digression on
"progress" in the modern world, where the pox, he hears,
was sent to Europe from America and probably ought to be
sent back:

> *The population there so spreads, they say*
>   *'Tis grown high time to thin it in its turn,*
> *With war, or plague, or famine, any way,*
>   *So that civilisation they may learn;*
> *And which in ravage the more loathsome evil is —*
> *Their real lues, or our pseudo-syphilis?* *

The "*Syphilis*" digression was by no means the only example of Byron's roundabout, colloquial or vulgar method of
flouting hypocritical convention. He pilloried Platonic love
as boring humbug and exposed the cant of a classical education, in which obnoxious passages were expurgated and
then:

> *They only add them all in an appendix,*
> *Which saves, in fact, the trouble of an index.*

He ridiculed the sentimentality of Romantic verse by deliberately defacing his own stanzas with workaday phrases
like "et cetera," "Well — well," "I'm afraid," "I can't tell
why," or by juggling with preposterous rhymes:

> *But — Oh! ye lords of ladies intellectual,*
> *Inform us truly, have they not hen-peck'd you all?*

Or by lampooning his own rambling style:

---

* *Lues Venera* or syphilis (1634), versus Byron's particular enemy, the
"clap" (1587)

> *My way is to begin with the beginning;*
> *The regularity of my design*
> *Forbids all wandering as the worst of sinning.*

Or again by making violent transitions from the beautiful to the cynical, so that contrasts are not slurred as in romance, but highlighted as in life itself:

> *'Tis sweet to hear the watchdog's honest bark . . .*
> *'Tis sweet to be awaken'd by the lark . . . .*
> *Sweet is the vintage . . . .*
> *Sweet is a legacy, and passing sweet*
>   *The unexpected death of some old lady*
> *Or gentleman of seventy years complete.*

All this buffoonery leads up to the sweetest thing of all: "first and passionate love." First love stands alone like "the unforgiven / Fire which Prometheus filch'd for us from heaven" — an event, says Byron, that was no doubt a fable of first love.

"Return we to our story," as Byron says after his latest digression. The "story" of Canto 1 describes two characteristic scenes, both of which give scope for his wit and gaiety. First, the seduction of Don Juan, an innocent sixteen-year-old (in itself a joke against the legend) by Donna Julia, aged twenty-three, whose husband Don Alfonso must be quite as old as Count Guiccioli. Second, the farcical exposure of Juan, who is given away by his shoes under the bed (Byron's lame foot again), after the frenzied Alfonso and his male servants have been foiled in their search for him in Julia's bedroom. There is no alternative but a convent for Julia (with which, incidentally, Teresa was soon to be threatened) and exile for Juan. His exile is decreed by his mother, Donna Inez, an all-too-obvious portrait of the Princess of Parallelograms: "Her favourite science was the mathematical"; "she was a walking calculation"; "Oh! she was perfect past all parallel." Donna Inez had tried to get rid of her husband Don José by proving he was mad:

> *But as he had some lucid intermissions,*
>   *She next decided he was only* bad;
> *Yet when they ask'd her for her depositions,*
>   *No sort of explanation could be had,*
> *Save that her duty both to man and God*
> *Required this conduct — which seem'd very odd.*

Life in *Don Juan* was always turning out to be odd. In
Canto II, Juan is shipwrecked on the way to his country of
exile, Italy, and a wonderful charivari ensues based on the
journal of Byron's shipwrecked grandfather. The hilarity,
the nonsense, the beauty always overtaken by sudden let-
downs, are maintained to the end, when Juan is washed up
on a pirate's isle and into the arms of the pirate's lovely
"gazelle-eyed" daughter Haidée. In describing a rainbow, for
instance, Byron opens with romantic similes — a banner, a
Turkish crescent of purple, vermilion and molten gold —
but closes with "a black eye." It is the poet, as always, who
has given a black eye to the reader.

These first two cantos of *Don Juan* came as two black eyes
to those critics who were hoping for more *Childe Harold*–
like cantos from the magical pen. They hit back savagely.

Blackwood's Magazine could scarcely believe that even
Lord Byron's "odious malignity" would produce such a
"filthy and impious poem," whose mockery of his injured
wife was "brutally, fiendishly, inexpiably mean." (The wit
of Canto I in fact made Annabella laugh.) The distinguished
historian Francis Cohen (afterwards Palgrave) complained
to Murray of the poem's "scorching and drenching" the
reader at the same moment, a state contrary to nature. In replying through Murray, Byron asked, "Did he [Cohen] never
swim in the Noonday with the Sun in his eyes and on his
head, which all the foam of Ocean could not cool?" "Was he
ever in a Turkish bath, that marble paradise of sherbet and
Sodomy?" Almost certainly Francis Cohen never was. Nor in
the other hot-wet predicaments which Byron suggested.

That old favorite, the *Gentleman's Magazine,* greeted *Don*

Juan with "the most decided reprobation"; the *London Magazine,* thoroughly foxed by "the quick alternation of pathos and profaneness, of serious and moving sentiment and indecent ribaldry," dubbed it "an insult and an outrage"; and the *British Reviewer,* if he had been Byron's next of kin, would have issued a writ *de lunatico inquirendo* against him. Among well-known moralists, the Reverend Caleb Colton, author of *Many Things in Few Words* (referred to by Byron as *Few Things in Many Words*), was one who loudly lamented the prostitution of so much genius: "The muse of Byron has mixed her poison with the hand of an adept; it is proffered in a goblet of crystal and of gold." His mind still on the Borgias, the Reverend Caleb applied to *Don Juan* words which had been coined for a work by Cardinal Bembo (to whom Lucrezia Borgia had written the love letters Byron had read in Milan) : "You can call this poem either the most obscene elegance or the most elegant obscenity."

Even William Hazlitt could never bring himself to accept "the splashing of soda-water," which inevitably followed "the classical intoxication." A professional courtesan like Harriette Wilson advised him to stop making a *coarse* old libertine of himself and to "take a little calomel." And an adulterous wife like Teresa Guiccioli was to forbid any more cantos after the fifth, unless and until she gave permission. But Byron believed in his "Donny Johnny," as did many others.

"Stick to Don Juan," wrote the new radical journal, *John Bull,* next year; "it is the only sincere thing you have ever written." He praised "the sweet, fiery, rapid, easy — beautifully easy, — anti-humbug style," adding, "I had really no idea what a very clever fellow you were till I read Don Juan." Byron's old friend John Galt, the novelist, perceptively called the epic "a poetical novel," predicting that Juan would end up a subscriber to the Society for the Suppression of Vice. Above all Goethe gave his august imprimatur by translating part of the poem himself. "We feel that English poetry," he wrote, "is in possession of what the Germans have never attained, a classically elegant comic style."

Some of Byron's enthusiasm for writing had been dulled by his publisher's early doubts about the poem. Nevertheless he persisted with the next three cantos. At least during the hours of composition his mind was freed from other anxieties. And in this poem he had accepted, albeit with many a wry grimace, the human condition.

Since Teresa was destined to be his last attachment — "my *last* love," "my last adventure," "my last passion," as he reiterated — the affair caused him as much anxiety as enchantment. He felt himself an aging Don Juan, his hair "half grey," his teeth remaining "by way of courtesy," in competition with an aged man-in-possession. This was a truly *"orrible systhème,"* as Mendalgo would have said, and not improved by Count Guiccioli's being called a "Cuckoo" with a "horned head" in a local broadsheet. Yet Teresa would not let her lover escape from the system.

In August they all three returned to Bologna. It was a measure of Byron's tension that a performance of Alfieri's *Myrrha*, a classical tale of incest, sent him into convulsions. Teresa, however, did not consider his convulsions a sign of madness, as Annabella had, but went into sympathetic hysterics herself.

Though his chains had now become part of him, he dreamed still of freedom. Perhaps he would emigrate with Allegra and Fletcher to South America: "those fellows are fresh as their world, and fierce as their earthquakes." And when there was news of social earthquakes in England, such as the "Peterloo massacre" of August 1819, he thought maybe he should return home. A visit to England "in the spring" became his annual refrain.

But it was still only early autumn in Italy. Surprisingly, the Count had offered him an apartment in the Palazzo Guiccioli in Bologna, far more commodious than his stuffy inn. For a few days the tension relaxed. Then the unaccountable Count asked Byron to lend him some money, Byron was advised to refuse, a quarrel broke out, Teresa's weakness since her miscarriage came to her rescue and she had another relapse. On 12 September she insisted on going with Byron to see a Venetian specialist who had already attended her in Ravenna on Byron's recommendation.

All these moves interested the Ravenna police. Without Byron's knowledge they began watching him closely. After all, he had been on their books since 1816 in Milan; and when a mysterious attempt was made in 1818 to shoot Wellington in Paris, the French police were informed by the Italian police that the would-be assassin might be Lord Byron.

Meanwhile Byron and Teresa visited Petrarch's home at Arqua on their way to Venice and wrote their names in the visitors' book together. It was Teresa's turn to suggest an elopement and Byron to urge caution — and to write in the third canto of *Don Juan:*

> *Think you, if Laura had been Petrarch's wife,*
> *He would have written sonnets all his life?*

After a delicious rest among the little artificial lakes and parterres of his villa at La Mira, they floated into Venice and slept together at Byron's Mocenigo palace. This was defying the *"orrible systhème"* with a vengeance. But notwithstanding the waves of hostile gossip (Lord Byron had "abducted" the Countess Guiccioli) and the alarm of Teresa's family, the lovers returned to La Mira. Byron remained, writing and making love until near the end of October. Teresa was flattered to find that he could "work better" while his beloved sat beside him and prattled. She might have been disconcerted had she known that he had acquired this habit with the whores of Venice.

A welcome visitor at La Mira was Thomas Moore. Byron took the opportunity of giving him a small white leather bag containing his memoirs. They were about his marriage (how it haunted him!) and Moore could sell it to anyone, edit it after his death — anything he liked. "I care not."

Not having seen Byron since 1816, Moore was struck by the new Juan look of "arch, waggish wisdom" in place of the Childe's "refined and spiritualised look." Byron was in fact still overweight. But his "Epicurean play of humour" was more active than ever, as he and Moore laughed over old times. Suddenly these stirrings from the past, added to the uncertainty of Teresa's and Allegra's future, changed his usual refrain of England "in the spring" into England *now*.

Count Ruggero Gamba, Teresa's father, had decided it was high time for his daughter to be brought home. Count Guiccioli accordingly descended on the Mocenigo palace, a series of emotional earthquakes took place as fierce as those in South America, and Teresa returned with her husband to Ravenna. What had Italy to offer Byron now? "I have done my duty," he wrote to Kinnaird, "but the country has become sad to me . . . and as I left England on account of my own wife, I now quit Italy for the wife of another."

But Allegra caught a fever. Their departure was postponed. By December winter had reached Venice. How could he drag the frail child over the Alps? And he would not start without her: "I have put off my intended voyage, till the spring."

Then Teresa caught something — or was it psychosomatic as Professor Marchand believes? At any rate, she caught Byron. In answer to urgent pleas from everyone, including even her father, Byron returned to Ravenna. He and little Allegra arrived at the Palazzo Guiccioli in the Napoleonic coach on Christmas Eve. For Teresa it seemed to be the solution. Byron was back in *serventismo* and this time it was with the husband's blessing and the family's full consent. For Allegra, however, the picture was still a shifting one.

It was apparent that Byron had reproduced in Allegra a new "baby B." Her beauty was his own over again. Like the first "baby B," she could twist anyone round her finger with her charm and determination. She was admittedly spoiled: "frowns and pouts quite in our way," her father wrote to Augusta. Teresa made a pet of her, taking her about in the carriage, and Byron sometimes found her an amusing plaything, with her Venetian dialect and comical "Bon di, papa." But the curious triangle may have been touched with jealousies: Teresa jealous of Byron's daughter by another, Byron jealous of Teresa's fondness for a child who was often in his way.

In the spring of 1820 he began considering Allegra's education. This should have involved Claire's rights as a mother. The poor woman had been imploring "Albè" with increasing desperation to allow Allegra, whom she had not seen for nearly two years, to visit her at the Shelleys'. But if Allegra was "obstinate as a Mule," as her father said, Byron was obstinate as a whole team of mules. He replied, via Mrs. Hoppner, to Claire's plea that he totally disapproved of "children's treatment" in the Shelley family. "Have they *reared* one?" (Little William had followed "Little Ca" to the grave.) His child should not perish of starvation, or green fruit, or be taught "there is no Deity." He would send her to England to be educated — or put her in a convent. On receiving this ukase Claire wrote bitterly in her diary, "A letter from Mad. Hoppner concerning green fruit and god — strange jumble."

The jumble in Byron's mind concerning Allegra was sorted out by the end of 1820, to the extent that a convent school near Ravenna was definitely decided upon. To choose the climate of the Romagna was as "strange" as the original jumble. For his Allegrina, whom he had once described proudly as "flourishing like a pomegranate," had sickened during the hot sultry summer with a fever which lasted on and off for weeks. True, her father took a villa for her in the country near Filetto. But suggestions that she should go to England or Switzerland were more sensible. Unfortunately they came from the Claire-Shelley-Hoppner circle, which Byron regarded rather as another "damned committee."

At last, on 1 March 1821, less than two months after her

fourth birthday, Allegrina was deposited by Byron's banker, like an unsatisfactory account, with the Capuchin nuns at Bagnacavallo. Byron himself had been happy with the Capuchin monks in Athens. Perhaps Allegrina would become a nun, "being a character somewhat wanted in our family," as he had once written to Augusta, or marry more respectably than she would in England as a little illegitimate. The main point was to have her brought up a Roman Catholic, which "I look upon as the best religion, as it is assuredly the oldest of the various branches of Christianity." Neither he nor Claire were ever to see Allegra again. Claire's deprivation was to be the result of Byron's harshness, Byron's the result of his own lack of concern.

In the midst of carnival time, 1820, Count Guiccioli, probably at Teresa's instigation, had invited Byron to rent the upper floor of his palazzo in Ravenna. This was convenient, though proximity to the odd old man made Byron uneasy. Was he going to spy on them? Nevertheless Byron moved in, together with "ten horses, eight enormous dogs, three monkeys, five cats, an eagle, a crow, and a falcon." This was the count that Shelley made during a visit seven months later, to which he had to add "five peacocks, two guinea hens, and an Egyptian crane" encountered on the grand staircase. Instead of the cramped inn where Byron had been staying, he could now walk in the paved garden with its roses, lemons and clipped evergreens, share the fine stables visible through an archway beyond, and again compose his daring epic beneath ceilings rosy with cherubs. He sent off Cantos III and IV to the less-than-eager Murray in February. In every other way, it seemed, he was back on the old beat, making love to Teresa according to the exciting yet not wholly satisfactory formula which he had described so vividly the year before: "*those moments* — delicious — dangerous . . . the hall! those rooms! The open doors! The servants so curious and so near."

When he heard that Hobhouse had been imprisoned for publishing a subversive pamphlet and Scrope Davies, like

Beau Brummel, forced to flee abroad for debt, he commiserated with Hobhouse in words that showed how dubious he still was about his own situation: "Brummel at Calais; Scrope at Bruges, Buonaparte at St. Helena, you in your new apartment, and I at Ravenna, only think! so many great men!" So many great men in exile.

Events were brewing in Ravenna which would send more "great men" into exile while liberating Byron at least to some extent.

The revolutionary underground was making itself felt. *Up with the Republic! Down with the Pope!* appeared on city walls. "This would be nothing in London," commented Byron, "where the walls are privileged. . . . But here it is a different thing; they are not used to such fierce political inscriptions, and the police is all on the alert, and the Cardinal glares pale through all his purple."

The new legate, Antonio Cardinal Rusconi, indeed was beginning to bestow some of his glares upon Byron. It was probably he who inspired the hitherto-complacent Count Guiccioli to break the liaison between his wife and this dangerously liberal foreigner. Thus politics were now to become interwoven with Byron's love life. In May 1820 the volcano on which he and Teresa had been dallying blew up. Her escritoire in the elegant boudoir with yellow, gray and black tesselated floor and lusty cupids was rifled. Soon afterwards her husband caught the lovers on the sofa. A screaming, sobbing, raging quarrel ensued; Teresa fled to her family in the Palazzo Gamba nearby and, after much further agony, persuaded her father to apply for a papal separation. Count Guiccioli's personal eccentricities were undoubtedly a help in the cause. On 14 July 1820 the Count's bastille fell to the Gamba onslaught and Teresa's separation was granted, on condition that she lived respectably henceforth under her father's roof.

The "horned Cuckoo" had played his hand with extreme clumsiness. His idea had been to throw out Byron not Teresa.

But when he ordered Byron to leave his upper-floor flat, his defiant tenant refused, having at great cost installed his enormous family of servants and animals. It was the lover, paradoxically, who was to enjoy the amenities of the Palazzo Guiccioli to the end of the chapter.

Count Gamba removed his family for the summer to his estate at Filetto (hence Byron's choice of a villa there for Allegra). Though Byron could not sleep under the Gamba roof he paid frequent agreeable visits, becoming "inoculated" for the first time in his life into a congenial family unit. His use of the word "inoculated," however, showed that the process was not entirely natural.

When the Gambas returned to Ravenna in the cooler weather he was "inoculated" ever more thoroughly into Carbonari meetings and plots, giving them money for arms and turning his home into an arsenal. They trusted him implicitly. In July the revolutionaries of Naples had forced a constitution on their Bourbon despot. A rising in the Romagna was secretly planned for September. Though it proved abortive, excitement continued to hiss and bubble in the streets of Ravenna; the graffiti proliferated; now and then a police officer would fall at his post. Byron out of compassion had one dying man lifted from a pool of blood and carried into his own house.

It was an atmosphere which suited Byron's muse: stirring outside events and an inner, inescapable relationship, which, while utterly necessary to him, he half longed to escape. He might even go to the Ionian Islands, he thought in January 1821: "Why not? — perhaps I may, next spring."

Next spring the Greek War of Independence was to erupt.

But for Byron the year 1821 was to be a record in torrential composition springing from great fertility of imagination and thought. Having completed his *Marino Faliero* in 1820 on the theme of tyranny, he wrote another historical Venetian tragedy, *The Two Foscari,* in 1821 with the emphasis on exile. A third poetic drama, *Sardanapalus,* contained even more of Byron. The allegedly effete, dandified Assyrian king

Sardanapalus proves himself to be a true war leader and dies heroically on a funeral pyre with his Greek slave Myrrha. The Myrrha-incest theme is present, if only in a dream, and whimsical echoes of Prometheus are still audible, Sardanapalus longing to retire to "a cottage on the Caucasus." A light satire called *The Blues* administered yet another rap to Annabella:

> *You wed with Miss Lilac! 'twould be your perdition:*
> *She's a poet, a chymist, a mathematician.*

As an inimitable satire of Byron's most hilariously savage brand, nothing would ever beat his *Vision of Judgement*. Poet laureate Southey had already published his own *Vision*, in which the preface pilloried Byron as leader of the "Satanic school" of poetry. Byron's withering reply took the form of a drama at the celestial gate, with George III just dead and trying to get inside (he died in 1820), despite Satan's claim to his person. There are lively doings with devils and angels (". . . for by many stories / And true, we learn the angels are all Tories"), the climax being reached when Southey is kidnapped from his home on Mt. Skiddaw by an enterprising devil. The bard immediately offers to write Satan's biography

> *In two octavo volumes nicely bound,*
> *With notes and preface, all that most allures.*

The uproar which greets Southey's attempt to read his verses aloud forces St. Peter to knock him headlong into Derwentwater, where he first sinks to the bottom "like his works" and then floats to the surface like "all corrupted things." Meanwhile King George has slipped into Heaven,

> *And when the tumult dwindled to a calm,*
> *I left him practising the hundredth psalm.*

Satan was much in Byron's thoughts during 1821, both satirically and seriously. In his third long poetic drama of

that year, *Cain, a Mystery,* he grappled with his own alter
ego, the evildoer who, seduced though he is by external
forces, nevertheless has some vein of wickedness within himself which responds to Satan's promptings. Like Childe
Harold, Cain is an exile, though the former is a pilgrim and
the latter an outlaw. Both are wanderers with no goal. Byron's
fourth drama and second "Mystery," called *Heaven and
Earth,* was finished in October. In each "Mystery" God is
castigated by Satan for creating only to destroy, as at the
time of the "pre-Adamite" creation or the Flood. Cain alone
feels compassion for the extinct animals that Satan shows
him (with the help of Cuvier's *Animal Kingdom* published
in 1817); Japhet alone, as he watches the ark floating to his
rescue, thinks with anguish, "Why, when all perish, why must
I remain?"

Both these provocative poems were to be published in the
following year and received with shock and abuse. Teresa
might well have asked herself why she had forbidden *Don
Juan* if Byron was to write *Cain* instead.

While Byron alternately composed and plotted with the
best, the disunited revolutionary movement staggered towards the precipice, as he had feared. There was everywhere
a fine revolutionary theme but far too many variations — the
Americani, the Massoni Riformati, the Guelfi, the Latinisti,
the Illuminati and many others. On 9 February 1821 bad
news arrived. The Austrians (or "Barbarians" and "Huns,"
as Byron called them) had outwitted the Carbonari by crossing the river Po before they could rise, and marching on
Naples. By the end of the month there was worse news: the
insurrection at Naples had been suppressed. The worst news
of all came on 10 July when Pietro Gamba was arrested by
the police and he and his father driven out of the Papal
States and into Tuscany and exile. In a tempest of tears,
changes of mind, mingled faith and doubt about Byron's will
to follow her, Teresa left Ravenna on 25 July to join her
father and brother in Florence. The alternative for her was
"exile" in a convent. The police had been as inept as Count

Guiccioli. For their real wish was to see Lord Byron an exile.

Byron remained alone in Ravenna. Like George III in his *Vision of Judgement,* his instinct was to slip into the peaceful heaven of his palazzo under cover of the general confusion and make music. Notwithstanding this temptation, he knew he must join Teresa. But he put off the journey for three months. In the end it was Shelley who made his departure possible by renting two mansions in Tuscan Pisa (where Shelley had now settled his own family) for Byron and the Gambas respectively.

Shelley was to provide Byron's last pleasant memories of Ravenna, as he was to be the central figure of his new life in Pisa. A visit to Allegra in her convent was Shelley's aim, before the Ravenna base was abandoned. In Shelley, unlike her father, Allegra inspired a poetic tenderness, as evinced in his *Julian and Maddalo:*

> *A lovelier toy sweet Nature never made,*
> *A serious, subtle, wild yet gentle being.*

Byron was a delightful host to his friend during part of August, convincing Shelley that he was "reformed, as far as gallantry goes," and but for "the canker of aristocracy" had become a man of "many generous and exalted qualities." Then Shelley covered the twelve miles to Bagnacavallo alone, won Allegra's confidence with a gold chain, admired her white muslin dress, black silk apron and trousers, raced madly with her along the corridors, listened to her mischievously ringing the convent bell, and finally decided that the nuns were taming her without unkindness.

On 28 August the mother superior invited Byron to see his daughter and her convent school. He failed to do so. Allegra had written suggesting he should bring some money with him for "gingerbread" at the fair, surely a natural demand in a small child. But it put him off. He squirmed at cupboard love even in a "baby B" aged four; or used the cupboard love to rationalize his own deeper resistance. Indeed he did not like Allegra, though he loved her in absence. Why risk yet another scene, after all the wearisome racket and rows he had endured before Teresa's departure? He had called his daughter's character "perverse" and her temper "violent" — and so no doubt they were, until the nuns took her in hand.

The common people of Ravenna lamented to see their handsome, liberty-loving, generous lord leaving them. Rightly, he did not suspect them of cupboard love. And how kind he was in bestowing the animals. Japhet would have been pleased to see that no animal was left behind except a goat with a broken leg, the crane which could eat only fish, a badger on a chain, the ugly peasant dog Mutz and two ugly monkeys, and these were consigned to his banker, just as Allegra had been eight months earlier. His travel-worn Napoleonic coach rumbled out of Ravenna on 29 October 1821. In some ways its owner felt equally faded. As he had written on his last birthday:

> *Through life's road, so dim and dirty,*
> *I have dragg'd to three-and-thirty.*
> *What have these years left to me?*
> *Nothing — except thirty-three.*

But he was wrong. The years had left him with his greatest poetry, as well as unimpaired political ideals demanding satisfaction.

EIGHT

A Nest of Singing-Birds
(1821–1823)

ON HIS JOURNEY from Ravenna to Pisa, Byron had a glimpse of his past, and his past glimpsed him, but without his knowing. Neither of these two encounters augured well for the future.

By chance the carriages of Lord Byron and Lord Clare passed each other between Imola and Bologna, allowing the two boyhood friends to converse for five minutes. What a five minutes. "I hardly recollect an hour of my existence which could be weighed against them," Byron wrote afterwards. Suddenly before his eyes was the "*male* thing" he had always loved best in the world. When they shook hands Byron thought he could feel Clare's heart "beat to his fingers' ends," unless indeed the pulse was his own. "It was a new and inexplicable feeling," Byron added, "like rising from the grave, to me." When Byron saw Lord Clare once more, in 1823, he felt that his powers of friendship stopped with Clare and perhaps Thomas Moore, excluding even Shelley, "however much I admired and esteemed him."

He had written just before the accidental meeting in 1821, "I never hear the word 'Clare' without a beating of the heart even *now*." The other Claire, whose name he never heard without a freezing of the heart, also passed his coach during this same journey, while leaving Pisa for Florence. "Just before Empoli we passed Lord B—— and his travelling train," she wrote in her diary. "As we approached Florence we entered also a thick white fog. . . . As if the skies were about to collapse on top of you." The skies were to collapse on top of Claire, Mary Shelley, and Teresa Guiccioli, in that order.

Proceeding to Pisa, Byron inspected the new home on the river Arno which Shelley had found for him, Casa Lanfranchi. He had "nothing to complain of" except the traffic on the busy riverside road called the Lungarno, certainly not of the walled garden bursting with ripe oranges, the lovely climate (no fires at the end of November), and the "famous old feudal palazzo" itself, with its ghosts and former "fierce owner or two," which may have reminded Byron pleasantly of Newstead. After what he called "all the bore and bustle" of moving, he was prepared to settle into a congenial routine.

Part of that routine was Teresa, whom he had not seen for over three months. He called daily at the Casa Parrà, where she was living with her father and brother Pietro, two or three minutes' ride from the Casa Lanfranchi up the Lungarno. The Tuscan government had granted them temporary asylum. What could be better? It would have seemed better to Teresa if she had not had to share "mio Byron" for the first time with a circle of English friends.

The Shelleys occupied a flat in the Tre Palazzi di Chiesa, whence they could see the white marble façade and decorative windows of Byron's palace — the one with private landing steps — obliquely across the Arno. Another pair of artistic friends, Edward and Jane Williams, had joined the Shelleys, he with ambitions to write for the stage, she a beautiful guitarist. Then there was Shelley's cousin Thomas Medwin, who was to show considerable literary skill in writing his *Conversations of Lord Byron*. A bogus Irish "Count," John Taaffe, was the "self-styled poet laureate of Pisa." So Pisa, wrote Mary, had become "a little nest of singing-birds."

It had also become a little nest of adulterers. The Williamses were not married (and incidentally Jane was Shelley's last attachment though not his mistress). "Count" Taaffe had withdrawn to Pisa after a love affair in Scotland with a married woman who tried to murder him. The circle included another Irish couple, "Mr. and Mrs. Mason," who were in fact Mr. George Tighe and Lady Mountcashell, the latter having run away from her husband. Her governess had been Mary Wollstonecraft, mother of Mary Shelley.

Byron fitted well into both nests; so well, indeed, that he was soon magnetizing Shelley's circle out of the nest at Tre Palazzi into his own at Casa Lanfranchi. The focus of Byron's attraction was his dinner party every Wednesday, during which his conversation would burst into reminiscences, jests, irony and argument continuing until three the next morning. In the daytime he would lead the all-male party out riding, often culminating in pistol shooting beyond the walls of Pisa. The governor had forbidden this suspect alien to shoot inside the city. A farm was found where there was not only shooting space for Byron and his friends but also a beautiful peasant girl, on whom Byron's heart might lightly perch.

In January 1822 a new "singing-bird," who had divorced his wife two years earlier, arrived in the form of John Edward Trelawny, nicknamed "The Turk." Known as "T" or "Tre" by Byron, he kept a vivid diary during these Pisan days; later he was to publish *Adventures of a Younger Son,* in which he invented a youthful career of piracy in the Far East, and a romance with an Arab girl, which concluded in her cremation on some nameless seashore; later still, as his feelings towards the dead Byron deteriorated, he published his wildly unfair but patchily brilliant *Records of Shelley, Byron, and the Author.* Meanwhile he presented himself at Pisa as a living "Corsair" who slept with Byron's poem under his pillow, stood over six feet high, stared out of flashing black eyes, squared a forceful jaw — and had learned his sailing expertise during a respectable though unrewarding career in the British navy, which he had left, still a midshipman, in 1812. He was now thirty.

Byron's performance at pistol shooting could be taken as symbolic of his position among his friends. His hand shook

continually, noted Medwin; nevertheless he was more successful than either Shelley or Trelawny, who could each hit
the target. "Shelley is a much better shot than I am," Byron
would say, "but he was thinking of metaphysics rather than
of firing." Similarly, Byron's dynamism at the Wednesday
dinners was compelling, despite his tendency — less and less
appreciated by Shelley — to lead the talk into ribald or
worldly channels as night and the liquor consumption deepened. Both Trelawny and Medwin later claimed to have
been astonished by Byron's leg-pulling and "mystification."
Trelawny found a mischievous Don Juan where he had expected a Childe Harold, a "solemn mystery." The way that
they all turned themselves into "vats of claret" shocked
Shelley, who began to retire from the "evenings" at an
earlier and earlier hour. His feelings for Byron were fast
becoming equivocal.

For Byron's genius as the author of *Cain* and *Heaven and
Earth* Shelley had unstinted praise. Published in December
1821, *Cain* was execrated and Byron denounced from a London pulpit as "a cool, unconcerned fiend." It sold well
nonetheless, if not as well as the romantic tales. In his own
words to Medwin, "My 'Corsair' days are over. Heigh ho!" It
was Lucifer's exposure of God's ways to man which must have
pleased Shelley in *Cain,* even though Byron had pointed out
in the preface that Lucifer's dramatic challenges did not
express his own beliefs. "It was difficult for me," wrote
Byron of Lucifer, "to make him talk like a clergyman . . .
but I have done what I could to restrain him within the
bounds of spiritual politeness." Again in February 1822 he
explained to the agitated Murray that neither Lucifer nor
Cain was speaking with the poet's voice. Lucifer was merely
"the first rebel" and Cain "the first murderer." Ironically,
Cain killed Abel out of disgust at the blood-sacrifice on
Abel's altar — Cain's altar being vegetarian like Byron's diet.
Nevertheless to his enemies — as to his friend Shelley — both
Cain and Lucifer were Byron speaking.

Shelley may also have responded to the melancholy of Byron's backward-looking Utopianism. Shelley's own thoughts were turning from the optimism of his *Prometheus Unbound* to the despair of his coming *Triumph of Life,* in which life's juggernaut crushes even its greatest sons — Napoleon, Voltaire, popes, emperors and no doubt Byron himself, because their philosophy "taught them not this — to know themselves." In Byron's *Cain,* it is already too late for man to know himself. The golden age is past. Cain is told by Lucifer that in the remote galaxies God has already created perfection — and destroyed it.

Shelley's delight in the two Byronic "Mysteries" soon changed to criticism of Byron's next poetic drama, also finished in 1821, *The Deformed Transformed.* The short sharp exchanges of the two poets about this work were reported by Thomas Medwin. "Shelley . . . tell me what you think of it," said Byron, handing Shelley the manuscript. Shelley took it to the window, read it, and came back. "Least of anything I ever saw of yours," he pronounced. Whereupon Byron tossed the manuscript into the fire. (It was published in January 1824 notwithstanding, so Byron's dramatic gesture must have concealed the fact that he kept the poem in his head or a copy in his desk.)

Shelley's outburst can hardly have been a simple reaction to the poem's intrinsic weakness. It was what Byron called "a Faustish kind of drama," based partly on "Monk" Lewis's derivative *Wood Demon,* partly on Goethe's *Faust;* and Shelley may have become bored with the Goethe-Byron syndrome. In *The Deformed Transformed* the sixteenth-century hero, a lame hunchback named Count Arnold, sells his soul to the Devil in exchange for the beauty, stature and strength of Achilles. The Devil kindly takes on Arnold's hump. Again Shelley may have turned against Byron's obvious obsession with his own deformity, combined as it was with enviable beauty. Mary Shelley was to write: "No action of Lord Byron's life — scarce a line he has written — but was influenced by his personal defect." The opening slanging match between Count Arnold and his mother recalls Geordie and Mrs. Byron. "Out, hunchback!" she screams, to which Arnold replies bitterly, "I was born so, mother!" and his mother shouts back, "Thou incubus!* Thou nightmare! . . . abortion!" — all perhaps rather tiresome to Shelley.

On a deeper level, Arnold's hump represents the deformed, diseased world in which we live. But in placing the hump where it belongs, namely on the shoulders of Evil, we cannot entirely get rid of it. The Devil will accompany Arnold wherever he goes, warning him at the outset:

> . . . *you shall see*
> *Yourself for ever by you, as your shadow.*

There is no escape, even for the idealist or poet. Achilles himself had a fatal weakness in one heel. And Manfred, for all his brilliant gifts, was born under a rogue star, misshapen and pathless:

> *A bright deformity on high,*
> *The monster of the upper sky!*

The key to Byron's unhappiness is perfectionism, the hopeless longing for a golden age. His own deformity must be associated not merely with personal ugliness and suffering but with the state of the world. The Sack of Rome by Charles V in *The Deformed Transformed* is also the revolution for which Byron eagerly waited, and the flight of the corrupt cardinals from Rome in the sixteenth century suggests the longed-for sack of corrupt ministers in the nineteenth century from London, Vienna and Constantinople.

Just as Byron's interest in *The Deformed Transformed* went far beyond mere "Faustishness," so Shelley's dislike of the poem was the symptom of a deeper malaise. The truth was that the exuberant genius of Casa Lanfranchi had unconsciously begun to clip the wings of the original singing-bird. Shelley found he could not write in Byron's ambience. "I have lived too long near Lord Byron and the sun has extinguished the glow-worm," he was to declare ruefully in

---

* Again the Gothick influence: an incubus was a medieval demon who mated with a woman.

1822. Significantly, the only poem he finished at this period was one in which Byron featured and which was itself more than a little "Faustish," being a translation of the *Walpurgisnacht* in Goethe's *Faust*. Shelley saw Byron in Mephistopheles. As Richard Holmes, Shelley's biographer, astutely observes, Shelley gave an unmistakable Byronic tang to his translation of the cynical fiend's remarks. Mephistopheles explains to Faust:

> *In truth, I generally go about*
> *In strict incognito; and yet one likes*
> *To wear one's orders upon gala days* . . . .
> *I could not, if I would, mask myself here.*
> *Come now, we'll go about from fire to fire:*
> *I'll be the Pimp, and you shall be the Lover.*

(Did Byron perhaps encourage Shelley over Jane Williams?)

Shelley denied any influence on Byron, though some people suggested that it was he who had turned their dear Corsair into a Cain. There is no doubt, however, that while Shelley did not sway Byron's religious beliefs (he once called Byron "little better than a Christian") he did affect his poetry. What Byron called the "very wild, metaphysical, and inexplicable" drama of *Manfred* was mainly composed immediately after his intimacy with Shelley at Diodati; and *Cain*, which Byron completed the month after Shelley visited him at Ravenna, was similarly "in my gay metaphysical style, and in the *Manfred* line."

Conceivably Byron might have succeeded in squaring the Pisan circle if he had had an affair with Mary Shelley. We know that her relationship with Shelley was failing (one of his nightmare hallucinations was to be of himself strangling her) and Professor Marchand believes that she might have fallen for Byron, given any encouragement. At Christmas the circle had planned to act *Othello* with Byron as Iago and Mary as Desdemona. But Teresa virtually vetoed the performance.

One result was that the tendency increased for Byron's

circle to become a male one. Even on Christmas Day the men
all dined at the Casa Lanfranchi without the women. Shelley,
with his dreams of a commune, cannot have approved. Nevertheless Mephistopheles got his way, by pretending that he
supported the Turkish harem system. "They lock them up,
and they are much happier. Give a woman a looking-glass
and a few sugar-plums, and she will be satisfied." Byron could
cite Bonaparte as another supporter. And so the ladies never
rode out on horseback. Teresa and Mary would share a carriage, for they were friends, and try to meet their men coming
home. "Our good cavaliers flock together," wrote Mary of
this man's world, and, quoting Scott's novel *The Antiquary,*
"they do not like *fetching a walk with the absurd womankind.*" The arrival of Trelawny strengthened the male element. He vigorously encouraged Byron and Shelley to build
two boats, a superior one for Byron and a smaller, of course,
for Shelley.

If Byron had all along somewhat overpowered Shelley with
the force of his success, he had also given Shelley just cause
for criticism and was soon to strain Shelley's feelings to
the breaking point, through the Allegra tragedy.

The thick white fog over Florence was not Claire's only
intimation of coming evil. She had a presentiment that she
would never see Allegra again. She was told by Elise that the
fiend Byron had boasted of his intention to make Allegra his
mistress in due course, since she was Shelley's child by Claire,
not his. In her misery Claire became hysterical, imploring
Shelley to help her kidnap the child, if he could not persuade
Byron to let her visit the convent. But when Shelley approached Byron he was put off with the ill-tempered comment that "women could not live without making scenes."

Shelley's patience was not inexhaustible. "It is of vital
importance both to me and to yourself, to Allegra even," he
wrote to Claire, "that I should put a period to my intimacy
with L B [Lord Byron]." Shelley even suggested settling his
difference with L B *"without words,"* that is, with dueling
pistols. L B knew nothing of all this.

There was one singing-bird missing from the Pisan circle whose punctual arrival might have drawn them together. It had been Shelley's idea to invite his friend Leigh Hunt to join them. Leigh at Pisa and his brother John in England would then launch a new magazine, the *Liberal,* which would earn the Hunts some much-needed money and become a vehicle for publishing Shelley's and Byron's latest poems, now that Murray was jibbing at the "Satanic school." Murray had been threatened with prosecution over *Cain* and understandably it was no longer bright morning between publisher and author.

Byron harbored kindly feelings towards Leigh Hunt, having visited him many times when his magazine, the *Examiner,* had landed him in prison for calling the Prince Regent "a fat Adonis of 50." Books had arrived for Leigh brought by Byron's own hand rather than by a footman, which deeply impressed this democratic denizen of Hampstead.

Nevertheless it would require Shelley's presence to weld Byron and Hunt together. Otherwise the "canker of aristocracy," which Shelley had detected in Byron, might cause him to criticize Hunt, as he had criticized that other member of the Hampstead set, John Keats. Admittedly it was Keats's poetry which Byron disliked. He considered it sentimental. Keats had said that his inspiration was a draught of "the true, the blushful Hippocrene"; Byron told Medwin that "the true Hippocrene" was gin-and-water. At Ravenna Shelley had discussed Keats's death with Byron, and how it was hastened by a savage review from John Wilson Croker in the *Quarterly.* Byron was sorry — though he could not resist a future jest at Keats's expense in *Don Juan,* Canto XI: " 'Tis strange the mind, that very fiery particle, / Should let itself be snuff'd out by an article."

All told, Shelley must be present when the Hunts — for Leigh's wife and children would come too — were introduced into the Pisan circle.

But when would they come? A disturbing message had

arrived in February 1822 to say that the exceptionally bad weather had prevented them from sailing. There they remained on the English south coast, spending the money Shelley had sent them and running into debt. Almost in the same breath as Shelley had written to Claire about calling Byron out, he had borrowed £250 from L B to lend Hunt. It was May before the Hunts were seaborne, an unlucky delay.

Meanwhile spring came to Italy and with it the end of the Pisan circle. What was known as the "Masi affray" broke it up.

Riding home on 24 March from shooting practice, the friends heard the sound of galloping hoofs behind them. It was Sergeant Major Stefani Masi of the dragoons, making a spurt for the city gate so as not to be late in barracks. He negotiated the ladies' carriage successfully but was then faced by a solid wedge of gentlemen blocking his path. Dashing through a narrow gap between the ditch and the outside gentleman, John Taaffe, Masi caused Taaffe's horse to shy. "Have you ever seen the like of that?" shouted Taaffe to Byron, pointing indignantly at the vanishing horseman. Byron gave chase. So did they all. A crowd collected like lightning round the Piagge gate. Shelley got there first (he must be first for once) and received a blow on the head which knocked him unconscious. Another gentleman had his nose bloodied, the courier suffered an internal contusion, Pietro Gamba belabored Masi with his riding whip, and Byron challenged him to a duel. Byron had failed to recognize the sergeant major's epaulettes and thought Masi was an officer — "but I am no great tailor in uniforms."

In the hubbub, Masi again broke through, hoping to reach his barracks. But someone — almost certainly Byron's coachman though he was never brought to book — suddenly darted out of the Casa Lanfranchi and stabbed Masi in the body with what Teresa described later as "a small fork." Crying out that he was killed, Masi rode a little way along the Lungarno clutching his side and then collapsed.

That night Pisa was in tumult. The foreigners were rumored to have headed a peasant revolt, resulting in the wounding of Byron and Taaffe and the death of Trelawny and Masi. In fact the sergeant major recovered; but the incident and its legal consequences were to close the frontiers of Tuscany against the Gambas, and therefore indirectly against Byron. Each of the households had servants imprisoned on suspicion of having wounded Masi, despite Teresa's loyal statement in court that she *thought* the blow had been struck by Taaffe. Jane Williams christened him "False Taaffe." Byron's servant Tita, whose deceptively ferocious moustaches always attracted attention, inevitably found himself in the dock. Though acquitted of the blow, he was convicted of carrying arms. His eventual release was followed by banishment; but not before Byron had sent him a twelve-course dinner to be shared with his fellow prisoners.

Tita temporarily joined the Shelleys at the Villa Magni in the Bay of Lerici, where they had removed for the summer sailing; he would return to his master as soon as Byron left Pisa. Trelawny had gone too, to superintend the boat building at Genoa. But Byron clung on, deeply unwilling as always to quit a proven perch.

His dualism of temperament had never been more striking than over his delay at Pisa. One part of him was all energy, the other all lethargy, notwithstanding the Gambas' precarious position vis-à-vis the authorities. Not to mention his own. As in Ravenna it was Byron they wanted to get rid of — the wicked lord who had murdered a mistress and made her skull into a drinking cup (or so a spy reported), who looked like the Vatican Apollo but behaved like Satan in Job (the impression of a Pisan student), a Satan who wandered round the world, firing pistols in farmsteads, creating uproar, and favoring *"all political novelties."*

Satan had in fact rented another villa near Leghorn from which to continue his wanderings. While he dallied in Pisa fate struck again.

Lega Zambelli, Byron's secretary, received a letter from his banker, Pelligrino Ghigi, at Ravenna. Allegra was sick. Not seriously. The nuns would keep him informed. She had typhus ("slow fever").

It was now many months since Byron had ignored that request from Allegra to visit her with money for the fair, and over a year since he had set eyes on her. But it did not even now cross his mind to make the journey from Pisa to Bagnacavallo. Messages came to Lega that she was better — worse — dead. She died on 20 April 1822, surrounded by wailing nuns, medical attendants and her favorite figures of saints and *bambini*.

Telling Byron was left to Teresa. He turned so white that she thought he would faint or lose his reason. In his torment he asked her to leave him and she crept away. He had recovered enough to write to Shelley a few days later: "I do not know that I have anything to reproach in my conduct and certainly nothing in my feeling and intentions towards the dead. But it is a moment when we are apt to think that, if this or that had been done, such an event might have been prevented." And to Lady Blessington a year later: "While she lived her existence never seemed necessary to my happiness: but no sooner did I lose her than it appeared to me as if I could not live without her."

The simple "this or that" which might have been done was Allegra's removal from the convent as the Shelleys advised, or visits by Claire, Byron and Teresa. A shred of excuse for him, though only a shred, has been discovered by his biographer Doris Langley-Levi Moore. She has recently examined all his finances, including the files of Lega Zambelli, and has woven the results into a narrative entitled *Lord Byron: Accounts Rendered*. In rendering account for his neglect of Allegrina he can plead that the good nuns of Bagnacavallo did not send an *express* letter until too late. Perhaps if the express had arrived in time, Byron would have set the Napoleonic coach rolling.

This would not have saved Allegra. Claire assuaged her agony by sending Byron a violent diatribe which shocked Shelley himself. Later she left for Vienna and a long life of cosmopolitan governess-ships, rounded off by conversion to the Roman Catholic faith and even a few months in a convent. "In the catastrophe of Allegra's death," writes Claire's biographer, Rosalie Glynn Grylls, "Claire rose to her full stature." The same cannot be said of Byron. Nevertheless he tried to have Allegra buried beneath an engraved stone in Harrow church, the nearest he could bring her to the happy last year of his own boyhood. The vicar and churchwardens, however, did not believe in calling attention to bastards, even noble ones. Allegra was buried without an inscription, probably beneath the floor of the church vestibule. All that remains today is one of her dolls in the possession of the Marquesa Origo and a plaque on the convent of Bagnacavallo erected in 1924, the centenary of her father's death. The plaque records that she was the daughter of Lord Byron, had been visited by the poet Shelley, and succumbed to a rapid fever at five years and three months. Byron wrote to Walter Scott, "Whom the gods love die young."

Among ironical comments on Byron and the death of Allegra, one verse in a long poem by Mrs. Frances Trollope, mother of the novelist Anthony Trollope, stands out. Mrs. Trollope's laudable purpose was to satirize the Harrow church vestry for their cruel cant in refusing a memorial to the innocent child. But not knowing all the facts, she unwittingly satirized her idol Byron also:

> *He saw her sicken and he watched her die,*
>   *The soft small hands' last pressure was his own.*
> *His the last glance of meaning from her eye,*
>   *And his to clasp her when the spark was flown.*
> *Then by her side in anguish down to lie,*
>   *Silent and tearless without sigh or groan.*
> *'Tis not for souls of lesser growth to know*
>   *Of such as his, how deep how strong the woe.**

* See *Salmagundi — Byron, Allegra and the Trollope Family* by N. John Hall (1975). Among the Trollope papers in the University of Illinois Library, Professor Hall has recently discovered a manuscript in Anthony

At last, towards the end of May 1822, Byron carried the Gambas away to his new summer villa for five weeks by the sea.

The Villa Dupuys in the village of Montenero above Leghorn had little to recommend it. Its walls were salmon-red and far from heatproof. Trelawny likened it to a suburban cockney box (villa) on the Thames. There was soon no water, which meant the servants walking a mile to fetch every drop for the house, so that the magnificent tuberoses, jasmine and heliotrope in the garden that Teresa had so much admired on arrival must all have wilted. Byron's mood, too, was subdued after Allegra's death. The evenings were best, when he could watch the fishing boats and distant isle of Elba, with its tale of exile dramatically ended; or cheat at checkers with Teresa — for she must not expect to be a kingmaker.

A token of her changing role might be seen in the resurgence of *Don Juan*. She could not keep Byron away from his greatest poem any longer. On condition that the new cantos were "more guarded and decorous and sentimental" than the old, she lifted her embargo.

Teresa's whole position, indeed, was settling into a domestic one. Though it was not true, as Medwin had said, that "Lord Byron is certainly very much attached to her without being actually in love," Byron's love had become as near humdrum as a poet's love ever can be.

Other developments in him which had long been visible began to stand out. His care for money intensified. Lady Noel, Annabella's mother, had died in January 1822 and he was henceforth to command an income of some £6,000 a year of which £2,500 was inherited from her — as well as her

---

Trollope's handwriting entitled "Salmagundi — *aliena,* 1834." Endorsed on the title sheet, "My mother's lines on the burial of Lord Byron's illegitimate daughter," it has proved to be Mrs. Trollope's long-lost poem of sixty-one stanzas, the one quoted above being the sixteenth — all in the manner of Byron's *Don Juan.* Anthony, then aged nineteen, has written comments on his mother's poem, some caustic. The "Salmagundi" or potpourri contains three other poems, two of which may be by Anthony.

name. He now legally signed himself "Noel Byron," or "N.B." to friends. "You see the great advantage of my new signature," he wrote to Moore; "it may either stand for 'Nota Bene' or 'Noel Byron.' " Hunt and Stendhal said he was delighted to share the initials of Napoleon Bonaparte.

Once he possessed real money his Gordon blood urged him to save it for a purpose. In *Don Juan* he ridiculed his new habit as senile miserliness:

> *So for a good old-gentlemanly vice,*
> *I think I must take up with avarice.*

That was a caricature of himself. His true impulse was to accumulate a sum large enough to cover his personal commitments — Teresa, Augusta and her children (Ada was already provided for) — and then to try his wings again either by promoting the revolution or emigrating to the New World.

While still at Montenero certain passing events caught his imagination. He was invited to come aboard an American squadron anchored in Leghorn harbor, where he was asked for the rose from his coat by an American lady, shown a copy of his poems by the captain, and offered a free passage to the States by the commodore. His journal, which he had restarted that May, noted the healthiness of his sales in Germany, France, and the United States, compared with England. And when George Bancroft, then a young American traveler but later to be the historian of his country, called on the famous poet at Montenero, he gave immense pleasure by telling Byron that Goethe and the Germans judged *Don Juan* "a work of Art." No wonder Byron preferred "a nod from an American" to "a snuff-box from an emperor."

An overdue visitor arrived at Montenero on 1 July. Leaving his family in Genoa, where they had arrived at long last, Hunt toiled up to the "hottest house" he had ever seen. The psychological atmosphere at the Villa Dupuys was no less heated, for Hunt's arrival coincided with a furious row among the Italian servants involving poor Pietro Gamba. Fletcher sent for a police officer; and the government's long-term decision to banish this tiresome family was updated and announced forthwith. Off they went, father and son, to Lucca, hoping to negotiate an asylum there. Byron and Teresa returned to the Casa Lanfranchi on 3 July. The ground floor had been turned over gratis to the Hunts, through Byron's generosity and Shelley's painstaking organization. Shelley, indeed, came on to Pisa from Lerici, leaving his beloved boat at Leghorn, to settle in the Hunts.

It could work only with Shelley there. Though Byron and Hunt got along well enough personally, there were too many divisive factors: the Hunt children, Hunt's invalid wife Marianne, the Byron animals, Byron's mistress Teresa, the Italian social scene of which Byron now formed a part and the "Cockney" literary background as represented by Hunt and his journal, the *Liberal*. These ill-assorted elements could hardly form a harmonious pattern.

Marianne's suburban insularity prevented her from trying to learn Italian and Teresa, whatever her willingness, was no nearer to speaking English. Hunt called Teresa "a kind of buxom parlour-boarder," ignoring the charitable status of his own tribe. Byron's reputation was sullied by Marianne and his walls by her infants. What did she think of Trelawny, he asked her one day; Trelawny had been "speaking against my morals! what do you think of that!" To which the suburban housewife replied tactlessly, "It is the first time I ever heard of them."

The Hunt children were being brought up according to theories of free expression, probably Rousseau's. Their precocity and uninhibited destructiveness horrified Byron, who called them a *kraal* of Hottentots and Yahoos. On the other hand, the graffiti perpetrated by his own menagerie cannot have been an improvement on those of the children; Byron's growling bulldog, Moretto, was stationed by him at the head way," and in the course of duty Moretto bit off the ear of the of the stairs and instructed, "Don't let any Cockneys pass this

Hunts' milking nanny goat, which they had brought with them all the way from England.

As for the *Liberal*, Byron correctly diagnosed that this avant-garde journal would fail, while his English friends, especially Moore, deplored the effect on his reputation of mixing with these "Cockney" types.

All in all, Hunt summed up the situation fairly: "There was a sense of mistake on both sides." And Shelley, who had originally intended to be the "link between the two thunderbolts," felt unable to meet Byron regularly since Allegra's death. At Lerici Shelley had seen her naked figure in the foam breaking on the beach. "There it is again! — there!" he cried to Williams, as the apparition clapped her hands at him. Nevertheless Shelley's "link," though now intermittent, would have been invaluable. Even that was not to be.

After saying farewell to the two thunderbolts Shelley returned to Leghorn, where Williams and a boy named Charles Vivian were waiting to help him sail his boat, the *Don Juan*, back to Lerici. The weather was thundery. Soon after midday on 8 July, however, it cleared and they weighed anchor. At 3 P.M. a storm wind began blowing in the Gulf of Spezia: "Look at the smoke on the water," said a boatman, "the devil is brewing mischief." They sailed straight into a violent Mediterranean squall and were never seen alive again. The legend that an Italian felucca rammed them, erroneously believing Byron's gold to be on board, can be disregarded. More acceptable is the theory of a fishing boat approaching them during the squall and offering to take them off. "No," shouted a shrill voice. And when Williams tried to reef the sails the same figure seized his arm. Shelley "knew himself." He would balk life of its Roman "triumph"; and if "deep night" nonetheless caught him " 'ere evening," we may be sure that the breaking foam was filled, as at Lerici, with magical hallucinations. Had not the man who built the *Don Juan* said she sailed "like a witch"?

Mary was recovering from a miscarriage, but accompanied

by Jane Williams she began a nightmare round of inquiries as soon as she realized the *Don Juan* was missing. A warning had been given by Trelawny to Byron on the eleventh: "His lip quivered, and his voice faltered," wrote Trelawny, "as he questioned me." Byron had no doubt that Shelley was "without exception, the *best* and least selfish man" he ever knew. A week later, on 18 July, the bodies of Shelley and Vivian were washed up on the beach near Viareggio, Williams's having come ashore the day before. Trelawny then took over.

Summoning Byron and Hunt, Trelawny stage-managed a pagan cremation on two consecutive days, 15 and 16 August. The putrefied corpses had to be dug up from the sand where the health authorities had buried them. "Are we all to resemble that?" cried Byron when he saw Williams's remains on the fifteenth; "— why it might be a carcase of a sheep." After throwing oil and wine on the pyre with the others, Byron dived into the sea and was violently sick. Next day was the turn of Vivian and of "Shiloh," as Byron used to call Shelley. (Shilloh was the new Messiah to whom the religious fanatic Joanna Southcote was to have given birth in 1814; instead she died of dropsy.) The volume of Keats's poems in Shelley's pocket — *Lamia,* the witch — was beyond preservation, but Trelawny kept the heart, which he later relinquished unwillingly to Mary.

Byron asked for the poet's skull; it was so thin, however, that it broke to pieces in the intense heat. Trelawny later pretended he withheld the skull lest Byron should "profane" it as a drinking cup.

After Shelley's cremation the purification of Byron had to be even more thorough. He swam a mile and a half out to his ship, the *Bolivar,* and back, so that his shoulders and arms were "St. Bartholomewed."* On the way home, wrote Hunt, "We sang, we laughed, we shouted."

In his latest canto of *Don Juan* Byron had claimed the right

---

* Teresa preserved a flake of Byron's burned skin.

> *To laugh at* all *things — for I wish to know*
> *What, after all, are* all *things — but a show?*

Trelawny had certainly made Shelley's funeral into a "show," but one at which even Juan could not laugh, except hysterically.

"We'll go no more a roving," Byron had written plaintively in 1818; since when, though his heart had come to rest on Teresa, his imagination had never ceased to rove. It was the expression of his chronic boredom. Now his goal would be England "in the spring," now the Neapolitan or the Greek rebels, now "Bolívar's country" in South America. After Shelley's death the thought of cruising in the Mediterranean disgusted him. There were other seas. Shelley himself had encouraged Byron to cross the Adriatic in the Greek cause.

Then he remembered that Teresa's tears had stopped him when he and Pietro wanted to go to Greece in 1821. Her present situation, eighteen months later, was even more dependent. Since she was living under her lover's roof Count Guiccioli obtained permission to cancel her allowance. The first of Byron's duties was clearly to return Teresa to her father's house. Having found no welcome in Lucca, the Gambas had taken a palace large enough for Byron and themselves in Genoa. There he must go.

Nevertheless Byron could not uproot in a hurry. And Hobhouse arrived in Pisa on 15 September. It took them a few days to recapture their old easy style. As in the case of Annabella, Teresa at first struck Hobhouse as unworthy of his dazzling friend — "a tolerably good looking young woman." But Hobhouse's visit was excitingly rounded off by a call from the Greek patriot Nicholas Karvellas. Was it to be Greece? Or, as Byron still told Hobhouse, "England in the spring"?

At length Byron's mountainous possessions (for he never threw anything away) were packed, his menagerie was caged, three cackling geese were slung behind his carriage against

Michaelmas Day, 29 September, and Lega Zambelli had paid for the Hunt children's damage ("To the glazier Mattei for repairing and replacing broken glass and windows in the house . . ."). They traveled to Genoa through Bagni di Lucca, and desolate Lerici. Here Byron, failing to recollect the lesson of his blistered back at Viareggio, raced Trelawny for hours through the "broiling" sea and consequently languished in bed for four days with "a violent rheumatic and bilious attack, constipation, and devil knows what." The Promethean theme came into his head again, for his sensations were "just as that damned obstreperous fellow felt chained to a rock, the vultures gnawing my midriff." They sailed on the fifth day and suddenly he found himself feeling better on sea air, cold fish and a gallon of country wine. The caravanserai entered Genoa on the night of 30 September and climbed up the hill to the suburb of Albaro. There Byron, nothing loath, parted company from the Hunts. They shared a villa with Mary Shelley, while Byron and the Gambas occupied the divided Casa Saluzzo. The three geese followed importantly at his heels, for he had not had the heart to wring their necks for Michaelmas. Once more Byron was in a white, many-windowed Italian palazzo, with a garden and a panorama of the Mediterranean. Teresa must have hoped he would settle down peacefully, despite ominous signs.

A howl of execration met the first number of the *Liberal*, published on 15 October. Byron's *Vision of Judgement,* they said, was "heartless and beastly ribaldry"; Shelley's translation of *Faust* was "a burlesque upon Goethe"; Leigh Hunt's verses showed "conceit, trumpery, ignorance." Defiantly, Byron transferred all his poetical manuscripts from Murray to the Hunts, calling Murray "a sad shuffler."

There was a conflict now between Byron's concern for money and his refusal to let his sales influence his poetry. To Kinnaird he would say, "All the bullies on earth shall not prevent me from writing what I like . . . 'coute qui coute.'" Yet the cost did matter. He had begun 1823 with an outright salute to lucre. Having worked out the precious ore of his passions in youth, the dross was now coming: "*I loves lucre.*" He added, "For we must love something." It sounded like another case of his heart resting on the nearest perch.

Trelawny could not understand what he was saving for. "He exhausted himself," Trelawny wrote, "in planning, projecting, beginning, wishing, intending, postponing, regretting and doing nothing." Except writing poetry. Trelawny had forgotten that.

In the new year Byron paid Mary to copy his *Age of Bronze* and *The Island.* The former, a satire on postwar Europe and the Verona Congress of 1822, showed Byron mounting an attack which still finds its target today:

> *Year after year they voted cent. per cent.,*
> *Blood, sweat, and tear-wrung millions — why? for rent!*

The Island, founded upon the true story of the mutiny on the *Bounty,* is more fact than metaphysics. The problem of evil in the Old Testament is nonetheless still here. The mutineer Fletcher Christian is on the surface a "Byronic hero"; but as Professor Paul Fleck points out, Christian is Satanic and irredeemable, while the other rebel, young Torquil, is guilty in the more human way of Adam, and is therefore redeemable by love. The third hero-type is William Bligh, captain of the *Bounty,* who is strong in the morality of the "Law," and like Moses would lead his people to the promised island — England — if only they would obey him.

The use of an island, whether "Old England" or Toobonai in the South Seas, as a symbol of perfection is a commonplace in romance. Paradise itself was "insulated" against Adam's sin. Byron was using the word *island* in the same sense when he spoke of Venice or Greece as his "greenest island." This metaphor for the ideal may have come to him on rereading Rousseau's *Nouvelle Héloïse* at Diodati. Here he found Julie cultivating her wild and secret garden at Clarens, which she called her "Elyseum," her "desert island." When St. Preux her lover first saw it he apostrophized it under the names of two South Sea islands, as it might be Toobonai: "O Tinian! O Juan Fernandez! Julie, the world's end is at your threshold!"

The world's end. Nothing short of that perfection would satisfy Byron, and he might have got his Juan there, had he lived to write all twenty-four cantos. Meanwhile Teresa cannot have failed to remark, apprehensively, that Juan had moved to the land of Byron's birth for the "English cantos." Here she could not follow him. But someone else could.

Marguerite Blessington arrived in Genoa that spring in the course of foreign travels with her rich husband, the Earl of Blessington, and a lifelong friend and gifted artist, the young Count D'Orsay. Born in Ireland and rescued from a cruel child-marriage, this brilliant woman of thirty-four was to edit Books of Beauty between entertaining the elite of London. She brought to Byron what Moore called a breath of "his native air." It was also a breath of the aristocratic womanhood he had once found in Lady Melbourne — beauty without flirtatiousness, brains without a trace of "The Blues." Byron rode, drove and dined constantly with these visitors, sending Teresa into convulsions of jealousy; for her perverse lack of the English tongue continued to isolate her.

Lady Blessington's *Conversations with Lord Byron in Italy* contains some of the best reporting published after his death, notwithstanding the smart French phrases he never used. To her we owe his admission that "there is something . . . in the poetical temperament that precludes happiness, not only to the person who has it, but to those connected with him"; his declaration that "there are but two sentiments to which I am constant, — a strong love of liberty, and a detestation of cant"; and his characteristic hope: "You will think me more superstitious than ever . . . when I tell you, that I have a presentiment that I shall die in Greece. I hope it may be in action, for that would be a good finish to a very *triste* existence."

If there was little of comfort here for Teresa, there was much for Greece.

NINE

"Sons of the Greeks, Arise!"
(1823)

BYRON's blurred hopes of action had focused at last. Two
forces were at work. First, the supersession of his vocation as
a poet; second, his allegiance to Greece. He said to Lady
Blessington, "He who is only a poet has done little for mankind"; he would therefore "endeavour to prove in his own
person that a poet may be a soldier."

The key date for his focusing upon Greece was the beginning of April 1823. A delegate from the London Greek Committee, just formed to help the struggling patriots, called on
him at Albaro. This was the incredibly energetic and peri-
patetic Edward Blaquiere, a young Irishman who had
studied the Spanish constitutional rising of 1822, and when
that was put down by Bourbon France, had turned his attention to Greece. Among Blaquiere's Whig and Radical colleagues on the London Committee was John Cam Hobhouse.
With Blaquiere came Andreas Luriottis, representative of
the Greek government. Immediately Byron was on fire. He
offered to go to the Levant in July "if the Greek provisional
Government thinks that I could be of any use." Pietro
Gamba, equally fired, was soon "dreaming of glory and
Greece."

At first Byron's imagination played around gifts for the Greeks of money, gunpowder, and medical stores. Thanks to his "avarice," £3,000 had been saved out of his last year's income. He also had humanitarian ideas of reducing the barbarities on both sides. During the first year of the Greek War of Independence some two thousand Greeks and two thousand Turks had been massacred.

By May his designs were expanding. On the twelfth he heard from John Bowring, secretary of the London Committee, that he, Byron, had been put up for membership. Bowring was a traveler, scholar and financier destined to be typical of the Victorian march towards respectability. In youth an ardent philhellene, with riper years he acquired a knighthood and a deep veneration for Queen Victoria. Accepting Bowring's invitation by return, Byron sent advice on Greece to the committee, for he was also in touch with Nicholas Karvellas at Pisa. If an international brigade were to be formed, the officers must not expect "to rough it on a beef-steak and bottle of port." Greece was poverty-stricken. On the other hand, her potential in wine, oil, and the like eclipsed that of the Cape and Van Diemen's Land "and the other places of refuge, which the English people are searching for over the waters."

In his enthusiasm, Byron was an apt pupil of George Canning, the British foreign secretary since the suicide in 1822 of the "tyrant" and "villain" Lord Castlereagh. For the purposes of British trade Canning wished to recognize the new South American republics. When in Greece, Byron was to tell a friend, "Mr. Canning may do much for Greece; I hope he will continue in office. . . . the great mechanical power of England, her vast ingenuity, gives him the control of the world." Byron's estimate of Canning was not far out.

Two young survivors from a German philhellene brigade, which had perished in Greece the year before, found their way to the great Lord Byron at the Casa Saluzzo. Their plight only increased his ardor — and his charitable disbursements. He saw no evil omen in the fact that previous philhellene committees had failed, one German and the other Swiss, yet both well organized. His own organization was proceeding apace.

That Pietro Gamba would accompany him went without saying. He also engaged Francesco Bruno, a young Italian doctor. Though scarcely out of medical school, Bruno was highly recommended and described by Byron as "an excellent little fellow." The presence of a personal physician seemed wise, since Byron's two exacting swims at Viareggio and Lerici respectively had left him with digestive troubles, and, after harsh dieting, a frame almost as "transparent" as in 1812. His boyish slimness amazed Lady Blessington and she thought him "too attenuated" for a Greek expedition. Still more "deranged" seemed his nervous system, for he would fly from depression to reckless gaiety and back to sadness. Dr. Bruno was hardly equipped to deal with such a complex patient. He was to be paid £100 and to live with the other gentlemen — quite a concession to a doctor in those days. But Bruno was intimidated by Byron's temper and taken in by a jocular threat that if he made the slightest mistake Byron's dogs would tear him to pieces.

These ravening hounds were the bulldog Moretto and a Newfoundland named Lyon, presented to Byron that May. Lyon was to prove a latter-day Boatswain in his enthusiastic devotion. Five horses were also to be shipped, four for Byron, whose lameness made them a necessity. His eight servants included Lega Zambelli, the steward, Tita, a Negro bought as a status symbol from Trelawny, and Fletcher, who still remembered Greece as "all rocks and robbers." Over them ruled an old seadog of a captain named Robert Scott, who drank his bottle of Jamaica rum every day but abominated drunkenness at sea. Byron had not been able to resist an offer of 400 guineas for his *Bolivar* by Lord Blessington, and therefore had to charter a brig for Greece, Captain Scott's *Hercules*. Two cannon were transferred from the *Bolivar* to the deck of the *Hercules*. Matching her legendary name, Byron ordered three Homeric helmets.

His contemporary biographer, Thomas Moore, tried to repel the ridicule which these helmets evoked in England by pointing out that even as a boy Byron had dreamed of raising a troop of horse in black armor, to be called "Byron's Blacks." Moore might have added that heroic helmets had been no rarity on the field of Waterloo, while the Greek leader Hypsilantes had raised a battalion that wore dashing black hats with the motto "Liberty or Death" beneath a skull. One of Byron's helmets was a green shako decorated with a figure of Athene, for Pietro; the other two were plumed, Homeric and gilded, the first for himself bearing the legend *Crede Byron*, the second for Trelawny.

Corsair Trelawny had been invited to join the expedition in June. He celebrated by writing to the builder of the *Bolivar* at Leghorn: "Lord B and myself are extraordinarily thick, we are inseparable . . . I am no expense to him, fight my own way, lay in my own stock etc." The corsair was indeed to fight his own way when they reached Greece. But Byron paid his passage. He had been recruited by Byron with the words, "You must have heard that I am going to Greece. Why do you not come to me?"

If only Teresa could have been asked the same question. But Byron dared not even tell her the news, from a mixture of pity, dislike of scenes, and nervousness lest she should again anchor him in Italy. Her agony was as great as he had feared when the faithful Pietro unfolded to her the terrible prospect. She too had a premonition that her lover would not come back.

The Byronic hero, into which mold the soldier-poet seemed to be fast returning, had never shown subtlety with women. He could love them romantically and lose them tragically, but was harassed and bored by the wide spectrum of intermediate sensibilities. How unfortunate that women were not satisfied with a mirror and sugarplums, as the two N.B.s, Noel Byron and Napoleon Bonaparte, had fondly supposed.

The parting from Mary Shelley was in some ways equally painful. Though her surviving son, Percy, would be rich when his grandfather Sir Timothy Shelley died, Mrs. Shelley now lacked even their fare to England. The sum of £2,000 had been left by Shelley to Byron, as one of his executors. Naturally Byron promised to see that Mary had all she needed. But what with his own preoccupations and dilatoriness, which in turn provoked tactless reminders by Leigh Hunt on Mary's behalf, Byron lost his temper. He lashed out in a letter to Hunt which the recipient described as "angry and extraordinary." It has since been lost. By the time Byron's temper was again under control, Mary had refused his help in favor of Trelawny's. It was scarcely making amends for Byron brusquely to decline Shelley's legacy and to give the destitute Hunt £30 to get him and his kraal to Florence.

Parsimony has often been blamed for Byron's behavior. In reality he had erred through his old devils of anger and egoism.

The last hours with Teresa were not shirked. From three to five in the afternoon of 13 July he lingered with her in the desolate Casa Saluzzo. Then, brokenhearted, she dragged herself to the Romagna, which her father had been allowed to reenter. Her lover embarked the same evening. She did not know that he had earlier written to several friends inquiring what were the prospects in Greece of women.

There was a dead calm that night, the thirteenth. Byron should not have been surprised at this fiasco on such an inauspicious date. He had to return next day with Pietro Gamba and Trelawny to Genoa, for a dinner of fruit and cheese in the garden of the Villa Lomellina at Sestri, where the Blessingtons, now departed, had stayed. He could not yet face the Casa Saluzzo. After again sleeping on board, the omens on the fifteenth were still adverse. A sudden gale battered them all night, forcing the unhappy old "tub" back into port, with its flimsy partitions kicked down by the terrified horses — "and troublesome neighbours they were in blowy weather," Byron wrote to Augusta — and its agonized cargo of seasick passengers. The hitherto "sad and solemn" pilgrim, reported Trelawny, cheered up somewhat at this exposure of poor human nature. While Trelawny super-intended the repairs on the sixteenth, Byron and Pietro re-visited the empty Casa Saluzzo before sailing. "Where shall we be in a year," Byron said, wistfully. On that very day a year hence, Pietro noted afterwards, Byron would be com-mitted to his tomb.

The auspices, at least for Byron's immortality, improved after they put into Leghorn on the twenty-first. Just before they sailed again three days later, Byron was handed a poetic tribute from the mighty Goethe himself, whom he regarded as "the greatest genius the age has produced." He had tried to dedicate *Sardanapalus* to Goethe but his instructions reached Murray too late; however, he succeeded in 1822 with his *Werner* (a Gothick drama of few attractions), which honor Goethe now repaid by sending Byron three verses of good wishes in German, beginning with the line, "A friendly word comes." Enchanted, Byron replied, "I could not have had a more favourable omen, a more agreeable surprise, than a word of Goethe, written by his own hand."

The omens from Leghorn were actually mixed rather than "favourable." A valuable addition to their party was a young Scot named James Hamilton Browne, who spoke Romaic and had lost his job in the (neutral) British service for be-ing too warm a philhellene. But the various Greeks whom Byron met in the busy seaport struck him, euphemistically, as "a little divided among themselves." A proof of their di-visions was given when he offered two Greeks a free passage on the *Hercules* to their native land. One of them, Count Skilitzy, was reported by his compatriots to be a Russian spy and the other, Captain Vitali, to be in Turkish pay.

Before sailing from Leghorn, Byron added to a letter from Pietro a postscript for Teresa in English. Too late, she was learning her lover's language. "My dearest Teresa — I have but a few moments to say that we are all well — and thus far on our way to the Levant — Believe that I always *love* you — and that a thousand words could only express the same idea. — ever dearest yours N.B." Poor Teresa could have done with those thousand words. But she had to get used to the idea of brief postscripts, unmistakably expressing his last — detachment.

As the tub rolled slowly down the Italian coast Byron mostly sat alone on deck, brooding or studying the bitter japes of Voltaire, Swift and La Rochefoucauld. The loss of Teresa was enough in itself to induce his melancholy. In addition, his recent intimacy with Lady Blessington had released a stream of poignant memories: nostalgia for gay Regency England, regrets over his failure in Parliament, resentment at his separation from Annabella. The resilient Lady Blessington, who was herself no stranger to past suffering, considered Byron's eternal lamentations over his marriage "unmanly," though she found him irresistible. "Incontinence of speech," she wrote, "is his besetting sin," and she scolded him for his indiscretions. Instead of *Crede Byron,* people would say, "Beware of being *Byroned.*"

Her warnings were ignored, for Trelawny reports that on the voyage to Greece Byron again talked of England and his wrongs, linking Shelley's name with his own as having been hooted out of their country by rancorous beasts and finally associating both names with the crucified Christ: "If the Christ they profess to worship reappeared, they would again crucify him."

It was not till they left Italy behind at the beginning of August that Byron's health and spirits lifted. He enjoyed a familiar pastime of telling ghost stories as they sailed at night past Stromboli, apparently in eruption. He was delighted, never having seen an active volcano before. Greece likewise he hoped to find in eruption, even though the flashes on Stromboli proved to be merely the lights in cottage windows. They had intended to make Messina their final Italian port of call, but they were sailing so well at last that they plowed straight on into the Ionian Sea.

"I am better now than I have been for years," said Byron,

recalling that on shore he always felt inclined to hang himself on waking. He and Trelawny swam in the warm waves, practiced pistol shooting at bottles and sometimes at poultry hanging in baskets from the mast, or played practical jokes. "Now, put your arm in, Tre," said Byron one day, offering Trelawny a sleeve of Captain Scott's flashy scarlet waistcoat and putting his own arm into the other sleeve; "we will jump overboard, and take the shine out of it." Into the sea they plunged, where Moretto and Lyon were already chasing the ducks and geese which Trelawny had let loose. "I hope you will both be drowned," roared the indignant captain. "Then you will lose your *frite*," retorted Byron, mimicking the captain's pronunciation of the word *freight*. Some of Byron's admirers have rejected this tale as a Trelawny invention. How could the soldier-poet be so irresponsible as to make the crew laugh at the captain and start what Scott called "a mutiny"? Nevertheless it sounds typical of Byron's attitude to authority in certain moods; and his mimicry was famous.

He could laugh at himself also. His two Greek passengers told him that their countrymen favored a monarchy — and who better than Byron for king? The monarch-designate took it pleasantly but lightly, according to Trelawny and Browne, saying that he would not refuse but if necessary would abdicate from his island throne, like Sancho Panza from *his* imaginary island.

They sighted the Ionian islands of Cephalonia and Zante on 2 August, followed by the violet-blue mountains of the Morea. When recruiting Trelawny, Byron had called Greece "the only place I was ever contented in." Now the memory of that contentment swept back even more sweetly and he said to Tre: "I don't know why it is, but I feel as if the eleven long years of bitterness I have passed through since I was here, were taken off my shoulders, and I was scudding through the Greek archipelago with old Bathurst, in his frigate." With old Scott they scudded past Zante and into Argostoli, the capital of Cephalonia. Both Browne and Prince Alexander Mavrocordato, Shelley's Greek friend, had advised Byron to make for Cephalonia, where the "neutral" British resident, Colonel Charles James Napier, was a strong philhellene.

Were there to be yet more bad omens? They anchored opposite a *hospital* and neither Napier nor Blaquiere was there on 4 August to greet Byron when he went ashore. Blaquiere had arranged to give him a picture of the general Greek situation but characteristically raced back hotfoot to England before Byron arrived. He had landed his big fish and now had other fish to fry. At this defection Byron evinced "surprise," which was a polite word for anger. Such behavior gave him his first clue to the London Committee's basic attitude to himself. He was window dressing.

Governor Napier's absence was temporary and accidental, though Pietro reflected Byron's fears when he wrote to Teresa, "I hope we have not made a mistake — I say hope, because we have not found him in the island." They had made no mistake. Two days later Napier arrived. He was to prove all that Byron hoped and more.

A Radical-Whig like Byron himself, Napier was the grandson of a duke (Richmond) and the father of two illegitimate Greek girls by a Cephaloniot woman. He was a professional soldier with a brilliant past in the Peninsular War and a remarkable future as the conqueror of Scinde. His sense of humor was alternately sardonic and robust, like Byron's own, and his instantaneous reaction to the poet was "I like him very much."

Let down by Blaquiere, Byron wisely decided not to visit the seat of war on the mainland of Greece until reliable information had been furnished from other sources. Napier was a good beginning. But from Napier he learned much that was disquieting. It appeared that the War of Independence was stagnating, whereas a civil war between the two chief Greek factions was well on the way.

The Turks still held the key fortresses of Patras and Lepanto as well as others in the west, Corinth in the center and Negropont in the east. Their fleet had not ceased to patrol the gulf and the Ionian Sea, whereas the Greek ships had shut themselves up in the harbors of Hydra, Spetsae and Psara until such time as the provisional government saw fit to pay their sailors. The raising of taxes for the war, however, had become virtually impossible, since the two factions needed every penny they could lay hands on to fight each other.

"This land of heroes," as Blaquiere had described Greece to Byron in April, was torn between the ascendancy of heroic civilians or *primates* in the west and of heroic soldiers or *capitani* in the east; between the western constitutionalists and the eastern militarists. Prince Mavrocordato, a young constitutionalist supported by Byron's friend Andreas Londos of Patras, seemed to dominate the scene during his year of office as president of the executive council. But believing that discretion was the better part of valor he had resigned before his term expired and taken refuge at Hydra from the suspected plots of his amiable colleagues. In any case, he had been unlucky in his valor. The appalling Battle of Peta, not far from Missolonghi in western Greece, had taken place on 16 July 1822, exactly one year before Byron set out to "electrify" (again Blaquiere's word) the land of heroes. It had resulted in the destruction of the German brigade of philhellenes by the Turks, and of Mavrocordato's military reputation. Mavrocordato's weakness was to overindulge in military ambitions. For he was by nature a humane, westernized politician. He wore a European stock, trousers and peaked cap. Behind spectacles, his sad wise eyes were those of a professor not a warrior. In his best-known portrait he sits in an armchair, holding a book.

Eastern Greece was the stamping ground of two very different characters, the famous *klephts* Theodor Colocotrones and Odysseus Androutses, the latter of whom was to change sides several times. You could translate *klepht* as robber chief or freedom fighter as you preferred. They wore the traditional jacket richly embroidered with gold and the fustanella or kilt, Colocotrones specializing in leopards' heads as epaulettes and Odysseus in jeweled pistols and daggers in his belt beneath the fur capote. Neither had any interest in Greek "regeneration" through a constitution, or central government or federation, as visualized by Byron, Shelley and the committee. "The world's great age begins anew," Shelley had written in his *Hellas,* dedicated to Mavrocordato. So far as the klephts were concerned, no new "great age" was required. All that they were after was simply the replacement of the Turks by themselves. And in fact they had been more successful than the civilian leaders of western Greece in dealing with the common enemy. Athens had fallen in June 1822.

However, there was one large body of warriors in western Greece who did compare for fighting power with the klephts — Byron's old acquaintances the Suliots. This fierce tribe of Christian Albanians had finally been driven out of their mainland fastnesses by the Turks in 1822, and many thousands of them had been settled by the efficient Napier in Cephalonia. Their clamorous descent on the *Hercules* the first morning in Argostoli struck horror into the hearts of all except Byron. Trelawny merely saw in these "Zuliotes" a devastating talent for scenting Byron's money, surpassing even the vulture's power "to detect carrion afar off." To Captain Scott they were "damned Zodiacs"; to Gamba they were impostors, since many non-Suliots and even non-Greeks had infiltrated their ranks. But to Byron they were the friends of his youth. Their jangling beads, ataghans, pistols, long guns, pipes to play or smoke, dirty fustanellas and lice-ridden capotes reminded him of wild songs and dances around bonfires in the Acarnanian mountains, when he had hired forty of them in 1809 to escort him safely back to Patras. He would repeat the successful experiment. He promptly took on a bodyguard of forty. And if they wanted his money, why not? They would be the nucleus of Byron's Blacks or the Byron Brigade, as it was now to be called. He had raised all his money for no other purpose.

The moneybags, upon which Lega Zambelli would coil

himself like a viper, were not to be quite such an anxiety to the master as to the man. By May Byron had collected from his English banker, Douglas Kinnaird, £6,000 in cash and letters of credit, soon increased to some £9,000. Thanks also to his devoted Genoese banker, Charles Barry, he was finally able to bring with him, according to Gamba, 40,000 Spanish dollars in bills of exchange and 10,000 more in specie. The problem of exchanging his bills was solved when Byron made friends with a merchant on Cephalonia named Charles Hancock and his generous philhellene partner at Zante, Samuel Barff.

By October Byron had only a fraction of the original dollars left, but meanwhile Kinnaird had sent him £600 or £700 more, and a promise to forward the proceeds of the long-delayed Rochdale sale, which he hoped would amount to £12,000. As we shall see, enormous demands were to be made on him, including £6,000 for the Greek fleet, and were largely if not fully answered. But despite vicissitudes, throughout his stay in Cephalonia he managed to believe that his money and his Suliots would work well together. On 17 December he was writing in his journal that a Suliot soldier might be maintained for five dollars a month, including pay and rations. "Therefore for between two and three thousand dollars a month . . . I could maintain between five hundred and a thousand of these warriors for as long as necessary." Byron rounded off this optimistic entry with the reflection that his own personal wants were very simple " (except in horses as I am no great pedestrian)," and his income "equal to the President's of the United States!" Thus he could "keep on foot a respectable clan, or Sept, or tribe, or horde, for some time." It was to be a horde.

While awaiting what he called his "advices" from the mainland, Byron decided to visit Ithaca on 11 August.

After a long hot mule ride right across Cephalonia to St. Euphemia, followed by four burning hours in an open boat, Byron, Gamba, Trelawny, Bruno, Browne, and the servants reached this dream-island. Homer's Odysseus had returned here after ten years of wandering, to find his faithful wife Penelope still on the lookout for him. We know that the Swiss tablet to the regicide's wife who stuck to her husband had reminded Byron of Annabella and upset him in 1816. His occasional strange behavior on Ithaca and on the way home may have had the same origin, though Byron did not draw a specific parallel.

There was no one to greet them when they landed. Byron wanted to sleep in a cave. However, the Continental gentlemen present disapproved of night air. A refugee Greek merchant put them up and next day, while Captain Knox, the governor, was being notified of their arrival, Byron slept at a cave's mouth under a fig tree. Here he had a dream or "beatific vision," from which he was loath to be awakened. But the ride to Vathy, the capital, over a saddle between two mountains was green with wild vines and pungent with cystus. Byron charmed Mrs. Knox by calling her Mrs. Penelope, and by treating each picnic party to drafts from the "Pierian Spring" served in the form of gin-and-water. "The few days which I passed with you in your beautiful island," he wrote to Captain Knox afterwards, "are amongst the whitest in my existence." He charmed — and somewhat alarmed — another visitor named Thomas Smith, by pouring out to him (despite Lady Blessington's warnings against verbal incontinence) all his thoughts of Annabella, Ada and his poetry as if he had known Smith for years. That night he was ill and would scarcely have survived, according to Dr. Bruno, but for his *benedette pillule* — blessed pills; next morning, said Smith, he came up from the beach like an old man "under sentence of death."

He greatly charmed the "free-thinking" bishop whom he had met fourteen years ago at Livadia and now ran into again, for the prelate gave him a hairy, garlicky kiss. But he found no matching charms in the antiquarian relics of the island. He was glad to discuss the Suliot refugees on Ithaca with Captain Knox, indeed he left 250 dollars for their succor; but he refused to be interested in the alleged "School of Homer," "Arethusa's Fountain" or any other spring but gin-and-water.

Did he not enjoy the "classical remembrances" of Ithaca? asked Browne. Byron replied with a sharp reference to "poetical humbug." And in Trelawny's hearing he utterly rejected "antiquarian twaddle" and the "emasculated fogies" who perpetrated it. "Let's have a swim. . . . Do people think I have no lucid intervals, that I came to Greece to scribble more nonsense? I will show I can do something better."

One "better" thing he did was to bring back the refugee Chalandritsanos family from Ithaca to Cephalonia, where he set them up with a regular allowance — a mother and two daughters. They had once been prosperous in Patras. Hearing of their renewed prosperity, a fifteen-year-old son named Lukas left the mainland, where he had been fighting with the klephts, and became Byron's page. He bettered himself, but not Byron.

The *benedette pillule* had to be administered again more dramatically on the sixteenth, when Byron returned to Cephalonia. After a broiling swim, a scorching crossing, a carousal at St. Euphemia and a reception at the monastery of Sami, where the party were to spend the night, Byron fled from the abbot's speech of welcome and groaning board with a groan no less emphatic: "Will no one relieve me from the presence of this pestilential madman?" Barricading himself into his room with smashed furniture, he tore his bedclothes and garments, shrieking at all comers, "Baih! out, out of my sight!" After Trelawny, Smith and presumably the terrified Dr. Bruno had all failed, Browne got the *benedette pillule* down his throat. Next morning he was all kindness to the abbot and monks (the only aspect of his visit now remembered at Sami) and rode cheerfully back to Argostoli singing Cockney rhymes.

The nightmare scene at Sami can be regarded as Byron's first convulsive fit brought on by overindulgence of all kinds in the August heat: "I was unwilling to lose so many hours of the day," he wrote, "on account of a sunbeam more or less." On the other hand it may have been one of his notorious rages exacerbated by an emotional experience. Before entering the monastery he had jumped into a stone sarcophagus lying outside the gates. Imagining a skull in his hand, he intoned "Alas, poor Yorick" from *Hamlet.* Alas, "poor B."

He slept late into the morning of 18 August. When Trelawny woke him it was out of yet another nightmare. "I have had such a dream! I am trembling with fear. I am not fit to go to Greece."

A very different Byron, practical and level-headed, took up the threads in Cephalonia. He had got into touch by letter with the famous Suliot leader Marco Botsaris, who was holding back the Turks above Missolonghi with 350 of his Suliots. Botsaris replied eagerly on the eighteenth, inviting Byron to join him with the Cephalonian Suliots, whom he was "so kindly" caring for. "Do not delay." Alas, poor Marco. A Turkish bullet got him three days later, before Byron could decide whether to delay further or not.

Delay it now had to be. For Byron had lost his two Greek advisers with the highest European reputations: Botsaris dead and Mavrocordato in hiding. While waiting for news from Tripolitza (the Greek capital) or London, he mingled with the male society of Argostoli. Neither of the Greek factions tried to seduce him through his passions, a welcome reprieve from temptation, even though, as he said, "I left my heart in Italy." He was agreeably surprised that the officers of the English garrison, far from avoiding the leader of the "Satanic school," invited him to dine. He replied to their toast in an engagingly nervous speech.

The garrison doctor, James Kennedy, an earnest Scot with Methodist leanings, organized a seminar on Christianity for his unregenerate friends. Byron went along. The metaphysical thirst which he had partially slaked in *Manfred, Cain,* and *Heaven and Earth* was reawakened — despite Kennedy's immense four-hour lecture before questions were permitted. Kennedy became his friend; and though Byron skipped the rest of the course, he stepped up his reading of the bedside Bible that Augusta had given him, until by the time he reached Missolonghi he felt he could take on that "very good Calvinist" Kennedy, and beat him.

As for Dr. Kennedy's frank remarks about Byron's sinful past, Byron would say half-seriously half-mockingly, "You cannot expect me to become a perfect Christian at once." Another member of the group, Colonel Duffie, regretted that Byron's inevitable conversion to Methodism was taking so long, since "his Lordship should now be writing some beautiful hymns." "When I do become one," said Byron, "I shall not be a lukewarm Christian." Others among his friends believed that Don Juan was to become a Methodist in the next canto and therefore his creator was cynically collecting local color. But though "Saint Kennedy" sometimes bored Byron, his "sermon with soda-water" continued to cast a curious spell.

Perhaps Kennedy's influence was partly due to a singularly appropriate book he had presented to Byron. "You have sent me an account of the death of Lord Rochester," wrote Byron, "as a fact, *par excellence,* having a particular reference to me." The Restoration poet, who died burned out at thirty-three, described his daily routine in words that might have been written by Byron:

> *I rise at eleven, I dine about two,*
> *I get drunk before seven, and the next thing I do,*
> *I send for my whore, when for fear of the clap . . .*

And so on. No doubt Dr. Kennedy hoped to be a Dr. Burnet to Byron's repentant Rochester.

Byron's fascination as a friend can be gauged from the playful nicknames he handed around: the important Count Delladecima was known as "Ultima Analise," because of his fondness for the phrase *in ultima analise* in conversation; and Charles Hancock became "Sir Ancock," after Dr. Bruno had addressed him as *Sigr. Ancock* in a letter.

Byron was by now a familiar figure in Argostoli, riding about in his nankeen trousers, green braided or plaid jacket, peaked cap with gold band and tassel, and blue spectacles. Sometimes his headdress was "feathered," which may mean the Homeric helmet. Every day he and Trelawny would swim from the *Hercules* to a rock on shore and sup under the olive trees. Once Byron held up his lame (trousered) leg to Trelawny with the remark, "I hope this accursed limb will be knocked off in war."

"I will exchange legs," replied Tre, "if you will give me a portion of your brains."

"You would repent your bargain," said Byron; "at times I feel my brains boiling, as Shelley's did whilst you were grilling him." Perhaps his "grilling" at Sami still haunted him. Moreover, there were no signs of anything being "knocked off in war" — except the heads of rival factions.

The demands of his unruly Suliots, egged on by shopkeepers, became extortionate. Gamba was given the job of packing as many as possible back to Acarnania with an extra month's pay and their weapons. Byron knew he might relent at the last moment. Nevertheless he was becoming disillusioned with a race which boasted so many shades of the word *no* that "perjury may slip through without being perceived." He had come to Greece, he wrote, "to deal with honest men and not with speculators and peculators," not to "join a faction but a nation." Trelawny, too, was becoming restive, but not because he had come to join a nation. He had come for adventure. At the end of August adventure beckoned.

The *Hercules* had completed her time in Greek waters, and with the departure of his floating home Byron decided to move into the "calm though cool serenity" of Cephalonia's green hills. Neither Trelawny nor Browne went with him. After Byron's death, Trelawny was to explain his departure as the explosion of pent-up irritation at Byron's delays. He realized, he said, that once on shore "Byron would

fall back on his old routine of dawdling habits, plotting —
planning — shilly-shallying — and doing nothing. It was a
maxim of his, 'If I am stopped for six days at any place, I
cannot be made to move for six months.' "

This second accusation against Byron of "doing nothing"
could not be countered by saying he was writing poetry. But
his temperamental objection to uprooting did not mean that
he was impeding the war. In the words of William St. Clair,
the philhellenes' historian, "Byron, almost alone of the philhellenes of the Greek War of Independence, did not rely on
an unspoken assumption of superiority in knowledge and
ability. He tried to inform himself about Greek conditions."
In fact, Trelawny and Browne had been dispatched to Tripolitza on a fact-finding mission. How best could Byron use
his dollars for the cause?

Byron's diminished circle moved on 6 September into
Metaxata. He called it "this beautiful village," for he could
see from the windows of his villa a pattern of orange and
lemon orchards, vineyards and olive groves sloping down to
the Ionian Sea. Zante floated on its blue surface like a green
cabochon emerald and in clear weather he could see the
Morea, whence so many strident and conflicting "advices"
were coming.

Since the two disastrous swims in the previous year he had
not slept well. He now rose at 9 A.M., measured his wrist and
waist to make sure they had not expanded (and if they had,
took epsom salts), breakfasted on tea and worked all morning with Pietro. The flat rock in the neighboring village of
Lakythra, where legend has it he sat writing his last poems,
was in reality the gray desk on which he drafted business
letters. But he had no regrets. If out of kindness to Teresa he
wrote in October, "I was a fool to come here," he said to her
brother in the same month, "How could I better employ my
time and money? I might have lived, or rather vegetated, in
splendour, in some uninteresting country of Europe; but
what are those pleasures . . . when once obtained? . . . If
Greece should fall, I will bury myself in the ruins! — if she
should establish her independence, I will take up my resi-

dence in some part or other — perhaps in Attica, where I once passed seven months."

That gave the lie to Trelawny's jealous letter to Mary Shelley of 6 September, in which he said that Byron intended retreating to Italy while he, gallant "Tre," continued the war. While at Metaxata Byron ordered all his Italian possessions to be sold, except the beloved Napoleonic carriage, two prints of Ada, and a few books, of which one was *Vathek.* No further hint was given to Teresa, after a note in September, that he would rejoin her in Italy. He might invite her to Zante. "Perhaps in the Spring . . ."

Meanwhile Pietro continued to insist on her lover's *"monkish virtues."* The "calm" serenity of Metaxata had been broken in October not by womankind but by an earthquake. Byron alone remained calm. With the dignity conferred by lameness he glided from the house, while his friends jumped out of windows or down the outside staircase into the courtyard.

His serenity was sometimes disturbed by the behavior of his Greek friends: by Greek sailors who cruelly murdered the crew of a Turkish treasure ship which went aground on neutral Ithaca; by Greek workmen who stood helplessly by when their comrades were buried in a landslide while roadmaking. Byron seized a spade and dug furiously. This was the kind of clear example he could set. If only he could do the same for the rival parties on the mainland. But — "between the two I have a difficult part to play; however, I will have nothing to do with the factions unless to reconcile them."

In letters he avoided saying anything about the Greeks "until I can say something better"; and even when he was forced to face the truth in his journal, he emphasized the psychological effect of "the shackles of four centuries," from which Greece could not escape in three years of liberation: "The links are still clanking, and the Saturnalia is still too recent to have converted the Slave into the sober Citizen."

The arrival of three newcomers to the island helped to clear his mind. In October a brilliant young philhellene called on him named George Finlay, who was to write a vast *History of Greece*. Finlay first startled Byron by his likeness to Shelley and then disturbed him by his evident overdose of "entusymusy." He was "too fresh from his studies in Germany," said Byron, putting Finlay wise about the Greek character. Finlay was astonished by the "affected voice and monotonous tone" in which the poet expressed emotional ideas, while allowing his wit and satire to run wild. "It seemed as if two different souls occupied his body alternately. One was feminine, and full of sympathy; the other masculine, and characterized by clear judgment. When one arrived the other departed." From this Finlay deduced that Byron's feelings for military glory would always be driven out by his "innate detestation of the trade of war."

A reluctant agreement had at last been wrung from Byron to visit the provisional government at Tripolitza in November. But by mid-November there was a new situation. The London Committee's subscription for Greece had failed. Unlike the foreign philhellenes, they had collected less than £12,000. The Greek government now fixed its hopes upon a loan of £800,000, easily raised in London, which was the speculative center of the world. They were sending Hamilton Browne to London as a negotiator along with their own two delegates. As Browne passed through Cephalonia, he handed Byron letters from the fugitive at Hydra, Prince Mavrocordato. The message was clear. Missolonghi in the west was in danger from the Turks, not Tripolitza in the Morea. And for 300,000 of Lord Byron's dollars the Greek fleet could sail from its eastern hideouts and rescue the west. It must be Byron (and his dollars) for Missolonghi.

The next visitor was Dr. Julius Millingen, an Englishman who stayed with Byron at the beginning of November. Millingen was as cynical about the Greeks as Finlay had been overenthusiastic. Nevertheless Byron persuaded the young doctor, whom he liked, to accompany him to Missolonghi as physician to the Suliots. Millingen's cynicism may have strengthened Byron's distrust of the "Eastern" faction. "The Greeks are perhaps the most depraved and degraded people under the sun," was one of his caustic remarks quoted by Millingen. At any rate the "Westerns" won out soon after Millingen's visit and Byron abandoned the idea of going to Tripolitza.

On 22 November there was a much more important arrival — Colonel the Honorable Leicester Stanhope, eldest son of Lord Harrington, veteran of the Mahratta War in India, agent of the London Committee and a typical specimen of all their sense and nonsense. If Byron had found Dr. Kennedy "very clever and eccentric," Colonel Stanhope was ten times cleverer and a hundred times more eccentric. An ardent disciple of the ancient Jeremy Bentham, most distinguished founder-member of the committee, Stanhope believed in Bentham's creed of Utilitarianism to the last drop of Greek blood. Never mind if the Greeks could not read — they should have printing presses before artillery; never mind if they "did not know a problem from a poker" (Byron's words) — they should have mathematical instruments before Congreve rockets; not butter before guns but pamphlets, newspapers and tracts, or, as the disgusted Napier put it, "water-colours, trumpets, fine drapes, to fight the Turks." Napier was particularly angry because the committee, while affording all these frills, could not afford to pay for his services as philhellene commander if he lost his commission in the British army. When Byron heard about the trumpets he wondered if they were meant to tumble the walls of Constantinople like those of Jericho.

Notwithstanding his eccentricities, Stanhope was a professional with a sense of order and drive lacking in the poet. He himself left for Missolonghi on 6 December, having pushed Byron nearer to his own point of departure. On the thirteenth Byron completed a loan of 200,000 dollars for the Greek fleet, Mavrocordato having reached Missolonghi two days before. Now everyone bombarded him with requests to hurry. He had been appointed commissioner to receive the committee's stores, and they needed him (and the stores) in Missolonghi. The Suliot corps had appointed him their commander and they too needed him (and his dollars). He was their "oracle," said Mavrocordato, their source of all "counsel and money," said Stanhope, tactfully inverting the order of Byron's gifts. They awaited him with "feverish anxiety."

Just before embarking on 29 December, Byron wrote to each of the three friends of his youth and young manhood, Moore, Hobhouse, and Kinnaird. All his messages had a certain prescience. "If anything in the way of fever, fatigue, famine, or otherwise, should cut short the middle age of a fellow-warbler," he told Moore, ". . . remember me in your 'smiles and wine' " — a graceful quotation from Moore's *Irish Melodies*. Hobhouse was given the news, with appropriate irony, that Mavrocordato expected Byron to *"electrify* the troops." But into the ears of Kinnaird he poured a trumpet call which he hoped would not only raise another £100,000 for the cause but raze the walls of the "city of Constantine" to boot: "I am passing 'the Rubicon.' . . . 'En avant,' or as the Suliotes shout in their war-cry — 'Derrah! Derrah!' which being interpreted, means 'On — On — On!' "

TEN

The Byronic Vision
(1824 and After)

"I WILL STICK by the cause while a plank remains which can be *honourably clung to*." Byron's metaphor of shipwreck, as he prepared to sail for Missolonghi, almost came literally true.

He had called on his banker at Zante for 8,000 more dollars, and perhaps a glimpse of the young Ionian poet Solomos, whom Blaquiere had promised and failed to introduce to him five months earlier. (Solomos, now Greece's national poet, wrote a famous lament on Byron's death.) Byron's party was in two ships, a mistico — perfect name for the raking, Byronic craft with sharp prow, shallow draft and great speed — for himself, his dollars, stores, page Lukas, dog Lyon, Fletcher, and Bruno. Pietro Gamba followed with more dollars, the baggage, Moretto, and servants in a heavy bombard. They set sail together, Gamba wrote, at 6 P.M. on 30 December, shouting patriotic songs to one another across the waves and, as the mistico outstripped the bombard, signaling with pistols the cheerful message, "To-morrow we meet at Missolonghi — to-morrow."

For the mistico, it was not to be Missolonghi "to-morrow," but after a dangerous five days; and for the bombard scarcely less. Byron counted on fourteen Speziot frigates, for which he had contributed part of his 200,000 dollars, holding back the Turks in the gulf, or at least keeping watch while he made the dangerous crossing. But there were no Speziots to warn him that the enemy was out. At 2 A.M. on the thirty-first a Turkish frigate loomed up before the mistico. Dead silence was maintained, notably by the sagacious Lyon, as the mistico slid away into the darkness. At dawn they saw one Turkish frigate chasing the bombard and another blocking Missolonghi, while a Zantiot ship signaled a frantic "Keep away." So "to-morrow" ended with their sheltering at Dragomestre up the coast, after landing Lukas near Anatolico, and escaping yet another Turkish ship. The boy was petrified of being captured at sea; and as Byron wrote to Stanhope on the thirty-first, "I would sooner cut him in pieces, and myself too, than have him taken up by those barbarians." Byron's message to Stanhope also contained the angry words "but where the devil is the fleet gone? — the Greek, I mean."

On 2 January 1824 a Greek escort vessel arrived at Dragomestre. But now the weather turned against them. Twice the mistico was driven on the Scrofe rocks between Dragomestre and Missolonghi. Byron prepared to life-save Lukas, who had unwisely returned. Suddenly Bruno rushed up. "Save *him*, indeed!" he screamed. "Dio mio, save *me* rather —." The candor of Bruno's egotism broke the tension and they all laughed. After entering a safe creek for the night, Byron horrified Fletcher by swimming for fifteen minutes in the cold sea, to kill the fleas in his clothes. Fletcher dated all future "pains in his bones" from this "freak" behavior.

On the night of the fourth they put into Missolonghi and Byron slept on board. For the sake of guarding his 25,000 dollars he had never left the mistico. When recounting his four escapes — twice from the Turks and twice from the rocks — it was always "the dollars" who had "another escape." The dollars on board the bombard had an even more alarming adventure. The bombard was forced into Patras, where all Byron's baggage and many lives would have been lost but for a "miracle" which he attributed to St. Dionysius of Zante. It turned out that the bombard's captain had once rescued the Turkish captain from shipwreck in the Black Sea. Pietro cemented this miracle with presents of liquor and a telescope — possibly one of the superfluous "mathematical instruments" from the London Committee. He reached Missolonghi a few hours before the mistico. Next day, 5 January 1824, was to be the most exhilarating of those remaining to Byron.

He landed on the beach from a Speziot gunboat at 11 A.M. In his scarlet uniform, the Greeks hailed him as Messiah and Delivering Angel. He in turn was delighted with the *rim-bombo del cannone* (Lega's words for the fleet's salute) and the picturesque crowds. He was taken straight to the house reserved for him, where the walls of his second-floor apartments were immediately decorated with a pattern of gleaming weapons, his bookshelves being relegated to a higher and less accessible position. On the first floor was "the typographical Colonel," as Byron called Stanhope, the soldier paradoxically believing in war by the pen, the poet in war by the sword. Prince Mavrocordato, whom Byron was meeting for the first time but who already in his eyes possessed "not only talents but integrity," gave him his thrilling marching orders: to lead in due course a brigade against the historic fortress of Lepanto.

Then came the antidotes to Byron's euphoria. Missolonghi's burnished lagoon, romantic in the rare burst of winter sunshine that had welcomed the Deliverer on 5 January, turned out to be rich in malaria as well as mullet. Byron was to find himself in a "pestilential prison." As the winter rains began their long seasonal deluge in earnest, he was to label Missolonghi "this mud basket." When he had talked in Cephalonia about putting "our shoulders *soberly* to the *wheel*, without quarrelling with the mud which may clog it," he did not foresee that they would be literally clogged by the mud of Missolonghi.

A disastrous side effect of the rains was lack of exercise for himself and of occupation for the troops. Byron could only cut down further on his diet of tea, cheese and vegetables in response to any gloomy readings of the tape measure. His eagerness to go riding drove him out to a distant olive grove approached by half an hour's row across the lagoon. At least some of the ground there was dry enough for a gallop, though he splashed into waterlogged ditches every hundred yards.

More worrying than his health (for he was no hypochondriac despite Stanhope's using that word) was the lack of trust accorded to Mavrocordato even by Europeans. Trelawny's reaction in the Morea was typical of this trend. Allying himself with the violent Odysseus, "a glorious being," and the first Byronic hero he had seen, Trelawny denounced the "super-subtle" Constantinople-educated Greeks, of whom Mavrocordato was leader, as "pre-eminent in all evil . . . and trained in the art of deception." Dr. Millingen at Missolonghi, though he had not met Trelawny, slung the same mud at Mavrocordato: "He could only advance by crooked ways . . . by tricks and cunning." The doctor added sourly that the "deceitful" character of the Greeks with whom Mavrocordato had to deal might render necessary his resort to trickery. "It was the current money of the country. No other would pass."

The current money of the country was in fact Byron's Spanish dollars. As he himself soon observed, "there seems very little specie stirring except mine"; and without his specie nothing else would stir, especially the Suliots.

To do them justice, these mountain warriors, who reminded Byron of Scottish Highlanders and their tongue of the Celtic, had eight months' pay owing to them by the government, besides a prejudice against attacking "stone walls." There were no signs of siege guns in the Byron Brigade, for the *Anne* with her expected cargo of artillery and engineers had not yet arrived, while the high stone walls of Lepanto were notorious.

By mid-January the sword and the pen were advancing in eager rivalry. Byron metaphorically waved his sword on the thirteenth, informing "Sir Ancock," Barff's partner, that five hundred soldiers would be supplied by him with rations and pay for a year, a further hundred soldiers to be paid by the government. Next day the pen was flourished by Stanhope, who published the first number of his *Hellenica Chronica*. It terrified Byron more than the enemy, though he had donated £50. In their devotion to utilitarianism, republicanism and rationalism, Stanhope and the committee seemed bent on alienating the European monarchies at a critical moment in the Greek struggle. They might alienate the literate Greeks also in proposing a reformed Greek alphabet.

The increasing strains on Byron's equanimity were shown in a flare-up with Gamba which did neither of them credit. The thoughtless Pietro had wasted 500 of Byron's precious dollars on things like broadcloth, exercise books, Hessian boots and horsewhips for the household: "The *latter*, I own that they have richly earned," Byron wrote, referring furiously to "Gamba's damned nonsense."

A prophecy by Lady Blessington was being fulfilled. She could imagine Byron rushing into battle, she had written in April, but not "enduring the tedious details, and submitting to the tiresome discussions and arrangements, of which as a chief, he must bear the weight." Byron was too much the aristocrat and poet to tolerate boring routine work, and so delegated it to inexperienced colleagues. When mistakes were made, however, he was too much the practical man to let them pass, and so flew into rages. Yet for the sake of the cause he faced the ups and downs of his situation with an ultimate good sense which no one had the right to expect of the temperamental Byronic hero.

Clashes in the congested town were becoming more numerous. Byron intervened in a row between Speziot sailors and customs officials, rescued a Turkish prisoner from Greek pirates, leveling his pistol at two of the pirates, who later invaded his house to snatch back their prey, and finally posted a permanent Suliot guard on the ground floor — all on 16

January. Two days later the Suliots rioted and a citizen was killed. If only the Byron Brigade could march out of Missolonghi before worse befell. "Derrah! Derrah!"

And gnawing away at his vitals like the Promethean vulture was an unrequited love for the boy Lukas. His ever more mechanical notes to Teresa may have reflected this hidden passion. Suddenly it rushed to the surface on his thirty-sixth birthday in a moving poem of ten stanzas. The deeply felt words of exhortation were all addressed to himself:

> *Tread those reviving passions down,*
> *Unworthy manhood! — unto thee*
> *Indifferent should the smile or frown*
> *Of Beauty be.*

> *If thou regret'st thy youth,* why live?
> *The land of honourable death*
> *Is here: — up to the Field, and give*
> *Away thy breath!*

On 25 January Byron did indeed seem to draw a little nearer to "the Field," for he was officially appointed to the Lepanto command. Under him were to serve the local *capitani* with their own followers, Gamba at the head of the Suliots, and a German lieutenant commanding the artillery — when there was any artillery to command. Next day, however, and for the next month, the prospect of any "Field" but that of diplomacy receded. Byron had to "give away" his breath, to quote his poem again, in pacifying the increasingly turbulent forces at Missolonghi.

An Ionian merchantman under British protection had been seized by a Greek privateer. Officers of the British brig *Alacrity* called on Byron demanding restitution of at least 200 dollars by Mavrocordato. The affair ended in Byron paying the 200 dollars to Mavrocordato. It was essential not to quarrel with the British. Byron had indeed made a great impression on the brig's captain, who promised to stand off Lepanto after the battle and pick up survivors. "For Heaven's sake don't come," exclaimed Byron, "for if they are sure of a place of safety, all my troops will run away." As for their commander-in-chief, he added, he at least had the advantage of not being able to run.

A few days later it was the Suliots who were misbehaving again.

> *The sword, the banner, and the field,*
> *Glory and Greece, around us see!**
> *The Spartan, borne upon his shield,*
> *Was not more free.*

The ancient Spartans, whose glory it had been to return from battle either as victors carrying their shields or as corpses carried upon them, were the legendary ancestors of the Suliots. In 1824, however, the latter-day "Spartans" were thinking less of fields and shields than of bread and butter. Not only did they demand — and receive — rations for their families and herds as well as themselves, but they refused to leave Missolonghi for Lepanto or even quit their barracks in the old seraglio, until their arrears were settled. The seraglio was needed as an arsenal for the foreign engineers. Byron threatened to dismiss his five hundred Suliots forthwith unless they obeyed orders. It was a perilous gamble but it worked. Afterwards he wrote to Hancock that "a man . . . had better end with a bullet than bark in his body." The bark was "China bark" or quinine; the bullet might come from a Turkish or Suliot musket.

Downpours of rain were to be expected in February. But not the flood of "incidents." However, for the first thirteen days developments seemed encouraging.

---

* Professor Jerome J. McGann, who is in course of editing Byron's complete poetical works for the Oxford University Press, has discovered that Byron's final version of this celebrated line was "around us see," not as hitherto printed, "around me see."

On the first, Commander-in-Chief Lord Byron, accompanied by Prince Mavrocordato and attended by General Gamba and Lukas ("not the Evangelist, but a disciple of mine"), were rowed many miles up the lagoon on a state visit to Anatolico. It was a diplomatic move, since the fierce chieftains of this town, having beaten off the Turks in 1822, held themselves in high esteem. Byron's reception was ecstatic. The *feu de joie* of bullets and cannonballs was so lavish as to put him in some personal danger. Both Gamba and Lukas fell ill after a soaking journey home. Byron remained fit and was able to nurse his "disciple," thus exemplifying another line of his birthday poem: "The hope, the fear, the jealous care."

Three days later Byron caught a cold during a frustrating incident on the beach at Missolonghi. The stores from the *Anne* arrived at last, but were left to spoil in torrential rain because 4 February was a saint's day. It was only after Byron himself turned to, that the Missolonghiots would help get the "combustibles" under cover. He attributed his cold to "swearing too much in the rain at the Greeks" — an excellent psychosomatic explanation of future ills also. The fire-master in charge of the engineering corps, which included English mechanics hired by the committee and foreign philhellene volunteers, arrived on 5 February.

This fire-master, William Parry, was in Byron's words "a fine rough subject," who had knocked about the world. He was soon having *"miffs* with Col. S."* But his warm heart and vivid language brought a human touch to Missolonghi in a time of need. One yarn of Parry's was a particular favorite with Byron: how Parry had visited old Jeremy Bentham before joining the *Anne,* and had been towed all over London in the wake of the energetic, loquacious prophet. Byron would roar with laughter and call again and again for "Jerry's Cruise."

It was to Parry that Byron said pointedly, "Give Greece arms and independence, and then learning; I am here to serve her, but I will serve her first with my steel, and afterwards with my pen." The pens of the London Committee,

however, had been busier than their steel. There were no
Congreve rockets in the *Anne*'s hold to fly over the stone
walls of Lepanto, and no coal to manufacture them; but "an
elect blacksmith" had not forgotten 322 Protestant New
Testaments. The Greeks venerated the rockets as Western
magic, whereas liturgical magic already existed in their own
missals. Such incompetence, said Parry, made Byron feel
"forlorn and forsaken."

Nevertheless he put a bold face on the immediate future.
He had given marching orders to a third of the capitani on
14 February and Gamba would lead an advance guard of
Suliots towards Lepanto, while Parry's artillery, promised for
the twenty-first (an empty boast), would follow with Byron
and the rest. Two Greek spies from Patras reported that the
walls of Lepanto, Arta and Prevesa were waiting to collapse
at the mere blast of Byron's trumpets.

Alas, on the fourteenth there was a spate of ills. Spies from
the Colocotrones faction in the Morea had infiltrated Missolonghi with stories that Mavrocordato would sell Greece to
the English if Byron, a pasha in disguise, did not sell her first
to the Turks. A truer report was that Colocotrones intended
to attack the reconstituted government. Before marching,
Gamba's three hundred Suliots insisted on a general promo-
tion, by which half the corps would become officers at en-
hanced pay.

This was the last straw. Byron flew into one of his more
spectacular rages so that the next day, Sunday, 15 February,
was a still worse occasion. At first he refused to have anything
more to do with the Suliots: "They may go to the Turks, or
the Devil, — or they may cut me into more pieces than they
have dissensions among themselves, — sooner than change my
resolution." Unfortunately for his peace of mind, the Suliots
caved in and six hundred of them were again recruited, half
under Costa Botsaris, half under himself. Thus Byron got the
worst of both worlds: continued responsibility for these "un-
governable" fighters but postponement of the fight for Lepanto until the new corps had been formed.

To fortify Byron against such stresses, Parry had mixed some stiff drafts of the "Pierian Spring." By 8 P.M. Byron was joking that "the author's brigade would be ready before the soldier's printing-press." But his mouth felt dry. Calling for cider, he drank it off, staggered and fell into Parry's arms in a convulsive fit — "whether Epileptic, Paralytic, or Apoplectic," he did not yet know two days later, when writing his journal. "It was very painful, and, had it lasted a minute longer, must have extinguished my mortality." His mouth was contorted, though he could still think — about Lukas. To the best of his belief it was his first fit and not hereditary, since his mother's attacks were *"hysterical."* He put it down to being "violently agitated" about public affairs and anxious in his "private feelings" (Lukas). His remedy was to clamp upon himself a regime of extreme abstinence. His doctors' remedy was to bleed him on the sixteenth — for twelve hours because they could not staunch the flow.

He had barely two days in which to recover. A furious altercation broke out at the arsenal on 19 February between a Suliot soldier and a Swedish philhellene engineer named Sass, who was first slashed and then shot dead. In order to save Missolonghi from massacre it was finally necessary to banish the intransigent Suliots. Byron gave them 3,000 dollars to go to Arta; and when they mutinied for arrears, another 4,800. "I boomed them off," he was to say cheerfully. In fact he bribed them to go. A Suliot bodyguard of fifty-six picked men was all that he retained.

Lepanto was postponed indefinitely and Byron thought no more about the author's brigade being ready before the soldier's printing press. In any case Stanhope left with his press for Athens, and six of Parry's hired mechanics fled to England. Byron did not blame them. They were not used to seeing "shooting and slashing" on their doorstep as if it were "a part of housekeeping."

On the day that Stanhope departed, 21 February, Missolonghi was visited by an earthquake. Byron was terrified for Lukas ("Whom did I seek around the tottering hall? / For thee") . But no one was hurt, he reported, except "those who got stuck in the scuffle to get out of the doors or windows" and were "rather squeezed in the press for precedence."

Mutiny, murder, stroke, earthquake, all in one week, all in "this hole." Yet he must remain in Missolonghi and "see this Greek business out (or it *me*) ."

The unwitting part played by Lukas is often underestimated in telling the story of Byron's last days. His hopeless love for the Greek boy did not strengthen his will to live. Despair wrung from him the tragic last verse of his last poem, in which, having remembered his self-sacrificing love for the boy through storm, fever and earthquake, he realized it was all no good:

> *Thus much and more; and yet thou lov'st me not,*
> *And never wilt! Love dwells not in our will.*
> *Nor can I blame thee, though it be my lot*
> *To strongly, wrongly, vainly love thee still.*

With his dog Lyon the opposite was true. All the dog wanted was to be allowed to love *him*. Byron would romp with Lyon for exercise, and Lyon would fetch the bottles he had hit with his pistol and lay them at his feet. His reward was to be told, "Lyon, thou art an honest fellow, Lyon. Thou art more faithful than men, Lyon; I trust thee more." And Lyon would spring up and kiss his master's hand. Lyon and Lukas. Perhaps it is not too fanciful to see in the beloved dog and the beloved page the good and bad spirits of his "private feelings."

From now until his death Byron felt the aftereffects of his illness, ranging from dizziness and flashing lights to irrational feelings of alarm. But there were pleasant moments, especially connected with women.

In pursuance of his humanitarian aim he had repatriated thirty Turks. Among them was a woman and her nine-year-old daughter Hatadje, a beautiful child who inevitably re-

minded Byron of his lost Ada. When Hatadje asked to stay
with Milord (and bedeck herself in silver and gold) he contemplated sending her to England as a Moslem "sister" for
Ada; alternatively to Teresa or Mrs. Kennedy. Not long after
Hatadje's appearance a pen portrait and picture of Ada herself arrived from Lady Byron via Mrs. Leigh. He had heard
with terror in September that Ada was ill and with joy in
December that she had recovered. Now it was reassuring to
know that she was merry and mechanical, not, as he had
feared, *"poetical"* — "it is enough to have one such fool in a
family."* When Stanhope called her the image of her father,
"his eyes lightened in ecstacy." A humble peasant woman was
to give him poignant pleasure while out riding by offering
him honey — for love not dollars.

Women could also still provoke his teasing instincts. He
liked to fire at the open turret of a house next door and bring
the women out scolding and gesticulating. When Fletcher
complained of no sex life, Byron dressed up a young soldier
as a Greek virgin and then had the would-be seducer accused
by "her" alleged brother. A third practical joke was to stage
another earthquake by making his bodyguard jump on the
floor above Parry's head, in order to frighten this victim of
the earlier scramble to escape. Byron's jokes gave pain and
were in fact signs of his own despondency.

But again, the political horizon underwent a real "lighten-
ing," if not in ecstasy, at least in hope. Soon after the earthquake young George Finlay had returned from the Morea
with letters from Trelawny and Odysseus. They suggested a
summit conference at Salona in March, when Greek unity
would at length be established. Byron was in a strong position. A huge Greek loan was being negotiated in London,
and he would almost certainly be one of the commissioners
for its administration. Perhaps he might bring Trelawny back
with him from the Salona conference. He needed "T" to clear

---

* Ada inherited a vein of mathematical genius, and as the friend and col-
league of Charles Babbage, anticipated with him the invention of com-
puters.

the decks in his disorderly household and make things ship-shape. His imagination began to soar. The Turks were said to be planning a westward march "in the spring." After the Byron Brigade had defeated them, he might go further west himself, to the United States, and negotiate the recognition of Greek independence. On 17 March he wrote his last note to his other T: "My dearest T. — The Spring is come — I have seen a Swallow today — and it was time."

It was time for the rain to stop. Instead, March was worse than February. "The weather has been, and is such," he wrote, "that neither Mavrocordato nor anyone else could go to Salona." The roads were rivers and the rivers lakes. "Derrah! Derrah!" What remained of the Suliot war cry? Only the eternal cry for dollars went "On — On — On." The Suliots were drifting back from Arta, having found no booty, and Mavrocordato could not feed them without Byron's dollars. Byron wrote to Barff on 7 April that Mavrocordato was "boring" him for more money. He had spent 59,000 dollars on them in three months. Could Barff raise £1,000 for them in the islands, against the London loan?

Not that he would keep for himself any of his personal loans if and when they were repaid. On 9 April he told Parry, as he had already told others, that he would *"re-expend"* it all in Greece, since "while I can stand at all, I must stand by the cause." That was virtually the last day, 9 April, on which he could stand.

April had opened grimly, with Missolonghi being terror-ized by Anatolico. Its primates were kidnapped, bazaars closed, the fort occupied by raiders. Byron's brigade helped to restore the citizens' nerve and his advocacy of "gun-boat diplomacy" cleared the fort. The weather cleared too; but he could not desert Missolonghi in its hour of need for Salona. So he rode out miles into the country, despite danger from bullets and further storms. On the ninth he was caught in a sudden squall. Hot and wet, he galloped to the jetty; cold and wet, he was rowed home. That evening he shuddered and ached in every limb. To Gamba he said, "I do not care for death; but these agonies I cannot bear." He had not learned the lesson of December when the same thing had happened at Metaxata and he had written, "Yesterday I was caught in the rain and I *ache*."

His last illness began next day, Saturday, 10 April. He rode out again with a headache but probably thought it "one of my thunder headaches." Afterwards he lay on his sofa thinking of a fortune-teller's prediction during his boyhood: "Beware of your thirty-seventh year." George Finlay came to say good-bye, before returning to Athens. Byron had liked talking to him about German philosophy, *Manfred* and *Cain*. Now he told Finlay and Millingen about the fortune-teller, declaring there were as many reasons to die a superstitious "bigot" as to live a "free-thinker."

For the next two days, 11 to 12 April, Byron was treated solely by Dr. Bruno, who diagnosed rheumatic fever, not serious. Since his patient stubbornly refused to be bled, Bruno administered "sudorifics" to cause sweating, purgatives, and hot baths. Byron was restless, irritable, sleepless, and sometimes delirious, though he took some broth "with relish." The rough Parry, however, recognized the symptoms and persuaded Byron to go to Zante to see Dr. Thomas there. But when a ship was ready on the thirteenth a sirocco blew up. Fate had permanently immured Byron in his pestilential prison. On this day a second jailer visited him professionally, Dr. Millingen. He agreed with Bruno that the patient must eventually be bled. And indeed if Byron had ever reached Zante or Dr. Thomas had reached him, it is unlikely that any treatment but bleeding would have been tried. Dr. Kennedy of Cephalonia also recommended it. Bleeding was the panacea.

On the fourteenth and fifteenth Byron's strength was ebbing. He fought tenaciously to keep his memory by reciting Latin hexameters, and when lucid dealt with his letters. As the cutting edge of his fine mind began to go, he wondered if he had been cursed with the evil eye. Would Millingen find "an old and ugly witch" in the town to consult? But by the time the obliging Millingen had actually found a witch, Byron had located the evil eye for himself. It had been put upon him in all good faith by two vampires, his doctors.

To continual pleas to be bled he retorted fiercely that "the lancet had killed more people than the lance"; or pointed out that bleeding a weak patient "is like loosening the chords of a musical instrument, the tones of which are already defective for want of sufficient tension." Bleeding would inevitably kill him.

His battle with the doctors over bleeding prevented him from taking them into his confidence on other subjects. Dr. Millingen reported to Dr. Kennedy that his patient had not once made even the smallest mention of religion. "Shall I sue for mercy?" he had muttered, and after a long pause, "Come, come, no weakness! Let's be a man to the last." This was Byron defying Arimanes like a true Manfred. It was left to Parry to hear more of the reality.

"I fancy myself a Jew, a Mahomedan, and a christian of every profession of faith," he told Parry, who sat by his bedside at Byron's request. The waves of delirium were uniting with the visions of Cain, and he went on: "Eternity and space are before me; but on this subject, thank God, I am happy and at ease. The thought of living eternally, of again reviving, is a great pleasure."

A cough attacked him on the seventh night which Bruno subdued with *benedette pillule,* though he insisted the pills were no longer blessed enough to save his threatened lungs. Byron agreed to be bled in the morning. Next day, 16 April, feeling better, he again declined the knife. Whereupon Millingen deftly transferred the argument from his lungs to his brain; without bleeding, his lordship might survive with his life *but deprived of his reason.*

Trelawny could have told Millingen that this was Byron's secret terror. He had read Scott's life of Swift during the voyage to Greece, "and was always talking to me of his horrible fate" — dying a grinning idiot.

Byron looked with mingled submission and revulsion at his

two doctors. "Come; you are, I see, a d——d set of butchers. Take away as much blood as you will; but have done with it." Millingen was satisfied. "I had now touched the sensible [sensitive?] chord," he wrote. Significantly, he and Byron had both used the word *chord,* he to describe his victory, Byron to symbolize a harp unstrung.

Between that Friday and the following Sunday, the eighteenth, the doctors took many pounds (the measure in those days) of Byron's blood, besides administering more purgative pills and doses of bark. Two blisters were applied above Byron's knees, for, said he, "as long as I live, I will not allow anyone to see my lame foot." Even on his deathbed the obsession gripped him. "Take care of your foot," he intoned mournfully to Pietro, when his friend hobbled into the sickroom after having sprained his ankle.

On the Sunday afternoon, Easter Sunday, a babel of agonized voices rose and fell around the dying man's bed — German and Greek from two more doctors, Italian and English. It was the kind of "lovely scene" that Goethe had suggested for Byron's next poem, an Old Testament epic with a powerful canto on Babel. *"Oh questa è una bella scena,"* said Byron to the weeping Tita. But to Millingen he spoke of Greece. "My wealth, my abilities, I devoted to her cause — Well: there is my life to her." Then he burst into excited war cries, half-Italian half-English. "Forward — forward — courage — follow my example." Poor Byron. He was dying with his body full of bark instead of bullets. The example he nonetheless set of courage on his deathbed could not have been bettered on the battlefield. And if he was never to shout the Suliots' war cry beneath the stone walls of Lepanto, at least his ravings showed that he would have made a heroic leader.

His head was bleeding from the application of twelve leeches and a tight bandage caused him excruciating pain. Parry loosened it and immediately he slept. When he awoke his thoughts were for "poor Greece! — poor town! — my poor servants!" His last words, murmured to Fletcher, were too low and faltering to be properly understood. Fletcher remembered the names of Ada, Augusta and her children, Lady

Byron, Hobhouse and some recurring worry about dollars. Yet again "drenched," as Byron complained, by the "Damned Doctors," he staggered into the next room and back with Fletcher's help. Then — "I want to sleep now."

It was 6 P.M. Missolonghi had maintained a voluntary silence all day, the Suliots exercising outside the town and no Easter Sunday festivities being held near the house. Letters with good news arrived from England: the loan was concluded, Byron was to be its commissioner and Hobhouse was coming out — all too late for him to take in. He slept exactly twice round the clock. Suddenly the silence was shattered by a violent thunderstorm. The Greeks in the streets looked at one another. They knew the sign. "The great man is gone." They were right. At 6 P.M. that Easter Monday, 19 April 1824, Byron died without regaining consciousness. He had just opened his eyes and shut them again at once, as if he had seen enough of the world.

The sword had worn out its sheath, as all Greece knew, in her cause. There was a memorial service in every important town, and in Missolonghi a proclamation by Mavrocordato of general mourning: at dawn on 20 April, a salute of thirty-seven guns to mark Lord Byron's thirty-seventh year; all offices and shops to be closed and Easter festivities suspended; black to be worn for three weeks. The skies darkened in sympathy and so torrential was the rain that the funeral had to be postponed until the twenty-second. Then Byron's bodyguard carried his coffin to the church of St. Nicholas. Spiridion Tricoupi, son of a primate, pronounced the oration. But the people wanted something more, and an urn containing the poet's lungs was afterwards placed in the church of St. Spiridion.

On 25 April or thereabouts, two characters who had let Byron down in different ways reappeared on the scene. Trelawny had been asked by Byron last August to "come back soon." He came back now, apparently to peer at his "best friend's" corpse before the coffin was closed, and to pronounce Byron an "Apollo" with "the legs of a sylvan satyr."*

Edward Blaquiere was the other arrival. He brought from England on the *Florida* a first installment of the loan whose success had been due to Byron's name. Ironically, the *Florida* turned round and on 25 May carried Byron's body home.

Any doubts about his resting-place had been resolved in his last moments. He told Fletcher, Parry, and others that he wished to be buried in England, contradicting a no doubt teasing remark to Millingen: "Let not my body be hacked, or be sent to England. Here let my bones moulder. — Lay me in the first corner without pomp or nonsense." Earlier, Trelawny had heard Byron's objections to having his "bones mingled with that motley throng" in Poets' Corner. In conversations with Lady Blessington, however, though fancying a "grassy bed in Greece," Byron expected "a marble tomb in Westminster Abbey — an honour which . . . I suppose could not be refused me."

It could be refused him and was. The Dean of Westminster declined the notorious remains while the Dean of St. Paul's, although regretting "poor Byron's" interment at "Huckley or Hockley in the Hole," evidently thought Hucknall a better hole for Byron than the cathedral.†

The news from Missolonghi swept through England in mid-May like the tremors of an earthquake. "Byron is dead." At first that was all they could say. Then Mary Shelley remembered him in poignant words — "Albè — the dear, capricious, fascinating Albè" — and Lady Byron in floods of unforgiving tears. Hobhouse recalled his "laugh," his "magical influence," his uniquely "devoted friends" — and alas, proceeded to show his own devotion and concern for his friend's reputation in a most misguided way. Largely owing to Hobhouse's efforts and despite Moore's protests, Byron's memoirs were burnt by two

---

* Doris Langley-Levi Moore has shown in *The Late Lord Byron* that Trelawny almost certainly did not arrive until several days later and therefore did not see the corpse at all. In any case Trelawny's own testimony elsewhere showed that Byron had *one* lame foot, the right. See p. 190.

† "The better 'ole," later to be a World War I name for England.

representatives of the family in John Murray's parlor. The
date was 17 May 1824 — Annabella's birthday.

If Byron's reputation demanded this ignominious holo-
caust, Hobhouse resolved to do his remains proud. He received the embalmed body and an urn containing the heart
and brain on board the *Florida* on 2 July, and arranged for
the coffin to lie in state in Great George Street, Westminster,
in the shadow of the Abbey. This was the nearest the dead
poet was to get to Poets' Corner until 1969, when a tablet
was unveiled, to the sardonic amusement of his ghost — or so
said the fellow-poet who presided at the ceremony, William
Plomer. Many Whig and Radical peers and gentlemen attended the lying-in-state by ticket and a sufficient number of
them — forty-five — sent empty carriages on 12 July to follow
the cortege as far as Pancras Gate. Having done their duty,
the empties turned back, leaving two carriages of male rela-
tives and friends to follow the hearse into the cemetery. Large
crowds of ordinary people had paid their respects in London.
Mary Shelley watched the hearse toiling up Highgate Hill;
and Caroline Lamb, without realizing who was inside, saw it
pass Brocket Hall.* After a rest at the Blackmoor's Head in
Nottingham, when the dust was shaken off the funereal
plumes, the poet joined some fifteen other Byrons in the
family vault at Hucknall Torckard, near Newstead, on 12
July 1824. Then, in Parry's words, "the tomb closed for ever
on Byron."

Parry was wrong. In 1938 the tomb was opened and Byron's
body viewed by a small group of persons. Among them, the
people's warden Arnold Houldsworth testified to the unmistakably Byronic countenance, despite the doctors' "hacking."
One of the surprises was to find the lame right foot cut off and

* According to Caroline's own account to Medwin, she was recuperating
from an illness and was in her carriage. On hearing that the hearse was
Byron's she immediately fell ill again. Lord Cowper, who owned Brocket
in the 1880's, told Wilfrid Scawen Blunt that Caroline was on horseback; she promptly fainted and crashed to the ground. Both these stories
may be apocryphal or highly dramatized.

lying at the bottom of the coffin. Byron had lost the cloven foot at last.*

A stained-glass window of the Road to Emmaus, erected in 1880, showed one of Christ's disciples with Byron's head. If he never trod the road to Damascus — no sudden conversion for him — he was often on the road to Emmaus, conscious of some half-recognized divinity at his side.

Byron is unique in two things: the inseparability of his life and poetry; and the impression he leaves of being "one of us." When alive he excited an equally passionate curiosity as man and poet. Today we cannot think of his poetry without his life, *Don Juan* without the goings-on in the Palazzo Mocenigo, "The Isles of Greece" without the Byron Brigade. "He was neither grave nor gay out of place," wrote Hobhouse, "and he seemed always made for that company in which he happened to find himself." If he had happened to live in our century he would have seemed made for it. As Goethe said, "Byron is not antique and not romantic, but he is like the present day itself."

Parry and Lady Blessington, linked by their knowledge of life's seamy side, each have something fresh to say about Byron's social attitudes. He believed in the popular "march of intellect" and its power to establish wider social graces, such as then existed only in country houses. To Parry he praised the new mechanics' institutes. Provided they were run by the workingmen themselves, the resultant "release of intellect" would produce a golden age — to which he would subscribe £50. "Poverty is wretchedness," he said, but even poverty was to be preferred to "the heartless unmeaning dissipation of the higher orders," of which, thank God, he was at last free. Parry was amazed at Byron's vivid interest in men of the lower orders, especially their jokes, anecdotes and slang. He liked to visit the engineering shops with Parry and learn how the machines worked.

This leads on to his curiously modern mixture of mys-

* The vault had been opened also in 1852 to receive Ada's coffin. See the Appendix pages 223–225.

ticism and space-age science. (He predicted a space age in *The Island* as well as discussing moon travel with Medwin.) Having seen through Herschel's telescope that the planets were worlds, he told Parry that every clergyman should have "a perfect knowledge of astronomy; no science expands the mind so much; it does away with narrow ideas." Byron was typical of his century in seeing God, as he told Dr. Kennedy, in "the Majesty of the Heavens." Beyond these expansive ideas, however, lay a contradiction which even the telescope could not cure. In a word, it was the split personality of the poet.

Lady Blessington got it out of him when they were discussing why poets made bad husbands. Suddenly he said: "It is as though creatures of another sphere, not subject to the lot of mortality, ·formed a factitious alliance . . . with the creatures of this earth, and, being exempt from its sufferings, turned their thoughts to brighter regions, leaving the partners of their earthly existence to suffer alone."

Here was Byron back in the theme of *Heaven and Earth,* his unfinished "Mystery" with no third act. Now we see why he was obsessed by the "seraph" myths of the Old Testament (myths which also fascinated romantics like Tom Moore and Alfred de Vigny) with their stories of angels marrying mortals and peopling the earth with beautiful giants or carrying their brides away to escape the deluge. They were poets. But their flight into space, to some undiscovered planet, some island in the sky — had it any reality? Byron's third act could never be written or his "Mystery" solved.

An influence on Europe as penetrating and prolonged as Byron's must be related to strong clear-cut themes, not to those fantasies which Lady Blessington elicited. His impact was in fact a double one: as the Byronic hero, and as the liberator.

France was to be his impresario of genius, though he never set foot there. The Romantic poet Alphonse de Lamartine was his contemporary, and Byron could quote Lamartine's

"Address" to himself of 1820. Though Byron did not much like being called *"chantre d'enfers"* — bard of hell (an English critic took this up saying his poems ought to be written on asbestos) — he could accept Lamartine's tribute to the "savage Harmony" of his verse and the enigma of the Byronic hero's soul: "Mysterious spirit, mortal, angel or demon." Byron inspired the music of Berlioz, and, as we shall see, the painting of Delacroix. France was at the heart of Byronism, excelling both in the myth business and in scholarship, besides mediating Byron to the rest of Europe through French translations of his poetry. "As a myth," writes Bertrand Russell, "his importance, especially on the Continent, was enormous."

The great Pushkin introduced Childe Harold's temperament to Russian literature in his *Prisoner of the Caucasus*. He heard with delight that his mistress, Calypso Polichroni, a fortune-teller's daughter, had been Byron's mistress also. Through Pushkin, the major poet and writer Lermontov found Byron. Lermontov not only rendered into Russian Byron's *Giaour, Darkness,* and *Don Juan,* Canto XVI, but also absorbed the idea of the Byronic superego into the depths of his own being — a being which in many ways resembled Byron's. He even had one leg shorter than the other. His finest poem, *The Demon,* describes the intense love of a demon for a Circassian woman in the Caucasus, the scene of Byron's *Heaven and Earth* and seraphic matings. Lermontov's demon is carried a stage beyond the cold defiance of Byron's Lucifer, since the Russian demon hates Heaven but yearns for reconciliation. The unwritten cantos of *Don Juan,* however, would surely have brought the Don, in his own satirical way, at least that far: "I shall end by making him turn Methodist," Byron told Lady Blessington; "this will please the English, and be an *amende honorable* for his sins and mine."

In Germany there was already a precursor of the Byronic hero in Schiller's *The Robbers,* which Byron read in 1814. Schiller's hero, Karl Moor, belonged to the earlier Gothick period of *Sturm und Drang*. When Byron's hero, Childe Harold, paid a return visit to Germany, so to speak, the poet Heinrich Heine adopted Byron's legendary collar and cape, becoming known as the "German Byron." As for Goethe's devotion to Byron, already noted, his biographer Richard Friedmann is puzzled to account for its extraordinary intensity. Was Goethe at that time "in need of a heroic demoniac figure"? Or perhaps (like Tommy Moore) Goethe loved a lord. Immediately after Byron's death, Goethe introduced into his *Faust* the flight of young Euphorion, Byronic offspring of romantic Faust and classical Helen of Troy, into the skies above Missolonghi, until, daring too much, he crashes into the sea.

Some expressions of French romanticism, as we have seen, had caused Byron to jib. He would have utterly repudiated certain Germanic developments of which he was part progenitor, along with Scottish Carlyle (self-styled Byron's "brother") and Nietzsche, another German admirer. Bertrand Russell has suggested that nationalism, Satanism, and hero worship were Byron's legacy to Germany. "The romantic revolt," he writes, "passes from Byron, Schopenhauer, and Nietzsche to Mussolini and Hitler" — but not with Byron's consent.

Poland's two national poets, Adam Mickiewicz and Juljusz Swowacki, both translated Byron, and the former not only affected a Byronic haircut but created a Byronic hero in his *Konrad Wallenrod*.

In Italy Byron's poetry directly inspired romantic opera. The great works of Donizetti and Verdi used Byron's early verse dramas as subjects — Donizetti's *Il Diluvio Universale* (The Flood from Byron's *Heaven and Earth*), *Parisina* and *Marino Faliero;* Verdi's somber *I Due Foscari* and romantically beautiful *Il Corsaro*.

This is no place to follow out the romantic Byronic idea in British life, literature and art. We need think only of Keats wearing the open-necked Byronic shirt in order to look like a poet, or Prince Albert wearing it on the morning after his wedding in order to dazzle Queen Victoria. Despite Byron's quirks of temperament, the steadfast Walter Scott was entirely subjugated by his friend's beauty and genius, writing after his death: "We feel almost as if the great luminary of Heaven had suddenly disappeared from the sky, at the moment when every telescope was levelled for the examination of the spots which dimmed its brightness." The voices alike of "just blame" and "malignant censure," said Scott, were at once silenced.

Disraeli took on Tita as his manservant and wrote *Venetia*, in which the hero, Lord Cadurcis, was Byron. Admittedly *Venetia* was a potboiler. But who could bring a pot to the boil better than Byron? Britain's greatest artist, J. M. W. Turner, illustrated many Byronic subjects, and exhibited those from *Childe Harold* with quotations from the poem.* John "Mad" Martin, an almost surrealist portrayer of doom, has left the paintings *Manfred on the Jungfrau* and *The Deluge*, the latter inspired by *Heaven and Earth*, while we have a drawing by J. H. Fuseli of Conrad rescuing Gulnare, and another by Ford Madox Brown of Bonivard's brother hanging naked in chains at Chillon.

Returning to France, the nineteenth-century painter Eugène Delacroix chose *The Giaour, The Bride of Abydos, The Corsair*, and the famous shipwreck scene in *Don Juan* as subjects. But it is his semi-allegorical masterpiece, *Greece on the Ruins of Missolonghi* (begun in 1827), which leads directly to the poet's second great source of influence — the legacy of Byron the liberator.

In his book on Russian literature, Maurice Baring has said that Byron always wrote about himself; therefore, though he

---

* Turner happened to be sketching by Lake Thun and in the Alps the same year as Byron was writing there, 1816. It is surely not a coincidence that John Ruskin's description in his *Modern Painters* of Turner's "Source of the Arveron" seems to echo Byron's poetry and journal. "Other ice is fixed," wrote Ruskin, "only this ice stirs. All the banks are . . . crumbling and withered as by the blast of a perpetual storm. He made the rocks of his foreground loose — rolling and tottering down together: the pines smitten aside by them, their tops dead, bared by the ice wind."

stormed the walls of "the city of romance" and planted his flag there, he never entered the citadel. His romantic imagination was limited.

There are two answers to this charge. First, despite his Continental reputation, Byron always denied that he was a romantic; and his half-finished *Don Juan* is indeed the antithesis of romance. Second, "the city of romance" where Byron planted his flag was a real one, Missolonghi, and he fell before he could wave it over Lepanto, Patras, and all Greece. Nevertheless his death achieved the final victory. The Greeks, however disunited, never forgot that Europe's most famous poet had chosen their cause to die for. When a new Greek edition of Byron's poems was published in Athens in 1974, a letter he wrote on 30 November 1823 to the provisional government, appealing for unity, was chosen as its preface: "You have fought gloriously; — act honourably towards your fellow-citizens and the world."

The world remembered Byron's sacrifice when Missolonghi was sacked by the Turks in 1826. Shock at this disaster led to the naval battle of Navarino in 1827, when Greek slavery was sent to the bottom of the sea together with the Turkish fleet. Byron's political hero, George Canning, had died just before, but it was his political strategy which achieved Greece's liberation.

The name of Byron, and a policy for liberation. These two marched together. In 1825 the unsuccessful Decembrist rising against the tsar of Russia possessed one without the other; most of the executed officers were Byronists. Without his name the ruins of Missolonghi would have meant no more to Europe than did the failure of the Italian patriots in 1821. And so when Italy reawakened many years after Byron's death, her new leader, Guiseppe Mazzini, associated Byron with the eternal struggle of oppressed peoples to be free. It was to him that Mazzini attributed Britain's mission of emancipation in the nineteenth century: "He led the genius of Britain on a pilgrimage throughout all Europe."

The pilgrim of eternity, as Shelley called him in *Adonais*, could be seen as the liberator of peoples from oppression, of society from cant, of language from banality, and of the poet from his ivory tower. "All contemplative existence is bad," he once told Annabella, "— one should *do* something." Goethe compared his literary style to a form of action — a wire cutting through a steel plate. If he never quite liberated himself, that was because he was still a pilgrim in time and space — though no one could express the difference between time and eternity more poignantly than Byron.

The sense of contrast would come over him as he laid down his pen and looked at the silent waters outside his window during his favorite hours between midnight and dawn; for he never took a house during his exile from which he could not see water. It might be the end of a letter to Tom Moore, generously defending the memory of Sheridan: "But, alas, poor human nature! Good night, or rather morning. It is four, and the dawn gleams over the Grand Canal, and unshadows the Rialto." No one "unshadowed" more things than Byron.

Or it was winter, and he had just finished an indignant letter to his publisher John Murray about the attacks on *Cain*. With a sudden change of mood he added: "I write to you about all this row of bad passions and absurdities, with the *Summer Moon* (for here our Winter is clearer than your Dog days) lighting the winding Arno, with all her buildings and bridges, so quiet and still: what Nothings we are! before the least of these Stars!"

By breaking his harp, as Mazzini put it, and going to Greece, Byron had brought his pilgrimage to an end in time, lifting it above the "nothings" of "poor human nature" into lasting significance.

APPENDIX

The Opening of Lord Byron's Vault,
15 June 1938

Notes by A. E. Houldsworth, People's Warden of
Hucknall Parish Church, 1938–1942

EARLY in 1938 the Vicar, Rev. Canon T. G. Barber M.A. expressed to me his desire and intention if at all possible to examine the Byron Vault. His declared reason for this being his earnest desire to clear up all doubts as to the Poet's burial place and compile a record of the contents of the vault.

To achieve this end, Canon Barber requested our local member of Parliament to assist in obtaining Home Office permission to the opening. The permission of the surviving Lord Byron (then Vicar of Thrumpton, Notts.) was also sought and in a letter of sanction his lordship expressed the fervent hope that great family treasure would be discovered with his ancestors and returned to him.

The date fixed for the opening of the vault was Wednesday, June 15th and arrangements were made to ensure strict secrecy in the proceedings. The doors of the Church were locked at 4.00 P.M. before work was started and no hint of the event being allowed to reach the public.

There were present: Rev. Canon Barber & his wife; Mr. Seymour Cocks M.P.; N. M. Lane, Diocesan Surveyor; Mr. Holland Walker; Capt. & Mrs. McCraith; Dr. Llewellyn; Mr. & Mrs. G. L. Willis (Vicar's Warden) ; Mr. C. G. Campbell, Banker; Mr. Claude Bullock, Photographer; Mr. Geoffrey Johnstone; Mr. Jim Bettridge (Church Fireman) and others not known to me. Probably the whole company numbered about 40.

About half-past six the masons had reached the stage of moving a large slab at the immediate foot of the Chancel steps. Considerable difficulty was experienced in prising this slab away, and when this was ultimately effected, it was found to be in the ceiling of the vault and consequently a ladder had to be requisitioned for the purpose of getting down into the vault. Dr. Llewellyn had provided a miner's safety lamp which was let down into the vault to test the air. This proving satisfactory, an electric lamp on a long flex was taken by a workman into the chamber.

The first view was of a surprisingly small vault containing three tiers of coffins placed on each other. The two top coffins evidently of a later origin than the rest were extremely ornate, being covered with purple velvet now much faded, lined with hundreds of brass studs and with coffin handles embellished with cherubim's heads. From a distant view the two coffins appeared to be in excellent condition. They were each surmounted by a coronet from which the velvet lining and ermine had disappeared. The coronet on the centre coffin bore six orbs on long stems, but the other coronet had apparently been robbed of the silver orbs which had originally been fixed on short stems close to the rim.

A closer examination in the vault proved that the centre coffin was that of Augusta Ada — Lady Lovelace — while the top left coffin was that of the Poet, though the coffin plate had disappeared as had also a good deal of the velvet which had originally covered the coffin. One or two coffin handles, these being embellished with Cherubim's heads, were also missing. At the foot of the staircase resting on a child's lead coffin was a casket which, according to the inscription on the wooden lid and on the lead casket inside, contained the heart and brains of Lord Noel Byron. The vault also contained six other lead shells all in a considerable state of dissolution —

the bottom coffins in the tiers being crushed flat by the immense weight above them.

All the male visitors in turn went down the ladder into the vault which was surprisingly free from smell except a mustiness. About half-past ten o'clock all the visitors had left the Church leaving only Mr. Willis, Mr. Johnstone, Mr. Bullock, Mr. Bettridge and myself. When the visitors had gone, I went down into the vault by the ladder, and examined the coffins.

The name plate, one handle, brass ornaments and strips of purple velvet had been taken from Lord Byron's coffin. These depredations must have taken place between the Poet's death and the burial of his daughter, Lady Lovelace after which the vault was sealed in 1852. I examined Lord Byron's coffin which looked quite solid, but which proved spongy, and with a slight pressure was able to lift the lid.

I then called Mr. Geoffrey Johnstone and Mr. Bettridge, and together we raised the lid, but found inside a lead shell which through corrosion or interference before 1852, already had a tear of more than a yard at the head. We turned back the lid of the lead shell, and found inside yet another wooden lid.

After raising this we were able to see Lord Byron's body which was in an excellent state of preservation. No decomposition had taken place and the head, torso and limbs were quite solid. The only parts skeletonised were the forearms, hands, lower shins, ankles and feet, though his right foot was not seen in the coffin. The hair on his head, body and limbs was intact, though grey. His sexual organ shewed quite abnormal development. There was a hole in his breast and at the back of his head, where his heart and brains had been removed. These are placed in a large urn near the coffin. The manufacture, ornaments and furnishing of the urn is identical with that of the coffin. The sculptured medallion on the church chancel wall is an excellent representation of Lord Byron as he still appeared in 1938.

When the Vicar returned to the Church I told him we had seen the dead Poet and he decided for the sake of posterity and the book he was writing, to see for himself. He descended into the vault and gazed on the body while we held up the lids. We subsequently photographed the coffins and all the coffin plates we could find, and finally left the Church in the early hours of the morning. I went home and had a bath and wrote notes on the proceedings from which the foregoing description is transcribed.

We did not photograph the body.

Of the people who saw the dead poet, only Mr. Johnstone and myself survive.

In his covering letter of 24 April 1975 to the author of this book, Mr. Houldsworth wrote: "These notes are purely matter of fact description, ignoring the atmosphere and expectancy of the opening. I have one possible amendment to my original description of Byron's body. His right foot was detached from his leg and lay at the bottom of the coffin. When I first lifted the lids I remarked to Jim Bettridge, 'Why, Jim, he hasn't a right foot.' This remark was in my original notes. Canon Barber, the Vicar, subsequently wrote his book, 'Byron, and where he is buried.' . . . His own description of his viewing Byron's body is somewhat romantisised."

On 6 November 1975, when Mr. Houldsworth gave permission for his notes to be printed as an appendix to this book, he added: "I regret that the other surviving witness Mr. Geoffrey Johnstone died on the 4th Nov and I shall attend his funeral tomorrow in the Hucknall Parish Church."*

---

* In fact my friend Mr. Cecil Roberts, the writer, is happily at eighty-three a second "survivor" who saw Byron's corpse, at the invitation of Canon Barber early on the morning of 16 June 1938, just before the masons sealed the vault. He describes his experience movingly in the fourth volume of his autobiography, *Sunshine and Shadow* (1972). "I have speculated very much," writes Mr. Roberts, "on who desecrated and opened Byron's coffin. Certainly vandals had been at work. The Canon thought that there had been only two possible occasions, when the vault was opened in 1852 to bury Augusta Ada, and when the chancel had been lengthened in 1888."

Bibliography

Blessington, Marguerite, Countess of. *The Idler in Italy*. 2 vols. London, 1839.

———. *Conversations of Lord Byron*. London, 1834. Reprinted: Princeton, N.J., 1969.

Buxton, John. *Byron and Shelley: The History of a Friendship*. New York, 1968; London, 1970.

Cline, C. L. *Byron, Shelley and Their Pisan Circle*. 1952. Reprinted: London, 1969.

Clubbe, John. *"The New Prometheus of New Men": Byron's 1816 Poems and Manfred*. Durham, N.C., 1974.

———. "Byron in His Letters." *South Atlantic Quarterly* 74 (Autumn, 1975) : 507–515.

———. "Byron and Scott." *Texas Studies in Literature and Language* 15 (Spring, 1973) : 18–33.

Coleridge, E. H. *The Works of Lord Byron: Poetry*. 7 vols. London, 1898–1904.

Dunn, Douglas, ed. *A Choice of Byron's Verse*. London, 1974. Paperback.

Elwin, Malcolm. *Lord Byron's Wife*. 1962. Reprinted: London, 1975.

———. *Lord Byron's Family*. London, 1975.

Gamba, Count P. *Lord Byron's Last Journey to Greece.* London, 1825.

Grylls, Rosalie Glynn. *Claire Clairmont: Mother of Byron's Allegra.* London, 1939.

———. *Trelawny.* London, 1950.

Gunn, Peter, ed. *Byron: Selected Prose.* London, 1972. Paperback.

Hall, N. John. *Salmagundi: Byron, Allegra, and the Trollope Family.* Phi Beta Mu, 1975.

Hobhouse, John Cam. *A Journey Through Albania.* London, 1813.

Holmes, Richard. *Shelley: The Pursuit.* London, 1974; New York, 1975.

Howarth, David. *The Greek Adventure—Lord Byron and Other Eccentrics in the War of Independence.* London, 1976.

Hunt, Leigh. *Lord Byron and Some of His Contemporaries.* London, 1828.

Jenkins, Elizabeth. *Lady Caroline Lamb.* 1932. Rev. ed.: London, 1974. Paperback.

Jump, John D. *Byron.* London, 1972.

———, ed. *Byron: A Symposium.* London and New York, 1975.

Kennedy, James. *Conversations on Religion with Lord Byron.* London, 1830.

Knight, G. Wilson. *Lord Byron's Marriage: The Evidence of Asterisks.* London and New York, 1957.

Lovelace, Ralph Milbanke, Earl of. *Astarte: A Fragment of Truth Concerning George Gordon, Sixth Lord Byron.* 1905. New ed., edited by Lady Lovelace: London and New York, 1921.

McGann, Jerome J. *Fiery Dust: Byron's Poetic Development.* Chicago, 1968.

———. *Don Juan in Context.* London, 1976.

Marchand, Leslie A. *Byron: A Biography.* 3 vols. London and New York, 1957.

———. *Byron: A Portrait.* New York, 1970; London, 1971.

————, ed. *Byron's Letters and Journals.* 5 vols. to date. I: *In My Hot Youth* (1798–1810). II: *Famous in My Time* (1810–1812). III: *Alas! The Love of Women* (1813–1814). IV: *Wedlock's the Devil* (1814–1815). V: *So Late into the Night* (1816–1817). VI: *The Flesh Is Frail* (1818–1819). London and New York, 1973–1976.

Mayne, Ethel Colburn. *The Life and Letters of Anne Isabella, Lady Noel Byron.* New York, 1929; London, 1930.

Medwin, Thomas. *Conversations of Lord Byron . . . at Pisa.* Edited by Ernest J. Lovell. London and Princeton, N.J., 1966.

Millingen, Julius. *Memoirs of the Affairs of Greece.* London, 1831.

Moore, Doris Langley-Levi. *The Late Lord Byron.* London and New York, 1961.

————. *Lord Byron: Accounts Rendered.* London and New York, 1974.

Moore, Thomas. *The Letters and Journals of Lord Byron, with Notices of His Life.* 2 vols. London, 1830.

————. *The Life, Letters, and Journals of Lord Byron.* Collected and arranged with notes by Sir Walter Scott [and others]. Reprinted from the Murray ed. of 1920: East St. Claire Shore, Mich., 1973.

Nicolson, Harold G. *Byron: The Last Journey.* 2d ed.: London, 1934. Reprinted: Hamden, Conn., 1969.

Origo, Iris. *Allegra.* London, 1935.

————. *The Last Attachment: The Story of Byron and Teresa Guiccioli . . .* 1949. Reprinted: London, 1971; New York, 1972.

Parry, William. *The Last Days of Lord Byron.* London, 1825.

Polidori, John William. *The Diary.* Edited by W. M. Rossetti. London, 1911.

Prothero, Rowland E., ed. *The Works of Lord Byron: Letters and Journals.* 6 vols. London, 1898–1901.

Quennell, Peter. *Byron: The Years of Fame* [and] *Byron in Italy.* 2 vols. in 1. 1935 and 1941. Reprinted: London, 1974.

Russell, Bertrand. *A History of Western Philosophy.* New York, 1945; London, 1946. Chapter on Byron.

Rutherford, Andrew, comp. *Byron: The Critical Heritage.* London, 1970.

St. Clair, William L. *That Greece Might Still Be Free: The Philhellenes in the War of Independence.* London and New York, 1972.

Stowe, Harriet Beecher. *Lady Byron Vindicated: A History of the Byron Controversy, from Its Beginnings in 1816 to the Present Time.* 1870. Reprinted: New York, 1970.

Strickland, Margot. *The Byron Women.* London, 1974; New York, 1975.

Trelawny, Edward John. *Records of Shelley, Byron and the Author.* London, 1858. Reprinted: 2 vols., New York, 1968. Paperback reprint: London, 1973.

Turney, Catherine. *Byron's Daughter: A Biography of Elizabeth Medora Leigh.* London, 1974.

Index

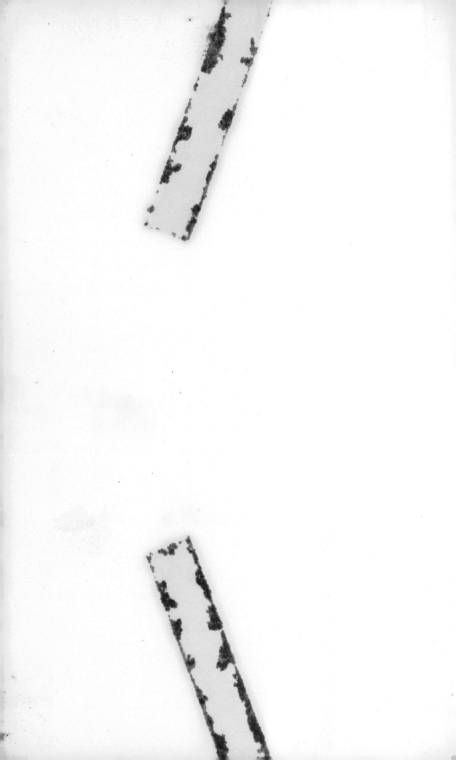